SOUL REFLECTIONS

Many Lives, Many Journeys

Other Books in the Sacred Psychology Series
by Marilyn C. Barrick, Ph.D.

Sacred Psychology of Love:
The Quest for Relationships That Unite Heart and Soul

Sacred Psychology of Change:
Life as a Voyage of Transformation

Dreams:
Exploring the Secrets of Your Soul

Emotions:
Transforming Anger, Fear and Pain

SOUL REFLECTIONS

Many Lives, Many Journeys

Marilyn C. Barrick, Ph.D.

Summit University Press

We gratefully acknowledge the following for permission to reprint excerpts from their copyrighted material: From *What We May Be,* by Piero Ferrucci, copyright © 1983 by Piero Ferrucci. Used by permission of Jeremy P. Tarcher, an imprint of Penguin Putnam Inc. From *Legacy of the Heart: The Spiritual Advantages of a Painful Childhood,* by Wayne Muller, copyright © 1992 by Wayne Muller. Reprinted with the permission of Simon & Schuster Adult Publishing Group. Poem by Helen Keller, courtesy of the American Foundation for the Blind, Helen Keller Archives.

SOUL REFLECTIONS: *Many Lives, Many Journeys*
by Marilyn C. Barrick, Ph.D.
 For information, contact Summit University Press, PO Box 5000, Corwin Springs, MT 59030-5000.
Tel: 1-800-245-5445 or 406-848-9500.
Web site: www.summituniversitypress.com

Library of Congress Control Number: 2003100014
ISBN: 0-922729-83-2

Front cover: The beautiful violet flower on the cover is a representation of the six-petaled seat-of-the-soul chakra as it appears in etheric dimensions of being. It is the place where we make contact with our soul and receive her impressions and guidance. This chakra's Sanskrit name is Svadhishthana ("sweetness" or "abode of the self"). The energy of the seat-of-the-soul chakra quickens our intuition and sense of freedom and is associated with diplomacy, mercy, forgiveness and transcendence.

SUMMIT UNIVERSITY PRESS

07 06 05 04 03 5 4 3 2 1

I dedicate this book
to lightbearers all over the world who yearn
to return to oneness with Spirit.

May the Sun of the Presence warm you
and ignite the fires of love in your heart.
As angels whisper their guidance,
may you incline a listening ear.
And may your soul and spirit be blessed
as you walk the path of loving-kindness.

May you see clearly through
the dreary fog of human expectations,
and may your soul and spirit
never falter during stormy weather.
May you be a swift learner of life's lessons
and the victor over dragons of the deep.

May you guide your soul through
the valleys of temptation,
and may the winds of adversity
propel you to a higher destiny.

Holding fast to the hem of God's garment,
may you become all of
who you really are.

Contents

Acknowledgments

It is with deep gratitude and hope in my heart for the victory of every soul on earth that I offer this book to my beloved guru Kuthumi, my friend and mentor Elizabeth Clare Prophet and the entire retinue of ascended masters who light the way for all of us. Without the inspiration and vision that comes from their guidance, I would not have the wherewithal to write this book on the soul.

I also owe a debt of gratitude to a number of special people, without whom this book would still be on my desk in manuscript form: my editor Karen Gordon, whose ability and skill fine-tunes my writing; Karen Drye, expert spiritual astrologer, without whom chapter 11 would not exist; Carla McAuley, for her erudite concepts and editing input; Lynn Wilbert, for her expertise in design and formatting; and Annice Booth and Nigel Yorwerth, for their valuable input.

I particularly wish to thank my clients, whose soul journeys that came to light during therapy have so greatly contributed to this book. And I lovingly acknowledge my friends and family for their never-failing support and confidence in me. A special thanks to my grandson Michael Hulme for his assistance and research on Tolkien's Lord of the Rings.

Preface

I am the master of my fate:
I am the captain of my soul.

–WILLIAM ERNEST HENLEY
"Invictus"

As I reflect upon the books I have previously written, on love, change, dreams and emotions, I realize that two elements draw them all together—God and the soul. I have always known God and I have always known my soul, but that was a private matter, or so I believed. Yet I have seen in my work as a minister and therapist that our souls have a lot in common.

We all live on planet earth, we all have parents, we all have friends or acquaintances, we all breathe air and drink water, and we all yearn inwardly for "the good life." However, as I moved along through life, I remember asking myself, "What is the good life all about?" Perhaps you have done the same.

Through trial and error I have discovered that it isn't about money or possessions or winning or losing. It isn't about being young or old. And it isn't about being loved, appreciated or admired by others. At the ripening age of 70 plus, I have come to realize that the good life is all about exploring, learning, loving, appreciating, enjoying and revering the *journey.*

What is this journey? It has taken many forms for me:

my soul loves the essence of God in nature, beauty, friendship, challenge, learning and what I experience when I reach for the stars. As a child I loved to talk to God, to feel the wind in my face as I biked, to play in the sand by the ocean and to meditate upon the stars. As a young girl I loved and learned, moved with the winds of change, dreamed my dreams and had my emotional ups and downs. As a young mother I nurtured, learned from and did the best I could for my children. As a grandmother I blissfully sit back and watch the show!

As I reflect on my personal life, I am grateful for the ongoing opportunity to learn and grow—particularly spiritually. And I am most grateful for the blessed opportunity, with my hand in God's hand, to forge my soul's higher destiny.

As a minister and therapist for many years, I have had the privilege of walking with God and being of help to people who have their own lives and dreams to pursue. Each and every person I have ever served has given me the greater gift.

My desire is that whoever reads this book will benefit from these pages of soul reflections—my own and those of others—plus the revelations and guiding inspiration of spiritual mentors. With love and gratitude for the opportunity to learn and grow from the thoughts, memories and visions of my fellow seekers on the path, I invite you to embark on what I hope will be a healing journey.

Introduction

Build thee more stately mansions, O my soul.

—OLIVER WENDELL HOLMES
"The Chambered Nautilus"

I believe that in the birthing and developing of the new millennium our souls are called to a higher destiny. We are all aware of forces seemingly beyond our control: changes in cultural values and mores, climatic conditions, earth shifts, violence between nations, and a general overlay of apprehension, confusion, resignation and depression among earth's people.

At the same time, the winds of Aquarius blow strong. We see creative advances in technology and sense an impelling urge toward humanitarian solutions. Many of us feel a yearning for spiritual awakening and divine guidance. We look to spiritual teachers, pastors, therapists and coaches for answers. Yet answers lie within—the enlightenment of the soul and spirit is an inner quest.

What do I mean by soul and spirit? Each of us (man or woman) is an expression of both the masculine and feminine aspects of the Godhead (i.e., the Father-Mother God*). Thus we have a dual nature, masculine and feminine: the spirit, masculine; the soul, feminine.

*In various cultures and religions known as God, Jehovah, I AM THAT I AM, Spirit, Great Spirit, Supreme Being, Brahma, the Tao.

What is the relationship of soul and spirit to our human self? I believe that we are spiritual beings created by God, clothed in veils of flesh for our earthly journey. Our soul is who each of us is as an individualized being of light, created by God. Our spirit is our unique essence—energetically, our inner powerhouse.*

Reflecting, then, upon our divine identity as spirited, soulful beings leads us to a deeper and more inclusive understanding of ourselves. The study of our psychology is about the inner life and the lessons of the soul. (The word *psychology,* derived from *psyche,* Greek for "soul," translates as "study of the soul.") An important part of the picture is exploring the impact upon us of our many lives and many journeys on the earth.

Each of us has journeyed long upon this earth and inwardly yearns to return to the heaven-world. Yet as a result of the density of the planet and our difficult experiences, many of us have become dispirited—sad, discouraged or apathetic—and have forgotten or lost track of our soul's true nature. This scenario is prominent in Gnostic texts and is the premise of the "Hymn of the Pearl," a text we will review and relate to our own journey in chapter 6, "The Quest for Enlightenment."

Psychologically, we as individuals are the sum total of who we are as a soul plus our physical genetics and life experiences. We carry the baggage of painful encounters, negative mind-sets, emotional hurts and physical wounds accumulated during our earthly journey. And we frequently get stuck in the resulting morass of pain and confusion. The good news is, no matter how deep the pain, we can bind up

*The word *spirit* (derived from *spiritus,* Greek for "breath," "vigor," "life") means "the animating force of life."

our wounds, discard the baggage and move on.

Through my life experiences I have been shown, over and over, that heartfelt appreciation brings comfort to the soul. Every one of us wants to be loved and respected, whether or not we say it out loud. The source of that inner need is the longing of our soul to be understood, appreciated and encouraged to fulfill her destiny.

The moment we decide to relate to others with love and compassion, we ignite a transformational process that gradually heals our wounds and helps us express who we really are.

The journey of our soul has lasted many lifetimes, and our teachers have been our life experiences and the people from every arena of life who have helped us with self-mastery and our walk with God. Many such stalwart souls have already returned home to the heaven-world and are known as ascended masters—advanced souls who have reunited with God. These illumined beings are our willing mentors and guides on the spiritual journey.

Elizabeth Clare Prophet, spiritual teacher and devotee of the ascended masters, describes them in her introduction to the magnificent book *Morya*:

> Those whose transition to the planes of heaven has taken them to the throne of God and to the dwelling place of his Lamb are called ascended masters. They have ascended to the plane of the I AM THAT I AM.* In the process of self-mastery in time and space, they have fulfilled all requirements of the Great Law for their soul's inner blueprint and divine plan....
>
> The stunning Truth of the ages is that the ascended masters are the true shepherds who come in the full

*The I AM THAT I AM is the individualized Presence of God focused for each individual soul, the God-identity of the individual. See Exod. 3:1–15.

> power of The Lord Our Righteousness promised through Jeremiah.
>
> In them we recognize and follow the excellence of their example of individual Christhood. We attach ourselves to them as our beloved and revered master teachers who show us how to multiply and perfect our own offering upon the altar of God....
>
> The ascended masters, our elder brothers and sisters, have so adored the living Christ that they have become one with him through the Lamb and share in the inheritance of perpetual communion with God....
>
> Their chelas [students] in physical embodiment are working side by side with other chelas who are continuing the mighty work of the ages in the etheric octave of the earth. This is the place... where we may "rest yet for a little season," either between embodiments or while waiting for the fulfilling of the divine plan of those coworkers yet striving to bring God's kingdom (his consciousness) into manifestation on earth by their witness unto the Truth.[1]

Ascended masters, our spiritual wayshowers, are souls like you and me who have balanced their karma, fulfilled their divine plan on earth and reunited with the I AM THAT I AM.

Among the ascended masters are great historical and religious personages: Enoch, Abraham, Moses, Noah, Joseph, Mary and Jesus, Gautama, Maitreya, Padma Sambhava, Kuan Yin, Confucius and many others who are our elder brothers and sisters on the spiritual path.

Like these great ones, we too are working out our karma and fulfilling a mission for the Creator. Our experiences on earth become an opportunity for our soul to progress in illumination and self-mastery. And the earthly tests we meet and pass are milestones on the journey. One day, by our own effort and the grace of the Almighty, each of us can realize union with God.

Death may claim the body, but the soul united with Spirit, the Infinite, can never die. As the Bhagavad Gita so beautifully expresses it:

> Never the Spirit was born;
> the Spirit shall cease to be never;
> Never was time it was not;
> End and Beginning are dreams!
> Birthless and deathless and changeless
> remaineth the Spirit forever;
> Death hath not touched it at all,
> dead though the house of it seems.[2]

All of us came from the heart of God in the beginning. We are destined to fulfill our purpose on earth and return Home in the victory of the ascension—if we will it so.

During our sojourn on earth, we are meant to be examples of love in action and to awaken people we meet to the inner spark of the divine. We are called to remind other souls of light (often called "lightbearers") of their soul's birthright and mission and that the ultimate goal of life on earth is to ascend to the heart of God.

This book on the reflections of the soul contains my gleanings from the fields of life as a woman, a spiritual seeker, a psychologist and an avid explorer of history and mysteries. What I have put into writing is the result of insights gained and lessons learned from my life experience and spiritual journey—and that of clients and friends.

I am forever grateful to Kuthumi, ascended master psychologist and tutor of my soul, whose path and teaching gives us clues to our soul's healing. As a prelude to this book, I would like to tell you about the soul journey of this great master, who is also known as K.H., or Koot Hoomi, to many on the spiritual path.

In his path toward self-mastery, Kuthumi was the sixth-century B.C. Greek philosopher Pythagoras, who founded his mystery school at Crotona, Italy, which was reminiscent of education described in Greek and Roman legends of the golden age. He walked the humble way of Christian sainthood as Francis of Assisi (c. 1181–1226). In his embodiment as Shah Jahan (1592–1666), he inscribed his soul's immortal love for his beloved in the Taj Mahal.

In his final incarnation, Kuthumi was known as Koot Hoomi Lal Singh, a revered Kashmiri Brahman. Born in Kashmir in the early nineteenth century, he attended Oxford University in 1850 and spent considerable time in Dresden, Würzburg, Nuremberg and finally Leipzig, Germany. There he visited with Dr. Gustav Theodor Fechner, founder of modern psychological research.

His remaining years were spent at his lamasery in Shigatse, Tibet, where he led a secluded life. Some of the master's letters mailed during this time to a number of his most dedicated students are in the manuscript collection of the British Museum.

Kuthumi and El Morya, known as K.H. and the Master M., founded the Theosophical Society in 1875 through Helena P. Blavatsky, commissioning her to write *Isis Unveiled* and *The Secret Doctrine*. The purpose of this activity was to reacquaint mankind with the wisdom of the ages that underlies all of the world's religions—the inner teachings guarded in the mystery schools since the last days of Lemuria and Atlantis.

In the late nineteenth century, Kuthumi reunited with Spirit in the initiation[3] of the ascension. Yet he is only a prayer away from each of us. In his tenderness and compassion toward all living beings, he answers prayers for people everywhere and assists the nature spirits who tend the earth.

Kuthumi maintains a spiritual retreat in the heaven-world over Shigatse. There he plays a majestic organ, drawing the harmony of cosmos through the fires of his heart. Through his celestial music he brings comfort, healing and peace to the soul at the time of death. As we go through this transition, he lovingly plays the organ to guide the soul moving from earthly existence upward to the octaves of light. And to this day, he inspires architects, poets and scientists with the mystical remembrance of their own soul's harmony in the celestial geometry and the rhythm of the stars.

Kuthumi, speaking through the messenger Elizabeth Clare Prophet,[4] has given us a beautiful teaching about the soul's journey to Selfhood, our soul's ultimate destiny:

> Self is interwoven with consciousness, and consciousness is the doorway to reality. In an impure state, consciousness puts out the light; in a pure state, it radiates light....
>
> Our subject, understanding yourself, is a broad one. We would softly yet skillfully pull the thread of man's consciousness through the eye of the needle into the world of crystal clarity....
>
> We come to fill the soul, the mind, the consciousness and the being of man with an awareness that will break the chains that have bound him to the limitations of his mortality.
>
> We wish to restore the boundaries of the temple of God in man and in woman and to reassert the individual's

> right to take dominion over his own life. We come to guide him in his search for ultimate reality and to assure him that we are very much present in the universe as his teachers, as his brothers and as his friends. As we represent God to the evolutions of earth, so may each individual.
>
> To one who is beginning to understand himself as a component of God, the world is a stella nova. He is refreshed in the dawn of each new day. The world is born anew all around him. His weary soul sheds its fantasies and frustrations. At last he opens his eyes to behold reality.
>
> From the beginning to the ending of time, God has sent ministering angels to instruct his children in the ways of self-mastery which would lead them to their reunion with him. He has sought the gradual and permanent elevation of all of his children into that vision of self that reveals the wholeness of the divine man, the Real Self.[5]

Awareness of the subtleties of soul and spirit broadens our vision of who we are and who we may become. In this book we will explore spiritual teachings about the journey of the soul—from heaven to earth and back again. I offer the reader therapeutic self-help techniques for healing the wounds of the soul incurred in hurtful life experiences (infancy, childhood, adolescence and adulthood) and for redeeming the wounded spirit masquerading as the inner critic.

We will broaden our view of the soul's journey by studying her connection with the stars plus many stories of saints and sages and valiant people in ancient and modern times. I bid you welcome to a vision of the homeward journey of the soul and a glimpse of the heaven-world that awaits each of us!

PART ONE

The Initiation of the Quest

1

The Merry-Go-Round of Time and Space

I saw Eternity the other night
Like a great ring of pure and endless light.
All calm, as it was bright;
And round beneath it, Time in hours, days, years,
Driv'n by the spheres
Like a vast shadow moved; in which the world
And all her train were hurled.

—HENRY VAUGHAN
"The World"

Many of my clients have asked me, "What is my soul? How does my soul relate to my conscious awareness of who I am? And why am I here on earth?"

I believe all of us have had similar questions, spoken or unspoken. The answers are both universal and unique because the soul originates in the Infinite but each of us walks our own path in the realms of time and space.

Some are blessed with a glimpse of the higher realms from whence we have come. One of my friends shared with me an extraordinary experience she had in meditation:

> I was immersed in a wheel or what I would call a circle of eternity, in absolute peace. I could see beneath me another wheel or circle, kind of like a merry-go-round, that represented points of time and space. I felt I could choose any point and go there whenever I decided to leave eternity. So I sat there and contemplated coming back into time. Of course I had chosen the time and place I had left, because it was God's will that I be there. But the experience of having made the choice myself stayed with me for a long time, as did the experience of eternity. I suppose that is what the Hindus call the wheel of karma.*

A Child's Glimpse of a Past Life

My teacher and friend, Elizabeth Clare Prophet, tells of her remarkable out-of-body experience as a child that set her imagination on fire and propelled a lifelong quest to understand the mystery of the soul, of karma and of reincarnation.

> One day when I was about four years old I was playing in my sandbox in Red Bank, New Jersey, where I was born. I was in my play yard that my father had made for me. It had a playhouse, a swing and sandbox enclosed by a white picket fence with an arch and gate. It was situated next to a delightful garden created by my parents.
>
> It was a beautiful day. Big white clouds were moving through a deep blue sky. And I was alone, enjoying myself in the sun, watching the sand slip through my little fingers, drawing designs in the fresh earth and making mud pies with cookie cutters and tin molds.
>
> Then all of a sudden, as though someone had turned

*Karma is the cosmic law of cause and effect: "Whatsoever a man soweth, that shall he also reap."

a dial, I was playing in the sand along the Nile River in Egypt and I was experiencing the beauty of that scene. It was just as real as my play yard in Red Bank and just as familiar. I was idling away the hours, splashing in the water and feeling the warm sand on my body. My Egyptian mother was nearby. Somehow this too was my world. I had known that river forever.

After some time (I don't know how much time had passed), it was as though the dial turned again and I was back at home in that little play yard. I wasn't dizzy. I wasn't dazed. I was back to the present, very much aware that I had been somewhere else.

So I jumped up and ran to find my mother. I found her at the kitchen stove and I blurted out my story. I said, "Mother, what happened?" She sat me down and looked at me and said, "You have remembered a past life." With those words she opened another dimension. And I have never been the same.

Instead of ridiculing or denying what I had experienced, she explained that the soul does not accomplish her mission in one life. She told me that my soul was eternal. She said that our body is like a coat we wear: it gets worn out before we finish what we have to do. So God gives us a new mommy and a new daddy and we are born again so we can finish the work God sent us to do and finally return to our home of light in heaven. Even though we get a new body, we are still the same soul. And the soul has a continuous recollection of the past but we do not.

She explained all of this to me in simple childlike terms I understood. It was as though I had always known it and my mother was reawakening my soul memory.

Over the years she was to point out to me children who were born maimed or blind, others who were gifted,

> some who were born into wealthy homes and some into poverty. She attributed their inequality to karma and to their past exercise of free will. She said that there could be no such thing as divine or human justice if we had only one life, that God's justice could only be known in the outplaying of many lives in which we see past actions coming full circle in present circumstances.
>
> Accustomed to praying to Jesus, my thoughts turned to him. I saw the logic of reincarnation and I said to myself, "God must have shown me this past life for a reason." But God didn't tell me the reason till I was well into adulthood. Then I realized that that life in Egypt was the key to the work I had to do in this life. No doubt through that glimpse into the distant past, there was transferred to me some substance of myself—perhaps some heavy karma that I had to balance today, thirty-three centuries later, or a mission I had not fulfilled whose time had come.
>
> Since then God has revealed to me other incarnations and taught me lessons concerning positive or negative momentums that I must build on or undo. Thus, I have seen the causes behind the effects of bad karma that I had to balance in this life, and I have seen how my good karma put the wind in my sails to achieve my goals and more. Karma, in fact, is why we are all here.
>
> You, too, have brought with you the momentums of your good karma as well as those of your bad karma that you must balance. You most certainly have positive or negative karma with family members and people you know or people you will meet. Life is a challenge and an opportunity.[1]

The ascended masters teach that our soul originates as divine potential, as a living spark of the infinite fire of God.

In the kiln of the Great Sculptor, we are molded into individualized beings and clothed with mortal bodies for our earthly journey. And we come to earth to fulfill a special purpose.

Every one of us is a beloved child of the Father-Mother God, destined to become a mature son or daughter who will one day return to the heaven-world—mission accomplished! We are here for a particular reason, to play a special role on the stage of life. And inherent in our God-given identity is a unique gift we are meant to offer to our country, family, friends and people we meet.

Think about it for a few moments: What do you believe is your special gift? Let your heart's intuition respond. And take a few minutes to write down what comes to you.

As you reflect upon your gift, meditate upon the "God child," the holy innocent, who lives within you. This is your soul as a divine being, a Christed one aborning in the manger of your heart. This glorious being, whom God created and blessed with a special gift, is who you really are.

Confused and Entrapped by Karma

Why have we forgotten that we are divine beings? The answer has to do with our history on earth. Our soul has lived many lifetimes on this planet in different mortal bodies. We have made many choices, some good, some not so good. In the confusion of returning karma, most of us have forgotten who we are and what we are meant to do here. We only dimly sense our origin and purpose as sons and daughters of God.

How did we get here in the first place? As souls of light, we exercised God's gift of free will to enter the physical plane. We came with our special talent that could help people on earth. And some came to rescue brothers and sisters of light who had lost their way and forgotten their mission. Today many of us find ourselves entrapped by confusion, unruly emotions and desires, and the karmic web we have spun.

So who am I? Who are you? Why are we here?

We are lightbearers; we carry the light of God within our heart and soul and body. Each of us is special in the eyes of God, whether or not we remember our divine origin. We may think of ourselves in terms of our "humanness" or who we seem to be from the reactions of other people. Yet our divine nature is still alive and well beneath the overlay of human memories, thoughts, emotional reactions and physical habits.

At some point, we awaken to wanting more out of life, something beyond the essentials of the human condition and what we have piled up in status or possessions. As we wake up, we begin to listen and respond to the still small voice of our soul. We may sense our connection with angels, masters, Spirit. And we begin to seek the path to the higher octaves.

As we do so, we may feel a conflict between who we really are and who we may think we are as a result of our karma. Our karmic condition in itself is confusing because it's a mix of experiences—the victories and the defeats of many lifetimes.

When we find ourselves confused about our identity, it is comforting to remember: You are who you are no matter who you may think you are![2]

A Cosmic Vision for Our Soul

In her reflections on the beloved master Morya, Elizabeth Clare Prophet portrays her vision of the divine destiny of the soul:

Morya is a master of change. He, the Magus, comes for the ordering of changes. He is the great astronomer-astrologer of the stars of your destiny. He knows every planet of your choosing . . . the worlds of maya that you have flung and hung in the sky of your solar system.

He knows the motions of causal bodies in orbit in the constellation of your personality. He knows the whys and wherefores of those effects that pound upon the rocks of the subconscious[3] until there is that resolution. And the rocks are smoothened and the sea is calm and only the gentle lapping of the tide signals the rhythm of a life restored.

If you are smart, my friend, you will seek him and find him. And when you do, you will implore his intercession in your life. For . . . he holds the key to the will of God in your life. He unveils the blueprint of the soul—i.e., the solar fire, the solar wind and warmth, the solar rains and earthly energy, the seas and the mountain ranges of your solar body.

All this is inside of you and more, my friend. He has shown me my inner universe and more. Oh, that you could imagine the wonder of all he holds in store! For thee, for thee!

I myself was not always so smart as to seek him with my life. . . . When I did, I sometimes momentarily lost the grasp of his hand or took my gaze from his. He did not let go nor lose sight of me, but the holding on and the attention to his face—ah, his blessed face!—that was up to me, you see. And it will always be, for you and me, until the grand assimilation of the worlds.

To find him, then, is just the beginning. But to hold him and to fix the gaze fast and tight and not lose sight of the goal—this and more is what the ending is.

Of what ending do I speak? It is the ending of the

> merry-go-round of time and space and the cycles of one's karma and that necessity of wearing these clay vessels that do not afford our souls the expression of our most grand and inner nature.
>
> We are natives of other spheres and so is Morya. He comes from the home we all once knew. By his striving and his overcoming he has arrived at a station in the higher octaves where life is lived in purer potential and God-free beings and the saints await our return. They are waiting for us to finish the work they have started during these long centuries of our incarceration on this earth.[4]

Strangers in a Strange Land

The unfinished story of karmic happenings on planet earth emerges from the teachings of ascended masters, saints and sages and from the recollections of people who have pursued the path of enlightenment. This story is the soul's reflection and memory of personal and planetary consequences of choices made during her sojourn on earth. How the story ultimately concludes is up to each one of us.

Once we embarked on our mission to planet earth, we found ourselves outside of the ethereal heaven-world, in a realm of lower vibration. As we gradually integrated with that vibration and a physical body, we felt separated from the Infinite. Here we were in this dense place, strangers in a strange land. We were not used to the heavy vibration. It was hard to remember why we had come. We felt alone and vulnerable but still determined to fulfill our mission.

We knew that once we left the higher octaves, the law of free will would become very important to us. It would be the major key to our return. By right use of free will, we could keep our vibration up, make good karma, fulfill our mission and make it back to the higher realms of light. By misusing free will, we would lower our vibration, make bad karma, forget our mission and get stuck on the earth plane.

Which was it to be? In the heaven-world, we knew we could be victorious. Yet when we got down here, it was far more difficult to discern good from evil and take right action than we had ever imagined.

Inwardly, we knew that our Father-Mother God, the angels and our Higher Self* still loved us. But they were in the etheric realm, the home of higher vibrations we had left behind. In the density of the earth, we didn't remember how to connect with them.

We dimly remembered we had vowed to work through these dense bodies. So we tried to pray, to meditate, to focus on God's love and to remember why we had decided to come in the first place. When we kept our vibration up through spiritual practices, we could make the contact. Then we didn't feel so alone.

When we didn't keep our vibration up, we felt bewildered, lonely and disheartened. We didn't remember we had a special gift to give. We couldn't easily find the people we were trying to help. And when we did, they weren't particularly receptive because they were now identified with the things of this world and the planetary lifestyle. Sometimes they didn't even recognize us.

A Web of Karmic Circumstances

In trying to fulfill our mission, we got entangled with the fallen angels who were running things on the planet. Now that was a big mistake. Those dark-angel types were all about power, tyranny and abuse, yet they had a charisma

*Real Self, Christ Self, Buddha Self, Atman, Tiferet

and charm that was beguiling. It was easy for the children of God on earth to fall under their spell.

You see, once the fallen ones cut themselves off from their divine source, they had only limited life (light) energy. When that energy was used up, they would no longer exist as individualized beings. So the only way they could keep going was to steal light.

How did they do that? They stole light through any kind of contact in which there was an energy exchange: by persuading the lightbearers to buy into their motives or mindsets, to react emotionally to their power trips or to be on the receiving end of a fallen angel's touch, especially intimate contact. The dark angels stole the light; the lightbearers got enmeshed with the darkness.

Those who came as rescuers got tricked in much the same way people already living on earth had been fooled. They didn't recognize the fallen angels as such because of the vibration of stolen light around them. Some were even in high positions as priests or priestesses or respected teachers of seeming virtue. But they recognized the lightbearers. And they targeted them because they carried the light.

These dark ones were slick and deceptive. We find clues and warnings about their ways in our most ancient metaphors. Remember the serpent's message to Eve? "Thou shalt not *surely* die," he said, implying that God would make an exception in her case. Just as Eve believed the lie and Adam followed her lead, we did something similar that lowered our vibration. Soon we no longer vibrated in consonance with the etheric realm. We couldn't hear or connect with God directly anymore.

In the midst of the ensuing confusion, we were spiritually, mentally, emotionally and physically abused by the fallen ones and their cohorts. Sometimes we tried to retaliate. But that made matters worse, and our consciousness descended still lower.

Wandering deep into the mists of maya, we slipped into forgetfulness. We forgot our inner compass, the higher intuition of our heart and soul. As we neglected to connect with our Higher Self, we began to lose our mastery of energy flow. Gradually we lost our spiritual bearings and forgot our purpose for being on earth.

Now we were at the mercy of our own density and entangled with the karma of the fallen angels. We only dimly remembered our origin in the heaven-world and that we came to earth on a rescue mission. If we did have a brief glyph of remembrance, it seemed like a dream. Eventually we considered ourselves human beings, inhabitants of planet earth.

Walking the Karmic Path

Our Father-Mother God never stopped loving us. Over and over again, they sent emissaries to remind us of who we really are. Avatars and ascended masters came to show us the way we once knew and had forgotten. Sages and spiritual teachers have offered enlightenment. Saints, past and present, have lived their lives as a demonstration of the path to reunion with God. And miracles, great and small, still happen every day.

It is up to us to wake up, to remember our divine origin, to reclaim our heritage as sons and daughters of God. Our Higher Self and the angels and ascended masters await our prayers and calls for help. And help comes forth in God's time and according to his will, whether or not we consciously perceive it.

In the etheric octave, the heaven-world, we knew God

through oneness with our I AM Presence.* Once we descended into the earth plane, we distanced ourselves in vibration from our Presence. And the law of cause and effect came into play. As the karmic wheel began to turn, whatever we sent out vibrationally, mentally, emotionally or physically returned full circle to our own doorstep. Our karma began to dictate our circumstances.

This is universal law as stated in the scriptures: "Whatsoever a man soweth, that shall he also reap."[5]

When we radiated positive energy, we blessed others and received blessings in return. When we emitted negative energy, we inflicted pain on others and received pain in return. Whatever we gave out sooner or later came back to us. These were cosmic lessons for the soul, especially since the returning negative energy became as a dark cloud between us and our I AM Presence.

The "Why Me?" Syndrome

Now this is likely the point where we began what I call the "Why me?" syndrome. It goes something like this: "Why are these awful things happening to me? Why me? Why isn't God, if there is a God, coming to my rescue?"

Of course God heard our cry for help. But by now we were firmly on a karmic path that only we could walk. We were still carrying the light and meant to return to our Creator, but we hadn't realized how dense this planet was going to be. It would take all of our higher attunement to fulfill our purpose—and we didn't even know what that meant anymore.

In despair we cried out, "I'm in so much pain. My God, why have you deserted me?" Then, of course, the fallen angels "sympathized" with our plight. When we bought into

---

*See footnote, p. xv.

their sympathy and our own self-pity, we aligned ourselves with the dark side and our consciousness kept plummeting. We began to feel petulant and angry at God.

Ultimately, many of us felt so bereft we didn't believe in God anymore. And in the process of disowning the Father-Mother God, we disowned our divine heritage. After a while, we didn't even remember it. That is the story of how it went for many of us.

If we want to get off this planet and return to the heaven-world, we need to redeem our karma because it acts as ballast tugging us down to the earth plane. When we transform that ballast into positive energy, our consciousness spirals upward.

As we strive for higher consciousness, we begin to pass our spiritual tests. We make headway in transforming the conglomerate of our darkness—our negative motives, thoughts, feelings and actions—known as the dweller-on-the-threshold.

If a story would help you understand the dweller-on-the threshold, think of the popular movie *Lord of the Rings* and the book on which the movie is based, *The Fellowship of the Ring,* by J. R. R. Tolkien.[6]

This poem from a description of the *Lord of the Rings* captures the mood of darkness:

Three Rings for the Elven-kings under the sky,
    Seven for the Dwarf-lords in their halls of stone,
Nine for Mortal Men doomed to die,
    One for the Dark Lord on his dark throne
In the Land of Mordor where the Shadows lie.
    One Ring to rule them all. One Ring to find them,
    One Ring to bring them all and in the darkness bind them
In the Land of Mordor where the Shadows lie.[7]

In Tolkien's classic story, the "One Ring" gives mastery over every living creature to the one who wears it. Thus its bearer is able to manipulate dark powers and enslave the world. And since the original Ring was devised by an evil power, the Nine Mortal Men who are given rings controlled by the Master Ring are inevitably corrupted.

The men who possess the Rings may start out being relatively good people, but as their consciousness becomes increasingly wed to the dark power of the Rings, their dark side (their dweller-on-the-threshold) grows in power. The men gradually lose their soul—and ultimately turn into soulless, evil beings called "Ringwraiths."

As the tale unfolds, the Master Ring, the Ring of Power, is in the possession of the Hobbits, short, mild-mannered, quiet beings. And the task of Frodo Baggins (the main Hobbit character) and the Fellowship of the Ring (those dedicated to halting the Rings' evil power) is to destroy the Master Ring by casting it into the fire from which it came. That action would end the evil power of all of the Rings.

Frodo and his faithful servant, Sam, try to take the Ring of Power to Mount Doom in order to destroy it. If they succeed, Sauron, the Lord of the Rings, and all the other evil beings will no longer exist, thus ending their corruption of all that is good in Middle-earth. The problem is that Mount Doom is right in the middle of Sauron's dark kingdom, and the evil ones will use all their power to repossess the Ring.

Out of the struggle to possess and control the Master Ring arises a war compared both in magnitude and complexity to the great wars of our times. In the movie, the outcome of the battle between good and evil is left hanging, awaiting the actions of the characters in the sequels to come—a drama we can equate with the battles of good and evil on earth today.

In the last of Tolkien's three-book series, *The Return of the King,* Frodo, the Ring Bearer, at the very moment he is about to cast the Master Ring into the fire decides that he wants the Ring for himself. His contact with the Ring on the long journey to Mount Doom has made him susceptible to desiring its dark, evil power.

This drama highlights the facing off of good and evil and what happens within a person who is struggling with it. In Frodo we see a well-meaning lightbearer increasingly mesmerized by the Master Ring (and his own dweller) and identifying more and more with its dark power. Ultimately, he barely escapes being taken over by evil.

As has been said, "Power tends to corrupt and absolute power corrupts absolutely."[8] The moral of the tale is that evil masquerading as good or benign is still evil—and the soul who is tempted by it can be lost.

We see a similar story in Robert Louis Stevenson's classic drama *The Strange Case of Dr. Jekyll and Mr. Hyde.* As you may remember, Dr. Jekyll discovered drugs that allowed him to transform his personality into the vicious, cruel creature he named Mr. Hyde. By so doing he could allow his evil, lecherous side to prowl and prey without the disturbance of conscience.

When the drugs wore off Dr. Jekyll would regain his normal identity. He thoroughly enjoyed this game of playing with the darkness—for a time.

Dr. Jekyll thought it was relatively harmless to play Mr. Hyde, to experiment with his wickedly criminal alter ego—until suddenly he discovered he could not reverse his identity. The monster, Mr. Hyde, had taken control. Try as he might, he could not reclaim himself as the kind, mild-mannered physician, Dr. Jekyll.

He had flirted with the dweller, thinking it a game. To his horror he discovered it was a no-win game. He had identified with the dweller one too many times and was now wed to the darkness he had courted.

If we would claim our soul's victory, we must recognize, confront and defeat the evil we have internalized. Only then can our soul be the victor in the midst of karmic circumstances. We are called to challenge the lure of evil, within and without. We are called to join forces with our Real Self. And we do so by praying from the depths of our heart and soul, "God, help me!"

When we pray in the name of the Christ for the dweller-on-the-threshold to be bound,* the conglomerate of our destructive "not-self" energies can be removed. Then we can replace those negative, incomplete or jagged patterns with positive energy through prayers, decrees,[9] fiats, mantras and affirmations. Thus we change our vibration and begin to replace who we are *not* with who we really *are.*

A Path of Spiritual Acceleration

Throughout the ages, saints and sages and advanced souls have come to help us outwit the dweller, to show us the path home to God. Sometimes we have followed their counsel and example, but often we have ignored it—to our detriment.

We also have our intuition, the gentle prompting of our Higher Self. All it takes to make the connection is a prayer, a quiet moment of meditation, a "listening ear." Yet we tend to rush around in our busy lives, asking other people what they would do, stacking up books and tapes as our sources of enlightenment—and ignoring our own inner resources.

*See the decree "I Cast Out the Dweller-on-the-Threshold," on pp. 308–9.

When we forget to connect with our Higher Self regularly, a sudden setback in circumstances, a negative mind-set, emotional distress or physical pain will tend to override that inner guidance. But often these are the very promptings we need to remind us to reconnect with God and our Higher Self.

When we do not trust our spiritual intuition or consider the advice of elder brothers and sisters on the Path, we can end up in trouble. And we create more negative karma. When we take time to listen to and follow higher counsel, we make good things happen and accrue good karma.

Every good deed creates good karma, which is an automatic deposit in our cosmic bank account. Thus we establish a higher vibration that keeps us in contact with our Higher Self.

We are still learning. We learn as we go. And we also have the example of those who have walked the upward path before us—heroes and heroines, saints, avatars, ascended masters. The lives and teachings of these adepts show us the intricacies of the path of spiritual acceleration. Their walk with God teaches us how to pass our tests.

Soul Testing: Thorny Situations

We are all on the path of initiation. And we move a giant step closer to our victory when we decide to view challenging situations in that light. Everything that happens to us—prickly encounters, stirring experiences, karmic dilemmas, unexpected good fortune or calamity—is a teacher.

Sometimes we pass the test, sometimes we don't. But we can learn from our mistakes. Whenever life doesn't seem to be treating us right, we can take the situation as an impetus to learn a lesson and thereby make progress toward a victory.

Yes, life is challenging, and sometimes it's difficult to welcome those initiations. Isn't it true that we have all faced situations where we couldn't see a single reason to be upbeat or pleasant, and then someone added insult to injury by scolding us for being negative?

We can lift ourselves out of the doldrums by remembering that whatever happens—go-aheads or setbacks, victories or defeats—it's either a karmic deal or a major test. And that includes interactions with difficult people. As El Morya has said, "If the messenger be an ant, heed him." When we view life this way, we move forward in the initiatic process. And we find it a lot easier to bless the human messenger who delivers that bundle of karmic payback.

Earth is a schoolroom, and we are intended to graduate one day. The lessons we learn along life's way propel us from one grade to the next. And inherent in every life circumstance is a key to our soul's victory.

So we do ourselves a favor by maximizing each opportunity. We can ask our Higher Self: How can I be my best self in this situation? What is the lesson for my soul? As we incline our heart and mind to God, we receive inspiration and intuitively sense what to do next. Then we can take enlightened action. This is a great way to pass life's tests!

Give Difficult Moments a Positive Spin

It isn't always easy to stay upbeat in the midst of a challenging circumstance. But we can make the effort to give ourselves, and people we meet, a positive spin anyway.

For example, we can choose to appreciate the finer qualities in ourselves and others. Everyone has a special something, a hidden beauty or uniqueness of soul if we just dig a little to see it. When we verbally appreciate that special quality, we make that person's day—and their answering smile makes our day.

As a child, I discovered that being happy about simple things had a certain infectious quality. My friends had so much fun teasing me about my Pollyanna nature that they too got happy. My intuitively giving difficult experiences a positive spin developed into a sense of humor that has been very helpful in life's prickly moments. That quality has been a boon to me all my life.

If you check in with your soul, you may discover a dancing being of light. If this isn't the case, it's time to develop insight into your soul's predicament. I remember a client of mine, Betty, who found her soul in tears, crying in despair. When she asked what was the matter, her soul responded softly, "I don't think anybody loves me—not even you. And I don't know what to do about it."

This was a wake-up call for Betty, who tended to gloss over her troubles. She realized that it was time for her to listen to, comfort and reassure the wounded part of herself. And she chose to do that in the therapy session. Here is a portion of that dialogue:

Betty touched the heart of the matter when she whispered to her soul, "I want you to know that I do love you, and I'm sorry I haven't been paying more attention to you. I know how much it hurts to feel unloved."

"Do you really love me?" her soul asked hesitantly.

"Yes, I do," Betty responded. "What am I doing that makes you feel unloved?"

"Sometimes you don't act like you love me," her soul responded, sadly and despondently.

"But I really do," Betty insisted gently. "How can I help you feel loved?"

"Remember when we used to look at the stars at night and pretend each one of them was an angel?" her soul asked.

"I felt so much love and light when we did that. And whenever we talk to God, I feel loved."

"That's true, and we haven't done that since I started my new job," Betty responded thoughtfully. "I've been so busy at work that I've neglected our spiritual time together. Is that what's the matter?"

"Yes, and it makes me feel better to hear you say it," her soul answered. "Don't you love God anymore?"

Betty was shocked. "Of course I love God. I've just been kind of overwhelmed at work."

Her soul's response was quick and to the point: "Couldn't God help us with that?"

Betty was silent for several minutes. And she told me it was difficult for her to stay with the pain she was feeling. I encouraged her to stay with her soul, who had such a deep yearning for closeness with God. So Betty resumed the dialogue.

With tears in her voice, Betty responded to her soul, "I feel your pain, my soul, and I am so sorry that I have neglected our time with God. I've missed him too. I thought I felt upset about the new job, but it's really about missing God."

"I get so scared when we don't talk to God," her soul replied. "Remember when we got so far away from God we thought he didn't exist? I don't ever want to go there again. And all those training seminars you're taking—I know they're necessary, but if we leave God out what's it all for?"

"What would I do without you to remind me?" Betty asked, as she hugged herself to hug her soul. "I love you so much."

"I love you too, and it feels really good when you hug me," responded her soul. "I'm okay now, but I'll keep reminding you if you don't mind."

"Absolutely, remind me!" Betty responded. "And let's set a regular time that we talk to God about what's going on in our life. Would you like to do that when we take our walks together?"

"Yes," her soul replied. "That would be perfect."

Betty completed the dialogue by meditating on Jesus and envisioning her soul surrounded by angels of love. When we talked about it afterwards, Betty told me it had been difficult at first, but as she stayed with it, she had felt warmth in her heart.

"When I'm in touch with who I really am, I get that warm feeling," she confided. "It's like I've been pretending I'm okay, and that's gotten me through a lot. But I can't do it alone—I need to feel the presence of God with me. So even though it was hard to listen to the pain of my soul, I'm relieved she told me the truth."

Gradually, through an ongoing process of loving her soul and communing with God on a regular basis, Betty began to feel a glimmer of joy—the first in many years.

This has been my experience with many people. When we listen to our soul and accept that we feel hurt, we make progress in our lives. Why? We are no longer using our energy to hide from ourselves. The realization that it's okay to be real with ourselves is a huge relief. It's the beginning of genuine healing. And when we invite God to help us, everything lightens up.

So when life is tough, be real about it. Take time to feel your feelings and come up with a game plan. Talk to God about it. Love and care for your soul. And when you have a victory, take a few minutes to celebrate, to dance a private jig of joy.

Fanning the flame of joy in your heart ignites happiness in your soul and in others. You experience the truth of the words of the ascended master Saint Germain: "Joy is the motor of life."[10]

The Art of Self-Mastery

Expressing joy doesn't preclude being grounded and relating to other people where they are. Another young client of mine had to learn the difference between joyful and upbeat versus flippant and flighty.

Jodi came to see me because she felt misunderstood by her family. As she told me, "They tell me I'm 'flighty'—that's their favorite word for me. And that really hurts my feelings."

"I can understand how it would," I responded. "Do you know why they think you're flighty?"

"It's because I like to do fun things," she replied quickly, "and my mind moves really fast from one thing to another. I don't like to be stuck in a rut. I'm just spontaneous, but they think I'm being irresponsible."

"Is there any truth to that?" I queried.

Jodi slowed down for a minute. "Well, sometimes I move a little too fast to do a good job of something that takes a lot of time and patience. I suppose that is being kind of irresponsible."

"Okay," I agreed, "that makes sense. What else might seem flighty from their point of view?"

Jodi thought for a moment. "I really can't think of anything else except that I'm just a different kind of person than they are. It feels like they don't accept who I am."

"That's hard, isn't it?" I responded.

"Yes," she sighed. "If your own family can't understand

you, who can?"

"Do your friends see you that way?" I asked.

She quickly said, "No, absolutely not. But then my family think my friends are flighty, too."

Since I knew that Jodi was on a spiritual path, I asked her, "What do you think is the spiritual lesson here?"

She contemplated before replying, "That's a good question. I think it has to do with knowing when I'm really being true to myself versus just doing my own thing in a way that hurts my soul or upsets other people."

"How do you know the difference?" I asked.

Jodi responded, "When I tune into my heart, I know the difference. But when I'm moving fast, I don't always take the time to do that. Maybe that's part of the problem."

I agreed. "That makes sense to me. What could you do about it?"

"Slow down!" she replied with a smile.

I smiled as I responded, "I recognize that one. I've needed to say that to myself periodically all my life."

"Really?" she brightened up. "It's good to know I have company. I guess it takes time and practice."

I agreed, "Yes, it does. I think it's because it is a deep soul lesson for many of us. When we catch ourselves moving too fast or flying too high, even spiritually, we need to slow down and tune into our heart and soul."

Jodi responded, "That's true. I have been flighty if I look at it that way. When I'm excited, I don't take time to tune into my heart and soul. I just kind of leap into action! I guess my family has a point, and I do love them."

"Of course you do," I answered. "So what would you rather do instead of leaping into action?"

"I think I'll put a sign on my mirror that says 'Check in

with your heart and look before you leap!' That would be a good reminder."

"Great," I replied. "What else might you do?"

"Pray," she smiled. "I know the angels and my Higher Self answer my prayers. I just need to shift gears, and it's already happening. I'm feeling good about this, and I can tell my soul is relieved."

Jodi called me several months later to tell me that her prayers and the note on her mirror were working. As she put it, "I'm not totally down to earth yet but my heart and soul feel happy. And it's been a month since anyone in the family called me flighty. That's progress!"

Jodi was experiencing the joy of true self-mastery. And she knew it. As she put it, "It's the greatest joy of all because it's a win-win situation—for myself, my soul and my family."

Jodi's story illustrates the importance of learning to be true to ourselves without alienating our family and friends. We can determine to respect other people's sensitivities while we pursue the fulfillment of our hopes and dreams. We can practice being thoughtful, diplomatic and compassionate in our interactions with others. And we can be practical, down-to-earth, no matter how high we may be flying inside.

The ascended master Morya once remarked that "your spirituality is expressed by your practicality."[11] That is a message to remember—and to live by.

Although most of us would like to live our lives that way, we do not always reckon with the residue we carry from early-life or past-life experiences. Let's look at how that carryover energy influences us at conscious and unconscious levels[12] until we deal with it.

2

Ready or Not, Here I Come!

Let us, then, be up and doing,
With a heart for any fate;
Still achieving, still pursuing,
Learn to labor and to wait.

—HENRY WADSWORTH LONGFELLOW
"A Psalm of Life"

Seeking to fulfill her destiny, our soul entered this lifetime, born as a babe, with a veil of forgetfulness drawn over her cosmic and earthly history. Nestled within sheaths of consciousness were memories of etheric experiences, past lives, earthly lessons learned and others still to be mastered.

As a lightbearer, our soul looked forward to gaining additional mastery, balancing her karmic ledger and fulfilling a higher destiny. However, that eagerness was somewhat tempered by a certain sense of apprehension.

Yes, we knew what we were coming into, but somehow the challenges looked simpler when we were in the etheric retreats, the spiritual schools our souls go to in between lives on earth.

In consultation with spiritual advisors, we considered

our karmic equation and chose our parents. And we said, "I'm ready. Here I come!" And all of a sudden, here we were in a brand-new body, born to our father and mother, having the opportunity, as it were, of a clean white page upon which to write our life story.

Our family was a product of our karma, whether auspicious or problematic. As little ones, we had an aura of innocence and a purity that radiated from within; we were open, dependent and trusting that we'd be loved and nurtured.

However, we carried with us age-old attitudes, ideas, emotional patterns and even physical habits. And these interacted with the patterns of the people around us—our parents, siblings, relatives and friends. These interactions became tests of our soul-mastery. When we passed a test, we redeemed misused energy and expanded our mastery. When we failed a test, we added to our pile of negative karma.

Interestingly, much of the karmic drama in our childhood family is reflected in our natal astrology. And the finer qualities of father, mother, sister and brother mirror back to us the finer qualities of our own soul. In these moments when we glimpse the face of God in another, we are prompted to exercise those qualities in our own life.

Our family's negative aspects are likewise a mirror to us, displaying unwanted qualities and providing us with an opportunity to self-correct and balance karma. The mirror can be either a direct mirror, where we see a negative pattern we are meant to correct in ourselves, or a reverse mirror, where it is our reaction to what we see that we are intended to modify. As the ascended master Serapis Bey says, "What you object to in others may well be the polarization of your own worst fault."[1]

In other words, we see people and events through the

lens of our own consciousness—no matter who or what they may be in their own right. That's why three people reporting an accident may give three different versions. Or a crowd watching a sports event may have widely differing impressions of the players.

We learn a lot about ourselves by paying attention to how we perceive other people. By noticing what we do not like in others and owning those perceptions as the product of our own mind, we create the opportunity for self-mastery. As we continue to confront ourselves in the great mirror of life, we can master the dimensions of self that the mirror reflects. What we fail to master, we magnetize over and over again—until we learn the lesson.

I remember a client of mine, Hal, an insurance agent, who was fixated on what he couldn't stand in his boss. When I asked him what the problem was, he grumbled, "He's totally critical, he's unreasonable and he's a real slob!" He added that the boss must like slobs because he hired so many of them: "Phil can't see the bottom of his claims stack, Brad's sloppy in his presentations and Judy's a gossip queen."

Actually Hal was worried about being behind in his own work and whether his own presentations were up to speed, yet he spent the majority of the therapy hour telling me everyone's faults. When I asked him to look at what he saw in these people as a mirror of himself, Hal was shocked. He was honest enough to admit that he could see himself in every criticism he had made.

Hal worked hard on correcting and improving his own efficiency and professionalism. And he gradually turned his critical nature into an asset by choosing to give kind and helpful input to his co-workers. He put it all in a nutshell with a parting comment after his last therapy session: "I feel really good about this self-improvement project, and it's making a big difference at the office!"

Circumstances as Soul Lessons

Most of us have had some kind of wounding—spiritual, mental, emotional or physical—as we were growing up. Typically, this resulted either from our own impulsive, thoughtless words and actions or from difficult encounters with family members, teachers, friends or acquaintances. People we admired usually measured up pretty well, and we felt good about that. But sometimes they didn't, and we felt hurt, betrayed or violated. Other people occasionally offered answers and helped us out. But when they didn't give us the time of day, we felt belittled and unworthy.

Thus our happy times were intermingled with inauspicious, not-so-happy times. Although we learned our ABCs and schoolwork just fine, we sometimes didn't really understand our life lessons. We reacted to difficult situations that came up in our family or with friends, neighbors or teachers. And we tried to fit in with the ideas, moods and behaviors of people important to us.

The younger we were, the more we took in from our family; like little sponges, we absorbed it all.[2] When we were hurt, we cried or got angry or tried to run away. We didn't like to be hurt; we wanted to be safe. So we watched our older siblings, parents and teachers to try to figure out how to stay safe.

We even tried to protect ourselves and those we loved by mimicking the behavior of grown-ups. Since we were children and not grown up yet, that didn't work out very well. But we kept at it because the adults were our models—and how else could we learn how to take care of ourselves?

I remember Allison, a five-year-old, who tearfully explained to me that when she tried to carry her baby brother down the stairs she was taking him to the kitchen for a snack. Her mother had caught her just before they both toppled off the top step. The mother made the appointment with me because she feared Allison was jealous of her brother. As I explained to the worried mother, Allison wasn't trying to hurt the baby, she was playing "mother."

Thus, as children, we developed our "child-adult"—an internalization of the ways grown-ups in our early life behaved. As we grew up and encountered situations that reminded us of childhood scenes, we either reacted as the hurt child all over again or as the child-adult we had tried to be.

The truth of the matter is, every person and every event in our life has been an opportunity for our soul to balance karma and to learn a necessary lesson. When we view difficult situations as tests of our soul mastery, we usually make good karma and often balance old karmic debts in the process.

Mindful of our origin in God and understanding our painful experiences as soul lessons, we realize the truth of the subtitle of one of my favorite books, *Legacy of the Heart: The Spiritual Advantages of a Painful Childhood*. As author Wayne Muller points out:

> When we are hurt as children, we can quickly learn to see ourselves as broken, handicapped, or defective in some essential way. As we remember with excruciating precision the violations and injustices that devastated our tender hearts, we come to view our childhood as a terrible, painful mistake. At times, the enormity of our childhood sorrow can fill us with a sense of hopelessness, disappointment, and despair....
>
> Yet, at the same time, I have also noted that adults

> who were hurt as children inevitably exhibit a peculiar strength, a profound inner wisdom, and a remarkable creativity and insight. Deep within them—just beneath the wound—lies a profound spiritual vitality, a quiet knowing, a way of perceiving what is beautiful, right, and true....
>
> Seen through this lens, family sorrow is not only a painful wound to be endured, analyzed, and treated. It may in fact become a seed that gives birth to our spiritual healing and awakening.[3]

When you think about it, tough situations, even "tough love," can challenge us to develop our inner strength. Unreasonable situations can show us the way of balance and wisdom. Unloving people in our lives teach us the value of kindness and empathy. When we view our trials with an awakened consciousness, we see the lessons and the opportunity.

Our soul earnestly desires to free herself from negative entanglements, to learn her lessons and express who she really is instead of reacting defensively. At inner levels of our being, we yearn to bond with our Higher Self. We want to serve God and be helpful to others. And, most of all, we want to complete our sojourn on earth and return to the heaven-world.

You may be wondering why, then, do we have traumatic experiences such as physical or sexual abuse, extreme poverty or homelessness, major illness or accident, the breakup of the family, divorce, separation from loved ones? What are we supposed to learn from those experiences? And why does a loving God allow them? These are questions people often ask when doing inner soul work.

As we begin to seek answers, we ponder free will and karma and how they apply to the journey of the soul. We understand that God is ultimate good and that our soul is created in his image—in that same state of purity and goodness.

However, instead of a built-in "be good" mechanism, we have been granted the higher gift of free will—the power to *choose* how we will conduct ourselves. Our parents, siblings, friends and acquaintances, even our "enemies," all have that same power of choice.

And so, our choices result in karma, good or otherwise, which we bear in our body, mind and soul and experience in the happenings in our lives. And sometimes we shoulder an extra pack—world karma—in order to help others. Whether that pack is personal or world karma, courageous souls, even in the modern world, have demonstrated the higher way of bearing the karmic burden. Let's look at the inspiring lives of Anne Sullivan and Helen Keller, two stalwart souls who faced a major dilemma.

The Remarkable Journey of Helen Keller

Helen Keller was born on June 27, 1880, to Arthur and Kate Keller in Tuscumbia, Alabama. She was a healthy baby but suffered a serious illness at the age of nineteen months. When she recovered from the acute condition, she was left deaf and blind.

The child was helpless to understand the outside world and completely dependent on her parents. Yet they could only communicate with her through touch. At times, Helen would scream in frustration and succumb to temper tantrums, a situation that became increasingly difficult for her parents to handle.

When Helen was six years old, her parents took her to see Dr. Alexander Graham Bell, who was an activist in education for the deaf. And as a result of that visit, they met Anne Sullivan, the woman who was to become Helen's dedicated teacher. Anne took on the challenge of trying to help the young child break through the world of silence and darkness that surrounded her.

Anne persevered through many difficulties, attempting to communicate with Helen in every way possible to help her relate to the outside world. Her first major task was simply getting the child to calm down and pay attention instead of indulging in frustrated screaming. Only then could she begin to teach Helen to associate the sense of touch with a particular object.

Anne started tapping out an alphabet code for the name of an object while Helen touched that object. At the beginning, Helen didn't understand and would try to pull her hand away. But one day, in the spring of 1887, a great miracle took place.

Anne and Helen were standing together beside a well. Anne was pumping water into one of the young girl's hands while repeatedly tapping out an alphabet code for w-a-t-e-r in the other. Over and over Anne tapped out the letters as young Helen struggled to break through her world of silent darkness.

All of a sudden, the tapping signal made sense to Helen. She realized that "w-a-t-e-r" meant that cool something flowing over her hand. She began to "see" through touch. The darkness of consciousness lifted on that sunny day in March. And both student and teacher were overjoyed. Before the day was over, Helen had learned 30 words.

After Helen's miraculous break-through, she proved to be a gifted child. She quickly mastered the fingertip alphabet and began to learn how to write. By the end of August of the same year, she knew 625 words.

Helen worked so diligently that in three short years, by the age of ten, she not only knew the manual alphabet but had mastered Braille and could also operate a typewriter. To everyone's joy, Helen progressed so well in developing the faculty of speech that she entered preparatory school when she was sixteen.

Anne Sullivan, her beloved teacher, continued to work with Helen, interpreting lectures and class discussion, all the way through college. In 1904, Helen achieved a glorious victory, graduating cum laude from Radcliffe College.

Helen Keller, the deaf and dumb child, became one of history's most remarkable women. She returned what she had been given by dedicating her life to helping the blind and deaf-blind. She gave lectures throughout the world to improve conditions for others like herself, thought to be beyond human help.

Helen's teacher, Anne Sullivan, will be recorded in history as "the Miracle Worker."[4] And the lives of these two remarkable women remind us that miracles still happen—when we are dedicated, patient and loving, and persevere in our quest.

Helen Keller wrote a poem about her experience that touches heart and soul:

> They took away what should have been my eyes
> (But I remembered Milton's Paradise).
> They took away what should have been my ears,
> (Beethoven came and wiped away my tears).
> They took away what should have been my tongue,
> (But I had talked with God when I was young).
> He would not let them take away my soul—
> Possessing that, I still possess the whole.[5]

Elizabeth Clare Prophet addressed her students about this true story of living love:

> God has shown me that every child that is conceived has a divine plan and a divine design—even if the do-gooders in society claim that the child is "unwanted" or "handi-

capped" and therefore should not be born into this world. The renowned pediatric surgeon and former U.S. Surgeon General Dr. C. Everett Koop says that in his experience disability and unhappiness do not necessarily go together.

He commented once that some of the most unhappy children he's ever known had their physical and mental faculties intact, and yet some of the happiest youngsters have borne burdens that he would find very difficult to bear.

Who are we to say that a life is not worthwhile? Only the soul herself can say. Helen Keller proved that life is worth living and fighting for. How can we ever forget the remarkable determination and the daring of the deaf, dumb and blind girl who overcame the utter darkness of her childhood to become an exceptional author, educator and lecturer?

People who are born into abject poverty and the worst of circumstances often rise to become great leaders and prime movers of the destinies of nations. Look at President Abraham Lincoln, born to uneducated parents and raised in a log cabin in the back woods of Kentucky. And the famous abolitionist leader Frederick Douglas, born and raised as a lowly Negro slave. And American inventor and technological genius Thomas Edison. Did you know that he attended regular school for only three months of his life and was thought by his schoolmaster to be retarded?[6]

When we see such examples, we realize there are forces more compelling than circumstance—the knowledge and drive of soul and spirit that give us direction and impetus. And by free will, each of us chooses our response to karmic circumstances. Helen Keller and Anne Sullivan have blessed all of us by sharing the wisdom they gained from addressing a major karmic challenge with courage. We can make the same choice—or not. It's up to us.

Experimenting, Discovering and Self-Correcting

When we make it a practice to comfort and bless those we meet along life's way, we walk a path of righteousness, the "right use of energy." We balance some bad karma and add to our storehouse of good karma, thereby uplifting our own soul as we help other people. And every decision we make counts. One of the ascended masters, Saint Germain, tells us he earned his ascension by making two million right decisions!

We are on that homeward trek. Many of us are meant to ascend at the end of this lifetime, unless we have a further mission to fulfill in the age of Aquarius. If we do have such a mission, it will likely involve expressing divine love in some creative way.

Spiritually, Aquarians are called to transform all that opposes true love (meaning hard-heartedness, hatred, even mild dislike) through the power of love. In the Aquarian age all of us have the opportunity to become "Aquarian love-conquerors."

Each of us is intended to love, guide and heal our soul through the aftermath of wrong choices made in the past. We are meant to learn our soul lessons, to pray for divine guidance and to be a living example of love to our brothers and sisters of light and those we meet along the way.

In order to make our ascension, we need to resolve all that holds us back from being who we really are as our Higher Self. Yet as we go through crises in our lives, we do make messes in the house of our being. When that happens, we need to clean it up just as we have our children clean up their rooms.

So we make choices, experience the results of those

choices and decide what we need to change. And by doing our best to understand, love and forgive, we touch our pain with love and begin to heal the hurts of our soul.

When we discover and discard false images and beliefs in ourselves, we can replace them with more of an inner knowing of who we really are. We can pray for the Holy Spirit as the violet flame* to transmute our emotional and physical burdens. And we can care for our physical body as the temple of our soul. All of this is our part in the healing of our psyche, our soul. And when we do our part, God's grace enlightens us and propels us all the way Home.

As we do inner soul work, we begin to realize that parts of ourselves from this and other lifetimes, components of our soul, are locked in the unconscious—frozen in time, as it were. Thus we find ourselves drawn repeatedly to certain situations, karmic relationships, traumatic happenings, until we see these events for what they are—cosmic lessons about how we have dealt with energy in the past.

Every problematic circumstance brings us face-to-face with the best and worst in ourselves. When the inner light bulb comes on, we see the situation for what it really is—an opportunity for interior correction and soul healing. The stage is set for our soul to confront ancient and present mistakes and imperfections, even traumatic experiences, and to accelerate her transformational journey.

Molds of Imperfection

Mark and Elizabeth Prophet explain how imperfections are initiated and sustained—until we do something about them.

---

*The violet flame is a high-frequency spiritual energy that transforms negativity into light and gives us a sense of freedom from inner burdens.

The moment man turns his attention from the pure, flowing radiance of his True Self, he forfeits the protection of the light focused through the lens of its perfect image.

Whereas the circle of the Macrocosm [the Body of God and the entire warp and woof of creation] is perfect, hence inviolable, the circle of the microcosm [man as creation within a framework of individuality] is incomplete unless it reflects the circle of the Macrocosm.

The microcosm is intended to mirror the Macrocosm. Thus the transfer of the Real Image to the soul occurs naturally when the soul is allowed to absorb the patterns [that are] released from the plane of the Superconscious Ego in place of those that originate in the plane of the [human] ego.

The invasion of the microcosmic circle can occur only when men relinquish their right to both conscious and subconscious control of their energies and worlds by admitting, in place of the perfect ideas of God, the thoughts and feelings of the mass synthetic consciousness.

Filling, as it were, brightly colored balloons of myriad shapes, these *thought* and *feeling* forms—which can be seen at astral levels by those who are clairvoyant—are actually floating grids and forcefields of the mass mind.

The invasion of the microcosm, then, takes place in the following manner: First, man opens the lens of his consciousness to imperfect images, which are sometimes seen and sometimes felt. Second, he allows his attention to focus upon them, whether consciously or unconsciously.

Third, over his attention flow the energies of the Macrocosm [and these fill] the molds of the synthetic patterns that make his world vulnerable to the influences of a synthetic society. By thus misdirecting the energies

> of the Macrocosm, man sustains imperfection in the microcosm.[7]

We can change these imperfections. We can determine to redeem every erg of negative energy we have emitted and to correct every insulting label we have stamped upon our soul or other people. We can envision who we really are as a son or daughter of God and determine to be that person.

With the clarity born of higher vision, we spot the weeds of negativity midst the flowers of right motive, right thought, right feeling and right action. As we weed and cultivate our garden of consciousness, our inherent spiritual nature begins to flower. And we feel a spark of joy!

Lessons of Unconditional Love

As we get acquainted with who we really are and fan that inner spark of joy, we partner with God in a healing process. We lay claim to the reality of divine love, the antidote to our painful experiences past and present, even back to the womb or perhaps another lifetime.

All of us have gone through many disappointments and hurts, challenges and stalemates, victories and defeats. All of these situations are a part of the fabric of life. Yet each drama, no matter how wounding or disconcerting, has ultimately been a multifaceted lesson of love:

First and foremost, to teach us to love ourselves as children of God even when we make regrettable mistakes.

Second, to help us expand in compassion for others so that we can respond lovingly when people disappoint or challenge us.

Third, to give us a golden opportunity to grow in loving-kindness, whereby we may bless fellow travelers along the way.

However, most of us have a hard time loving all of the people we meet. We know that's our goal, but it's easier said than done. Some people are not exactly lovable—and sometimes we aren't either. How do we love someone who is behaving in a very confrontational or uncooperative way?

We start by realizing that the tests of love are often painful because of the karmic baggage we carry. Yes, it's a wonderful feeling to love someone who loves us back, but what does it take to love someone who snubs us? Or even worse, someone who seems to go out of his way to mistreat us? Or what about loving our enemies?

What it takes is realizing that love is a state of consciousness. And when we are in that consciousness, we love because that is who we are. This is what allowed Jesus to look down from the cross and pray, "Father, forgive them; for they know not what they do."[8]

I remember the story of a missionary in South Africa during the apartheid uprisings whose reservoir of love propelled him beyond the call of duty. All the missionaries had been told to leave because it was a life-threatening situation. But this particular man chose not to leave, not to desert the people he so loved.

As he lay in bed in his hut one night, hostile Africans carrying spears, entered and surrounded him. As they raised their spears to kill him, he simply looked at each of them with deep love. He did not speak or resist. They stared at him, and, one by one, they lowered their spears and left the hut. He was unharmed. Love had conquered fear and hatred.

It takes the same unconditional love that the missionary felt for the Africans to love ourselves unconditionally—in spite of our weaknesses and foibles. When we do this, we accept the temporary flaws in the diamond of our being and find it easier to do the same with others.

How do we learn to love unconditionally? We decide to love ourselves as God loves us—we look upon our soul with gentle eyes; we live and breathe love until it radiates from every pore of our being. And we offer the fruit of love in kindness and compassion to others.

Wayne Muller clearly and poetically describes the beautiful practice of loving our soul as a divine child. He writes:

> We practice truly loving ourselves by learning first to imagine that the God-child is alive and present in the manger of our own heart, within our own body and spirit. Next, we must accept that part of our spiritual practice is to care for that divine child that lives most tangibly within us. If we are gentle, kind, and loving with ourselves, we may begin to see ourselves as God sees us, as a child of light, a child in whom the spirit of God has made its home.
>
> As a young child, we may have been hurt badly, our families may have brought us great suffering, and our hearts may have been broken. The practice of loving kindness insists that we meet this wounded child of God with tenderness and mercy; as God's child, we deserve all the love in the world.[9]

We can heal from painful experiences because memories, thoughts, feelings and bodily reactions are basically energy—and energy can move and change. If we rearrange or transform the energy, the memory fades, the painful thoughts, feelings and bodily sensations melt away.

Bring to mind a hurtful situation from your childhood or youth and remember how you reacted and how you felt. Perhaps you got really angry, tried to defend yourself or struck out at whoever was hurting you. Maybe you ran away, retreated into fantasies of getting even, criticized yourself and collapsed into helpless crying. Or maybe you simply "froze" and did nothing.

Make a note to yourself about that situation—what you thought about it, how you felt and how you reacted at the time. Notice how you feel right now when you remember it. And ready yourself for the meditation on loving-kindness I describe in the next section. This meditation can become a transformational process, a healing journey for your soul.

Transformation through Loving-Kindness

Loving-kindness is a magical concept. It's the kind of love that warms your heart and soul and everyone you encounter. I encourage you to try this step-by-step process to expand the light of loving-kindness within you:

Preparation

1. Take a moment to reflect on that hurtful experience from childhood, youth or adulthood you just remembered—or a different one if you prefer.
2. Allow the scene to come fully to mind. Notice your thoughts, "How could anyone be so cruel and hurtful? I was so little and vulnerable." Or "It was all my fault. I don't deserve to be forgiven." Or "It wasn't fair. Why did I always get picked on?"
3. Pay attention to your feelings, e.g., being hurt, helpless, frustrated, sad, afraid, angry, despondent, ashamed, having a sense of injustice, feeling unlovable, unworthy, lonely, and so forth.
4. Notice any tension or physical discomfort in your body. Whatever uncomfortable sensation you have right now is likely related to the memory.

5. Jot a note to yourself about that painful situation and the accompanying thoughts, feelings and physical sensations. Now you are ready to do a meditation for the spiritual healing of your heart and soul.

Meditation on Loving-Kindness

1. Close your eyes, clear your mind and take several slow, deep breaths. Imagine yourself as a bodhisattva of kindness,* a gentle being radiating brotherly love and magnanimity. See yourself seated under a magnificent tree in a beautiful garden. Center yourself in quietness and an inner sense of loving-kindness.

2. Envision brilliant white light flooding the garden, immersing and uplifting you. Feel the presence of angels and elementals (nature spirits).

3. Touch the area of your chest where you feel your heart beating (a little to the left of the center of your chest). Notice the gentle thump, thump, thump of the heartbeat as you remain attuned to the glorious white light.

4. Focus on your breathing as you continue to bask in the light and remain aware of your heartbeat.

5. Welcome the peaceful presence of Christ Jesus, Kuan Yin, Buddha Maitreya[10] or another master of your choice. Ask the master to guide your soul and teach you the art of loving-kindness.

6. Bring to mind the painful experience. Offer loving-kindness, understanding and blessing to the younger part of you in that upsetting scene.

---

*A bodhisattva is one who is selflessly dedicated to helping people on earth achieve enlightenment—in this case, by embodying the virtue of loving-kindness.

7. Notice your feelings and physical sensations as you love and comfort yourself and touch with gentleness the pain of your soul.
8. Reframe the old memory: See the situation as a cosmic teacher and yourself as an aspiring student seeking to learn the lesson.
9. Ask your Higher Self, What is the lesson my soul needs to learn? And listen for the still, small voice of your intuition to respond.
10. Forgive yourself and whoever may have been the instrument of your pain.
11. Envision yourself and everyone in that karmic situation understanding their lessons, forgiving and moving on.
12. Take whatever time you need to complete your experience. Breathe a prayer of gratitude, gently bring yourself back to the present and write a few notes about the experience.

This meditation on loving-kindness is a quiet and beautiful way to heal uncomfortable memories. As you sit as a bodhisattva of kindness in the garden of higher consciousness—observing your feelings and reactions, loving, accepting and forgiving yourself and others—you begin to understand and to master the soul lessons inherent in the experience.

Invoking Light for Transformation

Complete your healing experience by visualizing and affirming radiant white light for your transformation. You might like to give Kuthumi's "I AM Light" decree as a powerful affirmation of your divine essence. (When you say "I AM," you are saying "God in me is.")

I AM LIGHT

I AM light, glowing light,
Radiating light, intensified light.
God consumes my darkness,
Transmuting it into light.

This day I AM a focus of the Central Sun.
Flowing through me is a crystal river,
A living fountain of light
That can never be qualified
By human thought and feeling.
I AM an outpost of the Divine.
Such darkness as has used me is swallowed up
By the mighty river of light which I AM!

I AM, I AM, I AM light;
I live, I live, I live in light.
I AM light's fullest dimension;
I AM light's purest intention.
I AM light, light, light
Flooding the world everywhere I move,
Blessing, strengthening, and conveying
The purpose of the kingdom of heaven![11]

To me, this decree says it all. We are indeed outposts of the Divine, and the light of the Almighty is the antidote to all darkness, within or without. Invoking that light raises our consciousness, which is key to our successful return to the heaven-world. I give this decree when I need to buoy up my consciousness. I visualize brilliant white light all around me and repeat it three or nine times—or more!

We can also invoke specific vibrations of light (which appear on the color spectrum) for transformation and enlightenment. And ascended masters who are guardians of that particular dimension of God's light will respond to our call.

The violet flame, for example, is a spiritual light that appears as violet on the color spectrum. It is known in mystical teachings as the "cosmic eraser" or "universal solvent" because it transforms negative energies into pure light. Violet-flame angels and masters, such as Saint Germain and Kuan Yin, release the violet light when you give a simple prayer from your heart, such as:

> Beloved violet-flame angels, beloved Saint Germain and Kuan Yin, I call for the violet light to transform all negative energy in me into the purity of who I really am —a radiant child of God. I accept your loving assistance, and I send you my love and gratitude. And in accordance with God's will, I ask for this blessing to be given to all of God's people everywhere.

After your prayer, I suggest you give a mantra to the violet flame. Here is one that my clients find very useful to clear emotional debris and affirm the essence of their spiritual being:

> I AM a being of violet fire,
> I AM the purity God desires.

You can repeat this mantra over and over while visualizing yourself bathed in beautiful violet light. This is a spiritual method of transmuting (transforming) the burdens of your soul and spirit.

Another kind of spiritual light is a brilliant blue, which you can visualize and invoke by calling to the cosmic being Astrea. She will respond by wielding a blue-fire sword at inner levels to cut you free from old attachments and accumulated debris. You can give this prayer, or one of your own, as a fiery fiat:[12]

> Mighty Astrea, wield your cosmic circle and sword of blue flame to cut me loose and set me free from all density and negativity and ______________________
> ______[name whatever burdens you wish to be free of]______.

This fiat invokes the blue-fire power of God. Repeat it three or nine times as you envision a ring of blue-white fire around your aura and a blue-flame sword cutting you free from the burden of unreality. Coupled with your own faith and determination, God can free you from distressing energy.

Archangel Michael, defender of the faith and protector of the soul, also releases blue fire to guard us from negative energy, even physical danger. I remember a time a friend and I were driving in the mountains during a snowstorm. Suddenly, the car slid completely off the road and into a ravine deep with snow.

My friend and I both shouted to Archangel Michael as she floored the gas pedal, and miraculously the car zipped back up that steep, slippery slope onto the road. Although somewhat shaken, we kept right on driving. The whole episode took place in less than a minute. If Archangel Michael hadn't intervened to give us a blue-fire "push," our car would surely have turned over or been stuck in the snow.

Archangel Michael is a friend to all travelers. You can call to him to protect you and others when you are traveling in a vehicle or even when you are jogging or hiking. Here are two mantras you can give to invoke Archangel Michael's blue-fire protection:

TRAVELING PROTECTION

Lord Michael before, Lord Michael behind,
Lord Michael to the right, Lord Michael to the left,
Lord Michael above, Lord Michael below,
Lord Michael, Lord Michael wherever I go!
I AM his love protecting here!
I AM his love protecting here!
I AM his love protecting here!

I AM PRESENCE, THOU ART MASTER

I AM Presence, Thou art Master,
I AM Presence, clear the way!
Let thy light and all thy power
Take possession here this hour!
Charge with victory's mastery,
Blaze blue lightning, blaze thy substance!
Into this thy form descend,
That perfection and its glory
Shall blaze forth and earth transcend.[13]

When we invoke the light of protection, we clear the way for safe passage. The blue fire not only protects us, it also strengthens our will and clears our mind. We are in better command of ourselves, make wiser decisions and follow through more effectively. And we relate to others more authentically.

The Victory of the Ascension

Ultimately, when our soul ascends at the end of her sojourn on earth (the timing determined by our spiritual progress), our inner burdens drop away and we know ourselves as the magnificent beings of light that God created us to be.

Serapis Bey, hierarch of the Ascension Temple in the etheric realm over Luxor, Egypt, describes our appearance once we win the victory of the ascension:

> Although the form of an individual may show signs of age prior to his ascension, . . . all of these signs will change and . . . the physical appearance of the individual will be transformed into the glorified body. The individual ascends, then, not in an earthly body but in a glorified spiritual body into which the physical form is changed on the instant by total immersion in the great God flame. . . .
>
> The blood in the veins changes to liquid golden light; the throat chakra glows with an intense blue-white light; the spiritual eye in the center of the forehead becomes an elongated God flame rising upwards. The garments of the individual are completely consumed, and he takes on the appearance of being clothed in a white robe—the seamless garment of the Christ. Sometimes the long hair of the Higher Mental Body [the Christ Self] appears as pure gold on the ascending one. Then again, eyes of any color may become a beautiful electric blue or a pale violet.
>
> These changes are permanent. And the ascended one is able to take his light body with him wherever he wishes or he may travel without the glorified spiritual body. Ascended beings can, and occasionally do, appear upon earth as ordinary mortals, . . . resembling the people of earth and moving among them for cosmic purposes. This Saint Germain did after his ascension when he was known as the Wonderman of Europe.[14]

3

Setting Sail on a Healing Journey

O we can wait no longer,
We too take ship O soul,
Joyous we too launch out on trackless seas,
Fearless for unknown shores.

—WALT WHITMAN
Leaves of Grass

When we embark on the deep soul healing that propels us toward our ascension, our first ports are early-life experiences because they were formative. They set the sail for our soul's journey in this life. We remember good moments with a happy heart, but difficult moments bring tears to our eyes.

In working with people over many years, I have learned that the best way to heal early-life trauma is to transform those hurtful memories. How? By facing them squarely and creating a healing experience for your heart and soul. You can do that by lovingly fathering, mothering and mentoring your soul, your inner child, as you call to mind those painful experiences.

Inner child work has become popular over the past twenty years. It's a therapeutic method of working with the experiences of our younger self through imagery and dialogue. In this work we guide, comfort and help to heal younger parts of ourselves from the residue of hurtful events that lies unresolved in the subconscious or unconscious.

I equate the inner child with the soul. I have learned through many years of psychotherapy practice that disturbing thoughts, feelings and habit patterns often arise from our soul's painful encounters. These can surface from childhood, teenage or adult traumas in this or past lives.

I'd like to walk you through what I do in my therapy room so that you can follow a similar spiritual-psychological process. My clients find this process valuable in resolving spiritual, mental, emotional and physical trauma—and moving on with their lives.

In preparation for healing work, I offer prayers for protection and guidance and ask the Higher Self of each of us to help us in the healing process. Next, my client chooses three heroes or heroines, saints or sages, bodhisattvas or ascended masters to be role models. Psychologically, these beings represent the client's ego ideal. Their role in the therapy process is to help the client to father, mother and mentor his or her soul.

You might like to try it. Choose as *Father* a spiritual or heroic figure you view as strong, wise and honorable; as *Mother* one who is gentle, intuitive and loving; as *Mentor* one who is discerning, resourceful and patient. You will be calling upon their finest qualities to assist you in the healing of your soul.

They have also walked the earth and faced trials and dilemmas similar to those you struggle with today. And their wisdom and example can help you to be the mature adult—the strong father, loving mother and resourceful mentor to your soul.

At inner levels of your being, your chosen role models represent the qualities of the threefold flame, your spark of divinity. Father represents the fiery-blue power plume, Mother represents the glowing-pink love plume and Mentor represents the radiant-yellow wisdom plume. That spiritual flame is your soul's contact with her Source.

Take a few moments now to choose your Father, Mother and Mentor. And make a note to yourself as to why you chose each one. What are his or her special qualities? Write down what comes to mind.

Now I'll let you in on a secret, one you may have already guessed. The special qualities of your role models are attributes you already have—either developed as a part of your character and personality or as seed qualities sown at inner levels. You recognize them in people you admire because they are a reflection of your best self. Nurturing and bringing them to full bloom in your own life is a fulfilling process.

When we are transforming negative attitudes, thoughts, feelings or habits, we benefit from the example of enlightened ones. By developing their superior qualities in ourselves, we make real a higher vision for our own spirit and soul—for example, our spirit as an eagle soaring to the heavens, our soul as a bluebird of happiness nesting in our heart.

Schematic of the Psyche (Soul)

I often use Piero Ferrucci's schematic of the psyche to illustrate the compartments of the psyche, or soul. Ferrucci translated complex concepts, originally developed by Roberto Assagioli, into a common vernacular that all of us can understand and apply. The following diagram and commentary come from Ferrucci's excellent book *What We May Be: Techniques for Psychological and Spiritual Growth.*

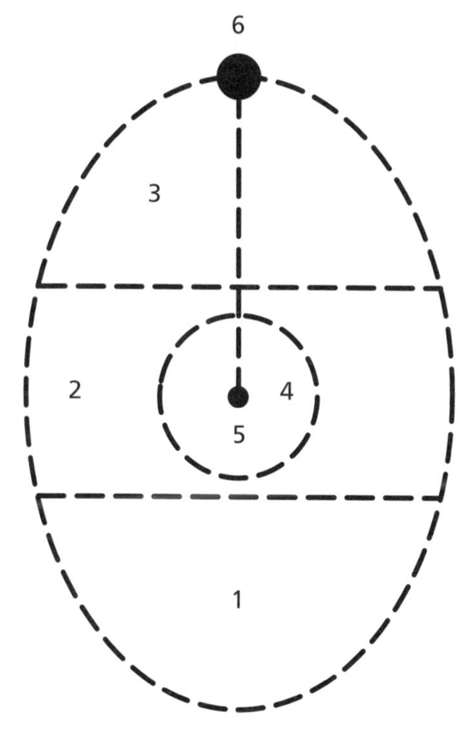

FIGURE 1. Our Psyche

Assagioli's so-called "egg diagram" (Figure 1) represents our total psyche. The three horizontal divisions of the oval stand for our past, present and future. All three are active in us, although in different ways. The *"lower unconscious"* (1) mainly represents our personal psychological past in the form of repressed complexes and long-forgotten memories.

As we have seen in the preceding chapter, if we wish to consciously encourage our growth we need to investigate our lower unconscious. Otherwise, it may be the source of trouble, storing repressed energy, controlling our actions, and robbing us of our freedom.

The *middle unconscious* (2) is where all skills and states of mind reside which can be brought at will into our *field of consciousness* (4), which—for you at this moment—is this book and the words you are reading.

Our evolutionary future comprises the states of being, of knowing, and of feeling which we call the *superconscious* (3). In the words of Assagioli, the *superconscious* is the region from which "we receive our higher intuitions and inspirations—artistic, philosophical or scientific, ethical 'imperatives' and urges to humanitarian and heroic action. It is the source of the higher feelings, such as altruistic love; of genius and of the states of contemplation, illumination, and ecstasy."[1] The exploration of the superconscious is one of our great tasks.

The distinction between the "lower" and the "higher" unconscious, or superconscious, is developmental, not moralistic. The lower unconscious merely represents the most primitive part of ourselves, the beginner in us, so to speak. It is not *bad,* it is just *earlier.* Conversely, the superconscious constitutes all that we still can reach in the course of our evolution. It is not, however, a mere abstract possibility, but a living reality, with an existence and powers of its own.

Our psyche is not isolated. It is bathed in the sea of what Carl Jung called the collective unconscious (7). In Jung's words, the collective unconscious is "the precondition of each individual psyche, just as the sea is the carrier of the individual wave."[2] Notice that all lines are dotted to signify that no rigid compartments impede interplay among all levels.

Who experiences all these levels? The *self* does. In the early stages of human development, awareness of the self is nonexistent. For most of us, it now exists in a more or less veiled and confused way. Our task is to gain

> experience of it in its pure state as the personal self, or "*I*" (5).
>
> The personal self is a reflection or an outpost of the Transpersonal Self (6)—enough to give us a sense of centeredness and identity. It lives at the level of individuality, where it can learn to regulate and direct the various elements of the personality. Awareness of the personal self is a precondition for psychological health.
>
> Identification with the Transpersonal Self is a rare occurrence—for some individuals, the culmination of years of discipline; for others, a spontaneous extraordinary experience. It was described in ancient times with the Sanskrit words *sat-chit-ananda*: being-consciousness-bliss. The Transpersonal Self, while retaining a sense of individuality, lives at the level of universality, in a realm where personal plans and concerns are overshadowed by the wider vision of the whole. The realization of the Transpersonal Self is the mark of spiritual fulfillment.
>
> Personal and Transpersonal Self are in fact the same reality experienced at different levels: our true essence beyond all masks and conditionings.[3]

Ferrucci's theory offers an excellent description of the soul in relation to the Real Self (Higher Self). And he describes our sense of identity—the personal self, the "I"—as an outpost of the Real Self. Our Real Self, the Transpersonal Self, is who we are beyond the veils of karma and mists of unreality and with whom we identify when we reunite with our spiritual essence.

Through transformational work,[4] we can access and transcend lower levels of consciousness. We can probe the depths of our unconscious records to resolve the residue of trauma our soul has experienced during her journey in time and space.

We are usually in touch with the middle unconscious, whether we realize it or not. I equate this concept with the subconscious—those thoughts and feelings that are just on the tip of the tongue, as we say.

What Ferrucci calls the field of consciousness is our conscious awareness of our thoughts, feelings and reactions, moment by moment, as well as of daily happenings and interactions with family, friends, community and national and planetary events.

The superconscious is the arena of our highest dreams and aspirations: the realm of inspirational images, creative ideas and practical, often ingenious, ways of making them happen. From the superconscious we generate enthusiasm, hope and compassion for all living beings. When we access this higher realm of consciousness, we are partnering with our Higher Self.

Healing in the Secret Chamber of the Heart

Think of a moment in your life that was hurtful. This scene could involve the same kind of painful encounter you worked with before but at a different time. Or this could be a completely different drama.

Whatever comes to mind, take a moment to go within and remember what happened in this second scenario. Remember the thoughts and feelings you had and the actions you took. Jot a note to yourself about what was happening, what you thought and felt, and what you did.

This time we will do our healing in the secret chamber of the heart. What exactly is the secret chamber of the heart? It is a sacred inner room, a space of beauty and holiness, a chamber of great light and peace where our spiritual flame of life, the threefold flame of divine love, wisdom and power (a radiant pink, yellow and blue), burns upon the altar of our inner being.

Saint Germain describes the secret chamber of the heart this way:

> Within the heart there is a central chamber surrounded by a forcefield of such light and protection that we call it a cosmic interval. This chamber is separated from Matter, and no probing could ever discover it. It occupies, simultaneously, not only the third and fourth dimensions but also other dimensions unknown to man. Thus the sacred altar of the heart serves as the connecting point of the mighty crystal cord of Light that descends from your God Presence to sustain the beating of your physical heart, giving you life, purpose, and cosmic integration.[5]

Although the threefold flame is ethereal rather than physical, some have seen that inner flame. Lord Lanto, master of the golden ray of illumination, determined that he would so expand his threefold flame that his disciples would be able to see it burning through his physical chest. And they did! We can pray to this ascended master to help us balance and expand our own threefold flame. As we do so, we become more loving, wise and strong in our higher convictions and benevolent actions.

The secret chamber of the heart is a protected and safe place to do healing work with our soul. Visualize the secret chamber as a beautiful inner chapel radiating glorious rainbows of light that emanate from the threefold flame burning on the altar in that sacred place. Your Higher Self is tending the flame at the altar and is always ready to welcome you.

Outside the chapel, envision a secret garden with beautiful trees, green grass, healing plants and fragrant flowers. And just beyond the garden, you catch a glimpse of a shining-white beach and the shimmering ocean. You can do your healing work in the chapel, the garden, on the beach or in the ocean—whatever setting seems most healing for your soul.

If you do not find it easy to visualize, you might simply imagine or sense the beauty and holiness of the secret chamber as the sacred center of your being. (Some people see images, while others just sense them.) Or you might remember a special place of your own that symbolizes that sacred center.

If you have some artist in you, you might draw or paint a picture of the secret chamber as you imagine it so that you will have an outer focus as a reminder.

Your secret chamber is a safe place for your soul to meet with your spiritual helpers—those enlightened beings you choose to be the protectors, luminaries and lovers of your soul. You can bring to them your hurts, your weaknesses and disappointments, your hopes and dreams.

Matthew and the Gang

I recall Matthew, an individual in one of my workshops, who experienced a remarkable healing in the secret chamber of the heart. Matthew's spiritual background was in Eastern traditions; thus, he chose Maitreya, Kuan Yin and Krishna as his spiritual helpers.

Maitreya is revered as the Buddha of loving-kindness, Kuan Yin as the bodhisattva of mercy and Krishna as the supreme personality of the Godhead. In the visualization of healing his soul, Matthew cast Maitreya as the loving father, Kuan Yin as the nurturing mother and Krishna as the mentor, representing his Higher Self.

What Matthew wanted to heal was his memory of being beaten up by a gang when he was in his early twenties. He had landed in the hospital with a concussion and broken ribs. At that time, he was a member of another gang who picked the fight in the first place. After that painful experience, Matthew quit drinking and separated out from gang life. However, the memory of the trauma stayed with him and still gave him the shudders some fifteen years later.

In the workshop, Matthew visualized the gang scene all over again, but this time he had Krishna at his side. And he imagined both gangs being immobilized by the light of Krishna. Krishna delivered a chastening to all of them, including Matthew, and exhorted them to lay down their weapons and become warriors of the Spirit.

In imagery, Matthew took the whole bunch to the secret chamber of his heart, where they experienced the loving-kindness of Buddha Maitreya. One by one, the young men took a vow of loving-kindness, and the two gangs knelt before the great Buddha. He received their hatred and anger, which they gave as a peace offering, and directed each one to ensoul loving-kindness.

Matthew's imagery continued with the bodhisattva Kuan Yin, who offered him the opportunity to extend mercy and forgiveness to the gang members. As he did that, he felt a gradual dissolving of the painful experience. After completing the workshop, he felt relief from the burden that had troubled him all those years.

Whether or not the other gang members repented in real life isn't the point. Matthew was redeeming what he had taken in from the gangs so many years ago. They had become phantoms of the mind, continuing to threaten him through memories and nightmares.

Matthew transformed his own fear and pain through the imagery work of accepting Krishna's counsel and Maitreya's loving-kindness. He completed his transformational experience by inwardly offering Kuan Yin's gift of mercy and forgiveness to the gang members and to himself.

Matthew followed up his workshop experience with decrees and mantras to the violet flame for the transmutation of any leftover debris. And he began a daily practice of sending *metta,* loving-kindness, first to his benefactors (the masters in the imagery exercise), second to a friend or loved one, third to an acquaintance, and fourth to the former enemy, the gang members.

Here is the classical pattern of *metta* phrases. (When sending *metta* to another person, substitute their name for "I.")

May I be free from danger.
May I have mental happiness.
May I have physical happiness.
May I have ease of well-being.[6]

Guided Imagery for Healing the Soul

With Matthew's experience as introduction, I offer the following guided imagery exercise in the secret chamber of the heart. This can be a healing journey for a wounded aspect of your soul that you embark on through a process of imagery and dialogue. If whatever you want to heal doesn't seem to connect with events in this life, consider the possibility that you are in contact with a hurtful event from a past life.

Begin by giving this prayer or one of your own before doing your imagery work:

> In the name of the Christ, I call to Archangel Michael to protect my soul during this healing work. I invoke the violet transmuting flame, the action of the Holy Spirit, to transform the old energy patterns, to free

myself and everyone concerned from all that would prevent our souls from being the pure sons and daughters of God that we were created to be.

I call for a beam of divine light to illumine the way to the door of the secret chamber of my heart. I call for the presence of beloved Kuthumi, master psychologist, to be with me, and I ask my Higher Self to take dominion over this healing process. I invite and accept the presence of my Father, Mother and Mentor helpers. And I am grateful for your loving assistance. Amen.

1. Seat yourself, hands in your lap with palms facing upward, feet flat on the floor. Or sit in the lotus position if you prefer. Center in your heart, alert, awake and relaxed as you invoke the presence of your Higher Self and Father, Mother and Mentor.

2. Tune into the beating of your physical heart and imagine your breath flowing through the heart. Focus upon a beautiful, peaceful scene in nature as you silently ask God to help you with this alchemy of healing your soul.

3. Visualize yourself walking down a pathway of brilliant light and approaching the door to the secret chamber of your heart. Knock softly upon the door. Your Higher Self opens the door and welcomes you.

   Bow before the Christ light, the threefold flame burning upon the sacred altar in this inner chamber of light. Greet beloved Kuthumi and your helpers who have come to assist you in your inner work.

4. Notice the four chairs on the opposite side of the room, facing a life-size screen. Sit in one of the center chairs, your Father and Mother helpers on one side

and your Mentor on the other. Kuthumi will tend the screen.

5. Remember the hurt you felt during that painful scene. Find the place in your body where it resonates.

6. Ask Kuthumi to project the drama that wounded your soul upon the screen and to bring the details to your remembrance. Let the experience unfold as you remember it.

7. Allow yourself to resonate to the hurt, the thoughts and feelings of your soul. Let the tears flow. And determine to make this a rescue mission, a healing experience for your soul.

8. Envision yourself as the loving adult entering the scene to help your soul. Ask your Father, Mother and Mentor to accompany you on this rescue mission.

9. See yourself and your inner helpers supporting, comforting and reassuring your soul. Give yourself a lot of love and a big hug.

10. Instruct the people hurting you in this scene: Explain that what they are doing is wounding to your soul. Tell them this is an opportunity to help your soul heal from this hurtful experience.

    Notice if they seem to be sorry or to be asking for forgiveness. Ask God to help you forgive them. If they do not seem penitent, ask the angels to take them to a spiritual retreat for further instruction.

11. Pray for forgiveness for anything you did wrong at the time. Teach your soul to say, "I am sorry, and

I ask God for forgiveness." Envision your soul accepting the return current of God's forgiveness. Stay with it until you feel complete.

12. Thank your inner helpers for their love and support. Conclude by inviting your soul to remain in the secret chamber of your heart with your Higher Self or the master you choose.

When you are ready, open your eyes and do some drawing or writing about your experience. You might draw a picture with your nondominant hand (the one you do not normally use) to describe your feelings intuitively. Respond by writing words of love and support with your dominant hand.

Remind your soul that whenever you are needed, you will be there to help. And give a violet-flame mantra to transform any residue of the record. When you feel complete with the experience, take a break: go for a walk, turn on some uplifting music or take a nap.

Role-Playing with Your Soul

Let's try one more way to resolve a disturbing experience: role-playing with your soul. Your soul is the inner infant, child, adolescent or young adult—whichever part of you carries the pain. If you have a stuffed animal, doll or a picture of yourself at that age, now is the time for it. These representations of yourself will stand in for your soul at the time of the experience.

If you prefer, you might use your jacket, purse or pillow to represent your younger self in the role-playing. Or simply place two chairs facing each other, one for you as the loving adult and one for the younger part of you. Using a doll, stuffed animal, personal article, pillow, picture or separate chair establishes a boundary between the adult and the younger, wounded self. You will be dialoguing about whatever the hurt part of you wants to talk about.

Okay, ready to try it? Begin by centering in your heart and asking your Higher Self to help you be the wise, strong, loving adult. Hold the stuffed animal, doll, pillow, personal article or picture on your knee facing you. Or place it in the chair across from you. Greet your younger self and ask three questions:

How old are you today?

What would you like to talk about?

What can I do for you right now?

Each time you ask a question, shift roles and respond as who you were at that earlier stage of life. Simply say your thoughts and feelings as if you were that younger you. (As you speak for the younger part of yourself, hold the stuffed animal, doll or picture against your stomach, facing out. If you are using the two-chair method, switch chairs so that you sit where your younger self has been sitting. And imagine your grown-up self in the other chair.)

As the younger self, verbalize your hurt feelings. And as the adult, respond as the loving, wise, strong self, your best approximation of your Higher Self. Remember that your goal is to heal your wounded self. Follow your heart and intuition, and do what you feel prompted to do.

A few tips: As the loving adult your goal is to listen, understand, comfort and say the truth, kindly and gently, no matter what your younger self says or does. As you continue to be supportive, he or she will begin to trust you enough to share more. If you get stuck, call to your inner helpers to assist you and ask your younger self, "What can

I do for you right now?" Then do whatever that is to the best of your ability.

As you go through this process, empathize with the thoughts and feelings of the younger you, whether they are pleasant or unpleasant. You are here to understand, to give comfort and guidance, and most importantly, to be a loving, caring listener.

Once you feel complete with the dialogue, tell your younger self that you appreciate the sharing. Make a commitment to talk again at a definite time. Invite that one to come to your safe place, the secret chamber of your heart, to be with your Higher Self, the angels and your divine helpers.

To follow up this inner work, imagine what you might be like today if you had had perfect nurturing in your infancy, childhood, youth or young adulthood. Write a page about this ideal nurturing situation. How might you re-parent yourself today?

What If Your Soul Is Hiding Out?

Sometimes we run into a snag because our soul will not talk to us. A very young child part may simply be frightened, and if we are gentle and loving, the little one will finally speak up. However, at times our soul is too angry to verbalize. It's an attitude of "I'm mad and I'm not talking!" Even then, under the anger is the hurt.

I remember a client who had that experience. Susan had to work steadily with her soul for three weeks before she could even make the contact. Her soul was hiding out. And when she finally came out, boy, was she mad—mad at being hurt, mad at being ignored, mad at being neglected. It took some time for Susan's soul to trust her outer self enough to reveal her deeper pain.

Resolving anger is a gradual process because there are layers of mind-sets and emotions. And nearly always accompanying the anger are elements of pride and hidden pain. The soul gets hurt, hides out, moves into "They can't do this to me!" and sooner or later erupts with anger.

At first when someone tells us they wish we would stop being angry, we tend to go through the denial bit: "Who me, angry?" Or if we take the situation seriously, we tend to blame someone else for our angry reaction. If we know that we were at least partly to blame, we feel even worse. Pretty soon we move into the victim stance: "I couldn't help it, that guy was just plain mean!"

We rev up righteous indignation: "It's not fair!" Here comes the anger again. But instead of letting it run its trip, we can determine to heal that knee-jerk reaction. We can recognize that though we were hurt, we have survived. Somebody doing something mean or unkind did not destroy us. We're still here.

At the moment we realize all this, we have an opportunity to do a turnaround. We can remind ourselves, "If I lived through this before, I can probably live through it again." We swallow our pride, invoke spiritual help and turn our attention to healing our wounded soul. Ultimately, as we heal from within, we begin to handle ourselves with more finesse, what the ascended masters refer to as "Christly aplomb."

As we shift our perspective, we are often able to acknowledge that the people who hurt us may have been doing the best they could. Wouldn't we like someone to give us the benefit of the doubt when we are hurt and angry? We would feel so much better if someone said, "Well, you must have been really hurt. And I know you were doing the best you could."

Let's take the cue and give others the benefit of the doubt. When we are generous, understanding and kind, we usually get a more considerate response from others. But even if that doesn't happen, we can feel good about our own self-mastery.

Dialoguing with Your Angry Self

A special aspect of inner soul work is dialoguing with the angry self and addressing the pain that underlies the anger. In my experience, this kind of pain frequently tracks back to traumatic events in our past, sometimes to ancient experiences.

The first step is to ask your Higher Self and divine helpers to assist you in the healing process. Make it a point to be centered in a loving, wise, strong adult stance. And try to embody the higher qualities of your divine helpers as you dialogue with your indignant self.

Think of your angry self as your wounded spirit, your injured masculine side. And once you are centered, encourage that part of you to talk about his anger and the underlying wound. Tell him, "I want to understand and help you. I'd like to know how old you are and what you are feeling right now." (You can do this through talking or writing.) Dialogue back and forth until you have an understanding of what the anger and pain are all about.

In the course of the dialogue, let your wounded masculine know that you understand how difficult the situation was for him and how upsetting it felt. He didn't know what to do and nobody was there to understand or help. Ask him, "What can I do for you right now?"

Switch roles and respond as the angry self. And whatever he says, remember it comes out of pain. Keep going with the dialogue. Always love and reassure, no matter what happens. You might say, "You aren't alone anymore because I am standing with you in that tough situation. I understand you are hurt and angry. I want you to know that I love you and I can help you. And our spiritual helpers will help us get through the pain. Tell me what happened, why you are so upset."

As you talk back and forth about the anger, you may find yourself drawn into the drama. It's difficult to stay one step removed when you are dealing with angry feelings. But stay with it. If you continue to be kind, interested and comforting, your angry self will gradually feel safe enough to let down the defenses and open up—and you will begin to understand the underlying pain.

When there is a lull in the dialogue, offer assistance: "I hear your anger and pain. How can I help you right now?" Listen carefully to the response, and be compassionate. If you aren't sure what to do, pray for guidance. And do what you believe your Higher Self or the angels would do.

A tip: Your job is to understand exactly what is going on so you can outwit the dweller that is provoking your spirit into misusing power. Once that masculine side feels understood by you, the anger will diminish and he will want to heal the pain.

Ultimately, as the anger and pain subside and you feel more at peace, ask your masculine side one more time: "Is there anything else you would like me to do for you right now?" Follow through by responding constructively to his request. Conclude the dialogue by saying, "I love you, I am committed to helping you and we are going to get through this together." Give yourself a bear hug, set a time to talk again and bring the interaction to a close.

To seal this work, envision walking with your masculine self to the secret chamber of your heart. Say good-bye and entrust your spirit to the care of your inner helpers. Make it a point to follow through with another dialogue at the time you set. This is how you build trust.

Healing the Ancient Pain of an Atlantean Soul

As you tend the wounds you have experienced in this life, traumatic experiences from previous lifetimes may surface. I'll give you an example from my practice:

Jeff, a thirty-year-old computer consultant, spent many weeks dialoguing, mostly listening, to his angry self's diatribe about everything, including God. He had come to therapy because he was getting in trouble at work with his trigger-happy temper. He had finally reached the point of wanting to get to the root of it.

He began by talking to who he thought was his four-year-old in this life (a time when he remembered having temper tantrums). He made some progress but soon realized that the expression of the pain was not entirely childlike. Some of it was more like the pain of a grown man.

In our next session, we changed tactics. Jeff asked the four-year-old part of himself if the pain went back before this life. At that point, his ancient self opened up, saying sarcastically, "Of course, it does! It's sure taken you long enough to figure it out!"

Jeff was a bit shocked but determined to persevere. "What happened to you? It sounds like it was really painful. Whatever it was, I'd like to help."

After a long silence, his ancient self responded, "I don't know if anyone can help me. I think God hates me."

"Why would you think that?" Jeff responded.

"You're pretty stupid or you would have figured it out," was the sullen reply.

Jeff wasn't sure what to do. He prayed and called on all his reserves to be steady and patient until this ancient self trusted him enough to open up. He replied, "I appreciate that you're talking to me, and I hear that you're hurting. I really want to help."

Silence for several minutes, but Jeff could feel a twisting in his gut and tears behind his eyes. I encouraged him to stay with it.

Finally his ancient self responded, "It hurts like heck to even touch the memory, but I appreciate that you asked. Do you really want to know?"

"Yes," replied Jeff. "I want to know what hurt you so bad. And I'd like to help."

"Well, I don't think you can do anything about it, but maybe I'd feel better getting it out," his ancient self said sadly. "It goes back to Atlantis, if you know what I mean."

"Not exactly," Jeff answered, worried that he was out of his depth but determined to stick with it. "Tell me what happened on Atlantis."

"Well, I was one of those scientists. We were on the edge of a scientific breakthrough, and then it all went wrong and we eventually ended up with cataclysm. Everything was lost." His voice faded, and he began to choke back tears.

Jeff had trouble staying in his loving adult because the pain went so deep and he was feeling it. I encouraged him to keep going. He reminded himself he was in the twentieth century now and fought to stay above the pain enough to help his Atlantean self.

"Hey there, buddy," he said, "I feel your pain, and I want you to know I'm here for you. I don't think you meant to be a part of that destruction, did you?"

"No, but that doesn't make any difference. I was one of the scientists," his ancient self replied despondently. "I can't forget what happened or forgive myself for not seeing it coming. And they told me God would never forgive me."

"Who told you that?" Jeff asked soberly.

"I guess you'd call them 'fallen angels,' but I thought they were fantastic scientists until everything fell apart," he replied.

Jeff took a moment to pray, "Father, what do I do now?" After a meditative silence, he asked his ancient self, "How about if we give God a chance to forgive us? We could at least ask, don't you think?"

"What's this 'us' stuff?" his ancient self replied sarcastically. "This was my doing."

"Yeah, but we're in this together, like it or not," Jeff said. "How about it?"

"You go first."

"Father in heaven," Jeff prayed, "I ask forgiveness for what we did so long ago on Atlantis, and I ask you to comfort and heal my ancient self who is so hurt and despairing."

Long silence. I was silently praying too.

"Me too," his ancient self said softly.

Jeff told me later this was when he began to feel less like he was buried under ten tons of cement. "That's good," he said to his soul. "I think God heard us, don't you?"

"Maybe," was all he heard in reply.

Jeff continued to pray, and he asked the violet-flame angels to flood him and his Atlantean self with that light for the transmutation and forgiveness for their part in the ancient drama. As he did so, he suddenly saw in his inner eye what seemed like an ocean of violet light all around him, and his ancient self reached out to be included. He put his arms around himself as waves of violet light flooded through them.

The powerful presence of God's light and forgiveness was tangible in the therapy room.

"I accept your forgiveness, God, and I thank you for your love," Jeff said. "And he does too."

His ancient self was silent, but Jeff could feel the change in his stance. "That goes for me too," he finally said. And I could tell that Jeff felt a lightening up.

Jeff continued to pray and to thank God. Through all of this, I had been silently praying with him and feeling, with a sense of wonder, the depth of his encounter with the presence of God. Finally, when Jeff seemed to be calming down quite a bit, I ventured to ask, "How are you doing? Would you like some water?"

"Okay, and yes, that would be good," he responded, with a sigh of exhaustion.

He drank a glass of water, and I suggested that he check in with his Atlantean self again.

"How are you doing now, buddy?" he asked gently.

"A lot better," was the reply. "I'm glad you hung in there with me. Do you think God really forgave us?"

"Yes," Jeff responded, "I do."

"I can hardly believe it," said his ancient self, "but I think you're right. They told me God hated me for what I'd done. I guess that was just one more of their lies."

"Sounds like it," said Jeff. "I know God loves us, and I think he's wanted to forgive us for a long time. But we didn't ask so he couldn't."

"It feels like a ton of weight off me," his ancient self replied. "What do we do now?"

Jeff looked at me, and I suggested, "Why don't you take your Atlantean self to the secret chamber of your heart to be with Jesus or whoever he feels close to?"

He looked relieved. "That's a good idea. I've always felt that Jesus loved me, even when I was doing something wrong. I think it made him sad, but I always knew he loved me."

"Okay, buddy," he said, "let's go to the secret chamber of the heart and see Jesus."

"Now visualize doing that," I said, "and stay with it as long as you like. When you feel complete, leave him in Jesus' care and we'll wind it up for today."

Jeff closed his eyes and went within. After a few minutes, he began to relax and look peaceful. He stayed that way a long time. Finally, he stretched and opened his eyes, smiling. "That was really something!" he commented. "I can't exactly put it into words, but Jesus was really there."

"Yes, I'm sure he was, and I'm happy for you," I said. "It seems pretty complete, but is there anything you want to tell me or ask me?"

"Just one thing," Jeff responded. "Thanks for holding the balance. I was scared to go that deep by myself."

"You're welcome," I replied. "God bless you."

"He already has," Jeff said and smiled again.

We concluded the session, and Jeff's inner experience stayed with him from that day on. He continued to dialogue with his ancient self when he felt prompted to do so, and he gave violet-flame decrees to transmute any related records. At a certain point, he realized that the deep core of anger he had felt was no longer there. He told me that as a consequence, he was finding it easier to work with difficult clients.

Incidentally, Jeff's temper tantrums as a four-year-old

were connected with this record—this was the age when the grief and anger from the ancient trauma first came up and he hadn't known what to do except have a tantrum.

As he told me, "I think my tantrums were the despair of my soul, but all I knew was I couldn't stand the frustration I felt inside. And the anger was a way of trying to protect myself; it kept everybody at a distance. But I don't need it anymore, now that God has forgiven me. I'm always going to remember the power of forgiveness, but you do have to ask, don't you?"

"Yes," I replied, "that's the first step, and then God meets us halfway. I think it makes God very happy when we ask for forgiveness and then accept it and forgive ourselves."

"I think so, too," Jeff smiled. "It's a good feeling to feel straight with God again."

As you can see from Jeff's inner work, we may have hurtful happenings early in life that tie into past lives. And then an adult-life experience awakens those painful thoughts and feelings from the past. When we do not consciously understand what is going on, we can be propelled into actions that get us into trouble. And then our soul and spirit are even more hurt and confused.

When we decide to face our negative thoughts and feelings, the memories can surface. We can deal with them and let them go. Our good memories, thoughts and feelings also play a part because they help us move toward constructive action. The trick is to make the shift, inwardly, from the negative to the positive.

When we seek to understand and give loving support to our wounded soul and spirit, we discover that the process is both enlightening and emotionally satisfying. And the uplift moves us to action! I encourage you to practice this kind of in-depth healing work.

One final suggestion: If you find it challenging to do this kind of healing work by yourself, I recommend that you consult an experienced therapist who combines psychology with spirituality. A competent therapist can provide you with emotional support and additional insights throughout your healing process.

PART TWO

Adventures of Soul and Spirit

4

Transforming the Inner Critic

What is this self inside us, this silent observer,
Severe and speechless critic, who can terrorize us
And urge us on to futile activity,
And in the end, judge us still more severely
For the errors into which his own reproaches drove us?

—T. S. ELIOT
The Elder Statesman

Now that we have experienced healing work with our wounded, angry self, let's take a look at a special case of this aspect of spirit, aptly called the "inner critic."[1]

When we were little, we were often on the receiving end of criticism, annoyance and "You had better shape up!" words and behaviors from other people. As children, we absorbed the critical comments, stinging rebukes and sharp corrections from those who were significant in our lives.

At first, we took it all in because the mind of the young child isn't selective; it simply absorbs. It's like having the voices of mother, father, sister, brother, grandparents and anyone else who made a strong impact on us echoing in the caverns of our being.

When we were a little older, we felt hurt when people around us were unkind, but we copied what they did. And most of all, we criticized ourselves. Why? Somehow it seemed safer to criticize ourselves before someone else did. Maybe it wouldn't hurt so much if we knew about it ahead of time, or maybe we could fix whatever was wrong with us.

We innocently put on the mask of the inner critic. It's the old saying "If you can't beat 'em, join 'em!" We may have felt vulnerable, scared, angry, rebellious or sassy—but we didn't dare show it. And underneath it all was just plain hurt.

An Early Warning Radar System

Even though our parents were good people, there were times they were annoyed or frustrated, even angry, with us. Right? Perhaps they didn't like it when we interrupted them, or when we were noisy, when we were stubborn or angry, when we couldn't sit still, when we didn't make A's in school. And some parents had enough problems of their own that they overreacted to everything. Sometimes, all it took was a look, and we knew we were in trouble!

The message we received, even when they didn't mean it that way, was "There is something wrong with you." So we tried to catch ourselves before anyone else could! We flagged ourselves as "bad boy," "dumb kid," "stupid girl," "jerk," "idiot," and other such labels. Our byword became the old childhood jingle "Sticks and stones may break my bones, but names will never hurt me."

The inner critic became our early warning radar system. By criticizing ourselves we attempted to anticipate the concerns of other people who were important to us. Over the years, that system of protection took on a life of its own.

The inner critic began to overprotect, to swing into

action with the slightest threat of a problem. And he is still trying to protect and defend us. He's like the fabled sorcerer's apprentice, running on his own track, without direction from our conscious adult self.

Psychologists call the attitudes, feelings, words and actions of others that we absorb as children *introjects.* We take them in and carry them with us for life—unless or until we decide to transform them.

When we were stuck in our inner critic, what we really needed was a loving, understanding adult to help us remove the mask and tend our wounds. Our wounded soul and spirit needed encouragement, understanding, a kind shoulder to lean on and a constructive way to handle the hurt.

Sometimes we received comfort and help, and sometimes we did not. When we didn't get help, the wounds were inflamed over and over again. Even as adults we carry them until they are healed.

Are you aware of your inner critic? It's that part of you that is never pleased with you, no matter how hard you try. It's the inner self-talk that delivers put-downs, thou-shalt-nots and pessimistic comments about you—and other people. The inner critic drives you unmercifully with its negative thoughts and commandments, allowing little time or energy for relaxation, joy or peace.

What Do I Believe about Myself?

In the course of developing the inner critic, we also developed a system of beliefs based on how other people related to us. Most of us still carry such false beliefs. Ask yourself, do you believe any of the following?

- I'm not lovable.
- Nobody understands me.

- There's something basically wrong with me.
- No matter how hard I try, I always mess up.
- Other people's feelings matter more than mine.
- It's my fault that other people don't like me.
- If I behave just right, other people will like me.
- I can't handle pain, fear, embarrassment, frustration, anger, loneliness, grief, etc.
- Nobody can ever know the real me.
- I can't change who I am.

Any of these beliefs may be firmly held by our younger self. Each of us could add to the list from our own perspective. We need to realize that we all carry such false beliefs. And unless we change our belief system to match the real us, we are heading for a serious identity crisis. Or we already have one!

We can learn to recognize and dismantle such beliefs and replace them with the truth of who we are, what is our responsibility and what belongs to someone else.

The basic truth is that each of us is a special child of God, made of the God stuff. We might say (paraphrasing a cartoon character), "I know I'm okay 'cause God made me and God don't make no mistakes!" That's one to remember. When we make a mistake, it doesn't mean that *we* are a mistake.

When we internalize disparaging comments, we feel ashamed of our very being. It's a kind of inner brainwashing that John Bradshaw refers to as "core shame."[2]

We may walk around feeling ashamed and down on ourselves. Or we may inflate our self-importance to try to feel better. But whether it is an inflated or deflated ego, it's still the same old *human* ego.

We can strive to remember who we are as our Maker created us to be and who we may become through bonding to our Higher Self. When the dial of consciousness turns, those false beliefs can give way to the realization of who we really are as a son or daughter of God.

A Profile of Your Inner Critic

False beliefs are a part of the inner critic's bag of tricks. And everyone's critic has its own style, history and appearance. I suggest you profile your critic through this exercise:

1. Write down whatever negative statements you make about yourself, especially when you make a mistake or fail to please someone important to you. That negative self-talk is your critic's special style of criticism.

2. Think for a minute. Where have you heard those statements before? Could it be father, mother, siblings, grandparents, cousins, babysitters, teachers or neighbors? Make a note of where and when you have heard those criticisms.

3. Give your inner critic form. What does he or she look like? Draw a picture or representation of him. Keep that image handy to remind you of who you are *not!*

Cast Off the Fetters of Who You Are Not

When the inner critic is in charge, it's like being chained to your mistakes, your worst moments or looking at yourself through a smudged glass of consciousness and seeing only the smudges. What you need is a raising of consciousness, a spiritual look at the person you really are and may become. An ascended master, Paul the Venetian, addressed this in a dictation* through Mark Prophet:

*Dictations are the messages of the ascended masters, archangels and other advanced spiritual beings delivered through the agency of the Holy Spirit by a messenger of the Great White Brotherhood.

I would like to speak to you for a moment, beloved ones, about those fetters which mankind have installed so securely about them as though they were afraid that if those fetters were cut, they would float away and drift into an empty nothingness.

I would like to tell you, beloved ones, that this is not true.... Mankind need have no fear that if they cut the fetters which bind them to the earthly consciousness, they will drift away. For the immortal consciousness of God is within the holy temple of their being, and as the psalmist of old said, "Whither shall I flee from thy presence?"[3]

Beloved ones, where can mankind go? Where can they flee from the face of God, seeing they dwell within him and are active in the principle of immortal life?

Pause, then, again and recognize that as you cut those weights and sins of human omission and commission from your consciousness, you will be enabling that consciousness to rise. And as it rises and looks up toward God, it cannot escape entering into some measure of the eternal mind.

That measure at first may seem small because it will be limited by the finite. It is as though a person stood before the window of a large shop covered over with the accumulation and dust of centuries, and then they dipped a cloth into water and began to make a small hole in the dust of this window.

At first, a small ray of light would come in. If they pressed their eye against this tiny hole, they would be able to see far and wide. But if they stood back from the window, the hole would still seem small.

And so it is with the window into eternal beauty. Men, as they temporarily press their eye against the small hole while they sit in heavenly places and are in our

> radiance in exalted consciousness, are able to momentarily catch a glimpse of the wonders of our octave.
>
> When absent, then, and separated as it were in physical form from one another and from those heavenly places of consciousness, it is as though they backed away from the window. And the hole fades into a limited nothingness and the shadowed window itself seems once again to occupy their consciousness.
>
> What is the remedy? It is so simple that I am sure you have immediately deduced it. It is to clean the entire pane of consciousness, and then you will be able to see all of the purity of God at all times.... You will immediately recognize that you have in the past [only] neglected to clean the consciousness of the eyes of your soul and to gaze at the purity and beauty which was all around you.
>
> And so, today, as I have carried you in a spiritual sense upon the magic carpet of the world's greater and larger view of beauty, I would like to point out that to God the world is a shining planet of splendor and perfection. Its people are pure and noble and grand, sons of God, radiant and shining with light.[4]

We can look beyond the frailty of human error, shine up the windows of our consciousness and see the nobility in self and others. We can transform that inner critic and claim our true identity, a transformational process that is healing to soul and spirit.

As we do this healing work, it is important to realize that we are also removing blocks to our soul's relationship with God. Those blocks developed when we identified with our lower nature and accepted the not-self. For many of us, that shift in identity occurred many lifetimes ago, and karmic circumstances in this lifetime simply reinforced it. Once we realize and accept the best of our soul and spirit, we begin to reclaim our higher nature.

Our negative momentums didn't begin in this life—they go back to previous lifetimes. Each of us has karma with family, friends, teachers, bosses, co-workers and acquaintances—even people we may not know in this life.

Unconscious Magnetism

Is there someone in your life that you have a hard time getting along with? If so, ask yourself, Does this person remind me of anyone I've known before? Is our relationship similar to one I've had before, perhaps as a child, teenager or young adult?

Make a note of whatever comes to mind. And remind yourself that the drama may go way back. Perhaps you gave that person a rough time in a previous life. Maybe that person giving you a hard time today is retaliating for some kind of pain you inflicted five thousand years ago.

Once we understand this, we can begin to heal our blind spots by focusing on what is going on around us. Remember that people who impact our lives for good or ill are frequently a reflection of our own character traits, either positive or negative.

This phenomenon is in keeping with the law of energy, "Like attracts like." We unconsciously magnetize people and events that resonate as we do. Seemingly random experiences are often a dramatic portrayal of something within ourselves that we need to celebrate or transform.

The problem is that the inner critic doesn't understand that like attracts like. This wounded protector simply absorbs a hurtful drama and blames everyone in sight. And once we are alone, the critic shifts the blame onto us. As the critic worries and criticizes us, our view of ourselves gets more and more jaundiced.

Spiritually, our inner critic is in bondage to the dweller-on-the-threshold, the conglomerate of negative energy we have absorbed, created and harbored throughout many lifetimes. That dweller has a consciousness of total negativity and destructiveness. And it seizes every opportunity our karmic predicament provides to devil us into submission and propel us into a downward spiral.

We can counteract that energy downer by calling to Archangel Michael to bind that pesky dweller. We can shout, "Archangel Michael, bind the dweller-on-the-threshold! Bind every negative aspect of the dweller! Free my soul and spirit! I claim my victory now!"

Shout it to the heavens until you feel the uplift of energy that accompanies Archangel Michael's response to your fiats. Seal your victory by affirming, "By the power of Archangel Michael and the grace of the Holy Spirit, I accept my freedom and my victory now!"

Let Your Soul Shine Through

The inner critic can also be likened to a shadowy figure at a masquerade ball. Hiding behind the mask is our soul who wants to toss the mask aside and be free. We are invited by our Higher Self to strip off the mask and let our soul shine through. This process is self-transforming, which is what inner critic work is all about.

When you begin to work with your inner critic, you may find the process somewhat difficult. But have you ever been in a terrible, "dragon" mood and someone put his arms around you and loved you—and you softened or burst into tears? That's the way it works. Your inner critic is playing dragon, yet your soul is mightily relieved when you ignore that mask and offer love.

So the first step is to recognize the mask. The second is to move from a stance of defensiveness to being real. And the third is to exchange self-criticism for loving-kindness. Once we practice loving ourselves, we naturally behave more lovingly to others.

How do we develop loving-kindness toward our inner critic? For starters, we cultivate softness—soft eyes, soft thoughts, soft feelings, soft words. Yet at times we need more than the soft, kind approach. We may need tough love, the kind of love that tells it like it is—with a genuine caring for soul and spirit.

We also benefit from understanding the difference between sympathy and compassion: sympathy is the drama where the guy is going down in the quicksand and you jump in with him to pull him out. You both go down! Compassion is where you throw him a rope and pull him out while you stay on firm ground.

When we are compassionate, we identify with the consciousness of our loving, wise, responsible self. We speak the truth gently. We express our concerns forgivingly. We practice loving-kindness, even in challenging situations.

The ascended master Kuthumi gave an inspiring message about kindness. I'd like to share his words with you:

> May you know the one great quality that is sought after that comes from the auric rings of Maitreya and his true bodhisattvas. It is the quality of kindness, almost overlooked in this hurried world, almost thought of as unnecessary. Yet what do you remember most about anyone? A kindness, a gesture, a sincere concern, a practical helpfulness, a perception of your need before you yourself know it.

> Kindness, beloved, is an aura of strength. Until you encounter someone who has that full-bodied flame, which surely relates to Maitreya, you may not even know just what the fullness of the cup of kindness can be.
>
> I speak of this, for it is well for the student on the Path to select a virtue . . . that he will make his own, his signet and his mark in life. . . .
>
> Many, many people are not happy, beloved. They surely are miserable in their souls yet cannot even articulate what pain they experience in aloneness. People who are surrounded by many yet feel unloved, for they do not love themselves as God—they have needs.
>
> I ask you to begin to rejoice in the givingness of self that meets the very specific need of anyone or everyone who is near you. This is the mark and the sign of a true teacher. You do not have to be perfected in elocution or the delivery of the Word, but you must be effective in opening up the heart and releasing that kindness, which all will feel no matter how limited your powers of speech or your vocabulary.[5]

I suggest you choose the quality of loving-kindness to reform your inner critic. Yet sometimes people say, "What do I do if I don't feel loving and kind?" The simplest answer is, if you don't feel loving, just behave lovingly anyway.

That's a major paradigm shift. Behaving lovingly primes the pump of our heart's flow of divine love, which blesses and heals all life. When we direct love to our own soul, we are reminded of our original purity, our oneness with our Higher Self.

Love is the fulfillment of our being. When we love ourselves, love our soul and heal our inner schisms, we feel loved and cherished at every level of our being. And we begin to remember who we are as sons and daughters of God.

Practicing Loving-Kindness

As we walk the path of loving-kindness, we heal our soul and offer a healing balm to those we meet along the way. As Wayne Muller puts it so beautifully in *Legacy of the Heart:*

> Beginning in this moment, starting with this very breath, our healing is up to us. As the rich mixture of sorrow and wisdom that saturates our life becomes more evident, as we mindfully explore the tremendous depth of who we really are, our challenge is to integrate these healing practices into our daily lives.
>
> Each emotional wound we have identified, every exercise, meditation, and practice of mindfulness ultimately serves to engender an acknowledgement and trust in a deep spirit of strength, wisdom, and wholeness we carry within ourselves.
>
> The fundamental thread that runs through the fabric of these teachings is the practice of loving kindness. Each childhood wound and every spiritual teaching has been presented to help us cultivate a particular aspect of mercy and compassion toward ourselves.
>
> At each juncture we have been confronted with a choice: Do we meet ourselves and our wounds with judgment or with mercy? Do we touch our childhood memories with anger, or soften them with love and forgiveness? Do we recall our violations with shame, or embrace them with genuine acceptance; do we react with fear and isolation, or with faith and courage? Do we add to the violence within ourselves, or do we cultivate unconditional love and kindness for all we have been and all we have become?
>
> Every day we live, each moment, offers a fresh opportunity to be more gently loving with ourselves and

others. We begin by learning to belong in the sanctuary of our own breath, to feel more at home in our own bodies, more confident in our rightful place as a member of the human family. This enables us to accept wholeheartedly ourselves and others just as we are, thereby planting the seeds of a genuine, secure experience of belonging.

Second, as we make a forgiving peace with the childhood we are given, we become more able to respond compassionately to those who, intentionally or unintentionally, brought us harm. As we loosen our habitual attachment to the old childhood stories, we begin to cultivate a mindful appreciation of our current gifts and capacities. We are free to be more creative and spontaneous in our generosity with ourselves and others.

In the same way, as we soften the tyranny of our judging mind, and as we let go of an exaggerated sense of our importance, we begin to experience a quality of mercy and inner peace. Through self-acceptance, mercy, and humility, we are set free to care for ourselves and others with less resentment, less anger, and less fear. As we slowly recognize that there may be enough love available for us all, we come to feel that our kindness and affection may be given freely without judgment or fear of depletion.

Finally, our healing is deepened through a mindful cultivation of simplicity, stillness, and non-attachment. These practices enable us to listen more precisely to the voices of our heart and spirit. We learn to name what is most deeply true within ourselves and to embrace what we have been given with gratefulness. As we become quiet and still, we gain access to an abundance of inner resources that give us permission to be kind and generous with ourselves and others.[6]

Our practice is to meet the inner critic with understanding, mercy and loving-kindness. As we do so, our spirit perks up and our soul breathes a sigh of relief.

Dialoguing with the Inner Critic

Many people find it helpful and enlightening to dialogue with the inner critic. As illustrated in the previous chapter, this can be done in writing or in the two-chair technique, where you alternate giving voice to your loving adult and the inner critic.

Be sure to ask how old this part of yourself is because the answer will help you choose the most beneficial approach. For example, if the critic is a young child, use simple words. If you are talking with a teenager, use teenage vernacular. And if that critic is an adult—or an ancient aspect of your soul—converse the way you normally do with other adults.

If at any time you as the loving adult begin to feel critical, stop and take a deep breath. Realize that you are identifying with the inner critic instead of staying centered in your loving adult. Separate out from the critic and determine to be your loving self no matter what the inner critic happens to be saying at the moment. Remind yourself that you need to be the encouraging father, mother and mentor, and ask your Higher Self to help you do it.

I'll illustrate this process with a dialogue from my clinical work. Daniel's parents divorced when he was eleven, and the divorce had been preceded by several years of stormy weather in the marriage. When Daniel came into therapy as a young adult, he was struggling with a lot of self-criticism. Psychologically, he was identified with his critical masculine side and split off from his more gentle, feminine aspect.

Spiritually, Daniel understood his masculine nature as his spirit and his feminine nature as his soul. He wanted to transform his critical nature into true manliness, and he knew he could soften that hard edge with love and compassion. The problem was he didn't feel any sense of love or compassion when he was hostile and angry. And as he explained, that was happening more often all the time. As he put it, "It's like my angry spirit is taking me over and I'm losing my soul."

After several sessions in which Daniel practiced centering in his heart and learning how to dialogue with neutral parts of himself, I suggested he dialogue with his angry critic. He agreed with a bit of trepidation because the day before he had lost his temper with a colleague at work. And that had resulted in a reprimand from his boss.

Before we began the inner critic work, I asked Daniel to close his eyes and let his mind go to an earlier time in his life when he felt the same way as he had yesterday.

Daniel put his jacket on the chair opposite him to signify his inner critic. He took a deep breath and addressed his critical self:

Daniel: Hi there. Thanks for showing up. I'd like to know what's bothering you right now and how I can help you. And by the way, how old are you today?

Critic: *(belligerently)* I'm ten years old, and what's it to you?

Daniel: I remember being ten. It was a tough time, wasn't it? It seemed like Mom and Dad were fighting all the time and nobody liked us. Is that the way you remember it?

Critic: *(long silence)* Do you want to know what I remember? I remember what a jerk you were. You never did anything right, and that's why you always got the brunt of their fights. And you're still doing it. Look what you did at work yesterday!

Daniel: Let's stick to the situation with Mom and Dad.

I didn't want to be in the middle of that, and you didn't either. Right?

Critic: That's true. *(silence)* How come we always got picked on?

Daniel: I think they picked on us because they were frustrated with each other. But it hurt a lot, didn't it?

Critic: Let's change the subject. It never did any good to talk about it. It's stupid to bring it up.

Daniel: I'm bringing it up because I want to help. I know you're trying to protect yourself and me. But it isn't working. And I don't think it's stupid to talk about it. Criticizing doesn't protect us; it makes us feel terrible.

Daniel was silent for a moment, and then to our surprise, his gentle side, whom he saw as his wounded soul, surfaced:

Soul: Thanks for noticing. You can talk to me if he doesn't want to talk anymore.

Daniel: Okay, let's talk. Who are you, and how old are you?

Soul: I'm the one who really got hurt. I'm ten, too. And he's just trying to protect me by mouthing off that way. I'd like you to know how I feel inside, if that's okay.

Daniel: Absolutely. What are you feeling?

Soul: Well, I'm really hurt and frustrated. Mom and Dad don't love each other anymore, and I don't think they love me either. I can't stand their fighting and hollering at each other. How can people stop loving each other and act so awful?

Daniel: It really was hurtful and frustrating. But I don't think Mom and Dad realized how much they were hurting us. They were too upset with each other. It was really lonely, wasn't it?

Soul: Yes, I just kind of hung out in my room by myself. Remember? It was worse at night when they didn't think we could hear them fighting. I didn't know what to do.

I couldn't fix it. *(Tears begin to slide down Daniel's cheeks.)*

The dialogue developed into a three-way interchange when Daniel's critic suddenly interrupted with an emotional outburst.

Critic: That's enough of this! See what you did? Let's just stop this right now. You're both acting like jerks!

The tears quickly dried up as Daniel's inner critic went into a full-blown tantrum. After some minutes of an angry diatribe, I suggested Daniel re-center and help his inner critic out. He took several slow, deep breaths, calmed himself down and took the plunge.

Daniel: Whoa there, buddy. I love you and I want to help you. But I need you to settle down so I can help you. *(He put his arms around himself and held on for the ride.)*
Critic: Let go of me. I hate you! You're no better than they are. Nobody loves us, and this isn't helping!
Soul: *(softly)* It's kind of helping me. I really need to talk about it, and I wish you could too.
Critic: What's the use? You're just being a crybaby. Why don't you just accept the fact that we're unlovable! We can live with it.
Soul: It hurts too much to keep it all in.

Daniel closed his eyes for a moment and then stepped back in as the loving adult:

Daniel: I know how it feels, and I want to help both of you. Buddy, how can I help you right now?
Critic: Give us new parents. How about that?
Daniel: I love you. I'll be your parent—how about that?
Critic: *(long silence)* What do you mean? My parents are

my parents, and they're both jerks!

Soul: Let's give him a chance. It can't hurt anything. And maybe he can help us.

Critic: *(silence)*

Daniel: I mean it, I love you. And God loves you. Our parents loved us, too. Mom told me about it years later. They were just stuck in their own stuff. No matter how they acted, it doesn't change who you are—and you *are* lovable. I think deep inside you know that. So how can I help you right now?

Critic: I'm thinking.

Soul: Give me a hug, and tell me I'm lovable. It's kind of hard to believe.

Daniel: *(puts his arms around himself and imagines giving his soul a hug)* You are lovable, and smart, too. And so is he.

Soul: I know. He's just scared to admit it.

Daniel: Well, it was scary. For a while, we thought we'd have to take care of ourselves, and we were too young to do that. That's when Granny and Gramps took us in for a while, remember?

Soul: Yes, and that was good. I knew they really loved us.

Critic: But it was still scary, don't you remember?

Daniel: I remember, and you're right. It was scary. But now I'm grown up, and I can take care of you. You don't have to worry about being alone again.

Critic: *(silence)*

Soul: That's kind of neat. I believe you, and he's beginning to believe you, too. He just hates to admit it.

Critic: *(unexpectedly laughs)* She's on to me, you know that?

Daniel: Seems like it! She's known you from way back because she's our soul. So what can I do for you right now?

Critic: Okay, I want you to tell me what a great guy I am, and I want you not to expect me to do all the adult things you do. They're too hard.

Daniel: That's a deal. You are a great guy, and I'll do the adult things. When I'm not sure what to do, I'll ask our Higher Self to help me. Okay?

Critic: And in return, what?

Daniel: You mean what do I expect? Well, I'd like it if you would stop criticizing me all the time. I do better with your love and support than with criticism. I love you, and I understand how difficult it's been. You are a special guy, and you've got a talent for self-analysis. I'd just like to hear some good stuff, too—like a compliment here and there.

Critic: *(silence, hint of a smile)* You really mean that, don't you? That's kind of neat.

Soul: *(joking)* We're just one big happy family, right?

Daniel: *(laughs)* Well, I can't promise no problems. But I can promise that I'll be here for both of you. And I'll keep asking God what to do. How about hugs all around? *(hugs himself)* Is there anything else I can do for you right now?

Soul: Just keep on loving me.

Critic: If I think of something, I'll let you know.

Daniel: Okay, it's a deal. Now I'm going to take both of you to the secret chamber of the heart, where our Higher Self will take care of you and you can be with Krishna. Would you like that?

Critic: Yeah, he's cool. Maybe he'll teach me to play the flute.

Soul: How about Mother Mary, too? She's good at hugs when you're too busy.

Daniel: Okay, Mother Mary and Krishna it is. *(Daniel makes a call to Mother Mary, Krishna and his Higher*

Self. Then he visualizes all of them in the secret chamber of the heart.)

Daniel felt good about this session. He was surprised and relieved when his soul surfaced because he had felt so out of touch with his feminine polarity. In the dialogue, the soul acted as mediator because the critic was too entrenched in criticism to change course. Daniel enjoyed interacting with his soul, his gentle side.

He continued to work with the inner critic, and gradually the critic turned into a supporter of his adult self. Daniel tells me he rarely gets on his own case these days. Instead, he focuses on championing himself through the rough times and giving himself the benefit of the doubt. If he's really done something wrong, he owns up to it and does what he can to make it right.

As you can see, heart-centered role-playing can be healing to soul and spirit, and it is a practice you can develop within yourself. However, if you need assistance or are dealing with serious trauma, seek the help of a good therapist.

A few points of advice: As a general rule, listen with an open mind and compassionate heart to whatever thoughts and feelings are aroused during the dialogue. Pay attention to healing the pain. No matter what comes up, respond lovingly and constructively. Simply pause and re-center in your heart when you find yourself at a loss. Use common sense and offer reassurance and loving-kindness.

Stay with it until you experience a positive shift in your inner critic; for example, he says, "I appreciate you hearing me out" or "Thanks for listening."

In Daniel's case, his soul started communicating and that gave his inner critic another perspective. Through facilitating and accepting the feminine and masculine sides of himself,

Daniel was able to reach resolution. Incidentally, this session was a turning point in his therapy and in his outer life.

We all have the feminine and masculine aspects of our identity. So it is important to love ourselves and to understand the impact of difficult circumstances we have been through. As was the case with Daniel, your soul can become your greatest ally. And don't forget to tend the inner critic, who masks your lonely, depressed spirit.

Complete your dialogue by inviting the inner critic to accompany your soul to the secret chamber of the heart. It's a safe place, a spiritual retreat for your soul and spirit.

As a follow-up, check in with the inner critic whenever you feel self-critical or negative. Gradually, as healing takes place, you'll begin to feel more positive about yourself and others. And life will take on a brighter hue.

Emotional First Aid

When you feel the inner critic being triggered or coming at you from another person, it's a good idea to give yourself emotional first aid:

1. Remove yourself from the situation that is hurting your wounded self and stirring up your critical nature.
2. Call to your Higher Self to help you let go of the turmoil and center yourself in peace and love.
3. Take a few deep breaths, inhaling through your nose, filling your abdomen and your chest, and exhaling slowly through your mouth. Focus full attention on your breathing, and see if you can take twenty counts to exhale the breath.

   Or take a walk or run, and deliberately focus your attention on the rhythm of the physical exercise.

4. Tune into your physical heart. If it helps you focus, place your hand over the area of your chest where your heart beats. Continue to be aware of your heartbeat as you connect it with the rhythm of your breathing. Imagine the breath flowing through the heart.

5. Remember a time when you felt joy, a sense of beauty, appreciation, inspiration, gratitude or just plain fun. Relive the experience and those good feelings as you continue awareness of your physical heart and breathing. Stay focused on all three for a full minute.

6. Ask your Higher Self, your heart's intelligence, What is a better approach for me to take in this situation?[7] Seek and follow your heart's direction on a regular basis. You will soon notice that you rarely need emotional first aid.

Twelve Steps to Transform the Inner Critic

1. Focus on the specifics that you want to transform. Be fully aware of hostile attitudes, negative thoughts, angry feelings and critical behavior.

2. Call to the angels to bind the inner critic pattern, and ask your Higher Self to help you be the real you.

3. Choose a specific virtue to replace the habit of criticism: kindness, helpfulness, civility, forgiveness, giving the benefit of the doubt, and so forth. Contemplate the positive intention, thoughts, feelings and behavior that accompany the virtue you choose.

4. Ask your Higher Self and the angels to help you trade in the old critical nature for the virtue you have chosen.

5. Imagine how you might meet a challenging situation once you are identified with your new virtue.

6. Write down, step-by-step, exactly what you would want to do, and practice privately at home.
7. Mobilize your will and determination, and try out the new virtue in a benign setting away from home.
8. When you feel comfortable with the shift in behavior in the benign situation, try it in a more challenging setting.
9. Give yourself permission to experiment and make mistakes. View each mistake as an opportunity to learn and grow. Analyze what happened, get back on track and try again!
10. Commend yourself every time you practice, and remember to be gentle with yourself, especially in trying situations.
11. Monitor your progress, especially as you graduate to situations where you used to react with the old, critic pattern. Concentrate on what you choose to do now instead of dwelling on what you did in the past.
12. Create an "I AM" affirmation to reinforce the virtue in your heart and soul, for example, "I AM loving and kind." Affirm it daily, and claim your victory!

I believe that transforming criticism is a joyful way to go because that critical reaction comes from pain. We feel so much better once we heal the pain and become proactive. Every time we replace criticism with a quality of our Higher Self, we become more of who we really are. And that feels great!

This transformational process reminds me of the classic movie *It's a Wonderful Life,*[8] where every time an angel earns his wings, a bell in heaven chimes. How about imagining that bell chiming every time you discard your mask and choose to be real? Imagine the joy in heaven, and hear those bells ringing now!

Mark Prophet on Removing the Mask

Mark Prophet, adept of the twentieth century, gave a great lecture on removing the mask and getting real. He said:

> It doesn't take long on Halloween or at a masquerade ball to pull the mask off, does it? Everybody says, "Surprise!"
>
> First of all, if we're going to take a mask off, we have to take the mask off of something. Now, what are we going to unmask? In this case we must perceive that there is something real about us. There is also something that is unreal about us. And the quicker we discover it and acknowledge it and learn to distinguish the difference, the quicker we will make progress in the light.
>
> Why is it important that we know the difference? It is important... because otherwise we are going to be feeding the mask and starving the real man....
>
> So there is a *real* you, and there is a *false* you. But I think that words are sometimes very inadequate tools to convey ideas, because the false you is really the mask that itself will be discarded. And we hang on to that mask!
>
> One of the great fallacies in this whole process of removing the mask is that we keep thinking that we are going to change the mask and make the mask look like the Divine Presence. But that isn't true at all.
>
> The mask is that *false* creation which we have *thought* to be our True Self—the creation that we are not only going to discard but never pick up again!... When you pull the mask off, you should see shining through a splendid, radiant divine being—the real you![9]

We can ask our Higher Self to help us pull off the mask. We can understand and love our own soul and the souls of those who have touched our lives in hurtful ways. And we can live our higher vision: spiritually, mentally, emotionally and physically.

On a spiritual level, we can learn the precepts of the spiritual path from the world's great religions and elder brothers and sisters on the Path. We can pray for our family, friends and neighbors and for the courage to understand, accept and forgive. We can invoke the violet flame to heal the records, memories and false beliefs of yesterday. We can ask our Higher Self to guide us every day, and we can honor our higher intuition.

On a mental level, we can study the lives of those who have inspired us. We can harness our intellect in the service of fulfilling our higher principles. We can banish negative thoughts by directing our attention to what is uplifting and inspiring. And we can send *metta,* loving-kindness, to ourselves, our family, friends, acquaintances, even our enemies.

On the emotional level, we can cultivate feelings of compassion for all life. We can choose to be kind, tolerant and forgiving—a major key to victory. As long as we refuse to forgive, we smart from the old hurts and remain critical toward self and others. When we forgive in all directions, we close that chapter of our life and move on. And as we emerge safely from the swirling waters of emotion, our soul heaves a sigh of relief. We have faced our fears and shored up vulnerabilities by being true to the best in ourselves.

On the physical level, we can be present with all our senses. We can establish a personal code of conduct that is in keeping with our highest values. We can explore positive options and follow through. We can walk our talk by being kind, cheerful and encouraging. We can relate to family and friends lovingly. We can choose the way of kindness and gentility toward all. We can choose to take the high road in our actions, no matter what!

Be Who You Really Are

As you identify with the real you, your best simulation of your Higher Self, you can wave a cheerful good-bye to the inner critic. You will be ready to do so because you are choosing to love, protect and mentor yourself and to be an instrument of loving-kindness to others. By doing so you ignite a spark of love that lights the way for people whose lives you touch.

Wayne Muller speaks of our personal healing as a love gift for the earth and her people:

> As we investigate the sorrows of childhood and their lingering effects on our minds and hearts, we gradually come to realize that we ultimately share our suffering with all the children of the earth.
>
> All beings who are born are given a portion of that pain, and all beings stand in need of deep healing, love, and care. Consequently, our healing is not just for us; the more we feel our place in the human family, the more we undertake our own healing as part of our love for all beings who suffer.
>
> As we extend our circle of kindness and compassion to include all living things, the more we engender the possibility of true, lasting peace within ourselves and for all humanity. . . .
>
> As we heal the wounds of the past, we carry less pain into the world, less confusion and anger, and we bring more clarity and peace. Here, our work is not simply for personal gain; it becomes our gift, our offering to the human family, to the earth, and to the divine spark within us all.[10]

5

Encounters with Dragons and Dwellers

Courage is the price that life exacts for granting peace.
The soul that knows it not, knows no release
From little things;
Knows not the livid loneliness of fear,
Nor mountain heights where bitter joy can hear
The sound of wings.

—AMELIA EARHART PUTNAM
"Courage"

History, myths and folklore are replete with stories of knights and ladies, dragons and serpents. Whether fact or fiction, these tales have lasted through the centuries because they echo our soul's awareness of the dweller-on-the-threshold.

Inwardly, our soul shivers with the realization that the dweller-dragon can be our nemesis if we ignore it. Yet by choosing to confront and slay that dragon we claim our soul's right of passage to higher realms. This is a formidable battle each of us is destined to win—if we so choose.

Saint George and the Dragon

One famous legend about that battle is the story of Saint George and the Dragon, dating from sixth-century England. It was popularized through Jacob de Voragine's *Legenda aurea* (1265–1266) and published as *The Golden Legend* in 1483. As the story goes, a formidable dragon in Sylene, Lybia, poisoned everyone who approached it with his breath. The people were so terrorized that they appeased the monster with a daily offering of two sheep. However, sheep grew scarce and a human victim, chosen by lot, had to be substituted.

The lot fell upon the king's daughter, who went to meet her fate. Enter George, a Christian knight who attacked the dragon, pierced it with his lance and led it captive with the princess's girdle (a belt or sash worn around the waist). George exhorted the people to be unafraid, to believe in Jesus Christ and be baptized. If they did so, he would take care of the monster.

After they agreed to his terms, George killed the dragon, and fifteen thousand men were baptized. (It's an interesting note that women are not mentioned except for the unfortunate princess!) Instead of taking a reward, George simply asked the king to honor the churches and priests and be compassionate to the poor.

George had been revered in England since the eighth century, and his personage took on new dimensions for England during the Crusades. At the siege of Antioch (1098) in the First Crusade, a vision of George preceded the defeat of the Saracens and the fall of the town.

King Edward III (reigned 1327–1377) recognized George as England's patron saint and founded the Order of the Garter under Saint George's patronage. Pope Benedict XIV made him protector of the kingdom. His fame reached its height in the later Middle Ages. By that time, not only England but also Venice, Genoa, Portugal, and Catalonia regarded him as patron saint because he personified chivalry and Christian ideals.

The most complete legend of Saint George is located in the early sixteenth-century stained glass at St. Neot's, Cornwall. And English poet Edmund Spenser wrote these words of praise:

> Thou, among those saints which thou doest see,
> Shalt be a saint, and thine own nation's friend
> And patron; thou Saint George shalt called be,
> St. George of merry England, the sign of victory.

How much is truth? How much is fiction? No one today really knows, but the legend of Saint George and the Dragon is clearly a metaphor for the journey of our soul.

Each of us is called to affirm our faith in God and slay our inner dragons. In fact, the dweller-dragon, biggest of them all, leads our soul as a lamb to slaughter until we do slay it. How do we do that? We begin by praying for guidance and rising to the challenge of recognizing and defeating the dragon's apprentice—the carnal mind.

Catch the Carnal Mind and Defeat It!

Elizabeth Clare Prophet describes a dramatic moment in the life of Godfre, an earlier messenger for the ascended masters,* that relates to the carnal mind—a mental aspect of the dweller:

---

*Godfré Ray King was the publishing pseudonym for Guy Ballard. He and his wife, Edna, founded the "I AM" Religious Activity in the 1930s. They are now known as the ascended masters Godfre and Lotus.

> There's a story that's told about Godfre when he was walking down the street in Hollywood. All of a sudden he stood with his feet anchored on the ground and made this fiat that his human creation would absolutely no longer have any force over him. Saint Germain said that it was a cosmic moment and that if he hadn't made that determination at that point in time and space, the whole I AM Activity could not have gone on.
>
> So taking that stand with that human creation, you definitely should use the full power of your throat chakra and register and record on your whole being that you're not having any human nonsense with that carnal mind ever again. And whatever patterns of it come up, you'll instantaneously allay them. It's a lifelong vigilance; it never ends.
>
> You make the fiat: "In the name of the Christ, I demand my carnal mind go into the flame! I demand my human creation submit to the Christ. In the name of the Christ, I demand action here. Blaze the light of the violet flame! Burn through and consume the cause and core!"
>
> And it's this determination, this absolutely steel determination. You can't just sit back and recite decrees and think that surrender is going to take place; it just doesn't. It's this furious determination that you have to have. This carnal mind has ruled your consciousness for hundreds of thousands of years and don't think it's going to give up without this fight.
>
> All of a sudden you decide you have had enough; it's not going to rule you any longer. And you make this fiat and nothing can cross that line ever again.[1]

When we decide to be the victor over the carnal mind or any other aspect of the dweller, we are tackling the core of our human miscreation. We are challenging the nucleus of the not-self, the anti-God, or anti-Self, and demanding that it come under the dominion of the Divine.

The dweller-on-the-threshold is the focal point of the consciousness behind our negative human creation. That dweller sits at the threshold of self-awareness, where elements from the unconscious move through the subconscious into our conscious world.

At the moment a dark motive or thought surfaces, we can call to Archangel Michael, defender of our soul, to help us. So we shout: "In the name of the Christ, Archangel Michael, help me, help me, help me! Bind that dweller! Bind the carnal mind! Transmute the darkness! I surrender it now! I claim the light! I AM the light! I claim my victory now!"

A Peek at the Loch Ness Monster

So the carnal mind is the mental aspect of the dweller. Let's look at the emotional aspect, which can feel like a monster railing at deep levels of our being. Illustrating this point, Mrs. Prophet gave an interesting commentary on the Loch Ness monster:

> I remember when on our way home from Ghana in 1972 we went to Scotland with our beloved Mark. We took a train to northern Scotland and we went to Loch Ness. Loch Ness is a very deep body of water, the habitat of the legendary Loch Ness monster. And the Loch Ness monster is supposedly a remnant of some prehistoric type of water beast or leviathan, as is mentioned in the Bible. Supposedly it looks like a giant sea dinosaur that swims about. This "Nessie," as they call her, is supposedly a female.
>
> And so, people come from all over the world watching for the Loch Ness monster. I can remember how we drove round and round the loch looking for the Loch

Ness monster, and the idea is that you can see its head peeping above the water.

Well, Mark said he saw it. I didn't see it. I missed it! But nevertheless, there are books printed with pictures that people supposedly have taken of Nessie. This goes back several hundred years that people have been watching for the Loch Ness monster.

Of course, the loch is very still; it's an inland body of water. And so, seeing it may mean seeing just a little sliver of its tail or a sliver of its head or a sliver of its back.

But that body of water, or any body of water, represents the emotional body, its surface being the line that is drawn between the conscious and the subconscious mind. Whatever is below the surface is below the surface of our awareness. We may get rumblings and soundings that it's there, but until it finally emerges and manifests itself in some way, we don't necessarily know the definition of the dweller-on-the-threshold—somehow the marks of identification are missing.

It's right there ready to come through the door of consciousness, but at that threshold, at the line separating the planes of awareness, the guardian action of the Christ mind, the holy angels and one's free will stands to prevent the dweller from actually surfacing and moving into action in our world.

Now, there are individuals, of course, who do not stand guard, and therefore they become suddenly and ferociously the instrument of a "sea monster" that is out of control. And so, you see, the more people become psychologically disturbed and have divisions in the four lower bodies,* the more they are apt to manifest aberrations

*The four lower bodies are the four sheaths surrounding the soul, the vehicles the soul uses in her journey on earth: the etheric, or memory, body; the mental body; the desire, or emotional, body; and the physical body.

by which the dweller may gain entrance to their world through the lever of the conscious mind. . . . Once in control of the conscious mind, the dweller takes over the whole house.

Supposedly, in our society, the difference between someone who is sane and someone who is insane would be the control or noncontrol of that Loch Ness monster, that dweller-on-the-threshold, which dwells in the sublevels of the emotional body. The person who makes the conscious decision not to allow the carnal mind to vent itself in the ups and downs of life is sane because he, and not the beast, is in command.

Many people are entirely dominated by the carnal mind and extremely sane at the same time, or at least sane appearing. When you get to know them, you don't think they're quite sane, but they do manage to run banks and big businesses and all kinds of corporate enterprises on this planet; and the planet manages to survive, and we survive. And sometimes we wonder why and how it all works.

Well, there comes a time in the life of the individual who contacts the spiritual path, the masters or their representatives when he comes face-to-face with Christ and anti-Christ—Christ in the person of the man of God and anti-Christ in the personal dweller-on-the-threshold within himself. And he may see both face-to-face.[2]

Christ and the Dweller

Mrs. Prophet explains that this was the case with Saul on the road to Damascus. Master Jesus forced Saul's encounter with his dweller, temporarily blinding him as the light confounded the darkness. Jesus made Saul choose between his dweller (the anti-Christ, or anti-Self), who was persecuting the Christians, and his Real Self, personified and represented in the ascended master Jesus Christ.

By choosing his Lord, Saul chose the path of discipleship leading to individual Christhood. In return, the Master bound Saul's dweller until he himself should ultimately slay it. Imbued with the power of Christ in Jesus, Saul, now called Paul (having put off the old man and put on the new), went forth to witness to the truth of Christianity. This remarkable spiritual experience shook Paul free from his dweller and awakened him to his Real Self and the truth of the mission of Jesus Christ.[3]

What will it take for us to shake the dweller and awaken to our Real Self? We can open our eyes to our negative character traits. We know we don't want them, so we squash them every time we see them. When they reappear now and then, we squash them again. This is the road to victory. When we try,* God helps us overcome and claim that victory at our own pace.

There is a point on the road of self-mastery where the soul is called to slay that dweller totally and utterly. This test came to Jesus in his forty days in the wilderness, three years before his crucifixion and resurrection. As recorded in Matthew 4:1–11:

> Then was Jesus led up of the spirit into the wilderness to be tempted of the devil. And when he had fasted forty days and forty nights, he was afterwards an hungred.
>
> And when the tempter came to him, he said, "If thou be the Son of God, command that these stones be made bread."
>
> But he answered and said, "It is written, 'Man shall not live by bread alone, but by every word that proceedeth out of the mouth of God.'"
>
> Then the devil taketh him up into the holy city, and

*The spiritual meaning of the word *try* is "*T*heos (God) *r*ules *y*ou."

> setteth him on a pinnacle of the temple, and saith unto him, "If thou be the Son of God, cast thyself down: for it is written, 'He shall give his angels charge concerning thee' and 'in their hands they shall bear thee up, lest at any time thou dash thy foot against a stone.'"
>
> Jesus said unto him, "It is written again, 'Thou shalt not tempt the Lord thy God.'"
>
> Again, the devil taketh him up into an exceeding high mountain, and sheweth him all the kingdoms of the world, and the glory of them; and saith unto him, "All these things will I give thee, if thou wilt fall down and worship me."
>
> Then saith Jesus unto him, "Get thee hence, Satan: for it is written, 'Thou shalt worship the Lord thy God, and him only shalt thou serve.'" Then the devil leaveth him, and, behold, angels came and ministered unto him.

Mrs. Prophet teaches that Jesus was actually confronting the planetary dweller-on-the-threshold in the person of Satan. This planetary momentum of the dweller-on-the-threshold is the collective undefined unconscious of all evolutions of the planet.[4]

Jesus dealt again with that planetary dweller-on-the-threshold in his confrontation with the chief priests and Pharisees, the elders of the people and the powers of Rome. This face-off with forces of darkness was possible because he had already slain his personal dweller. This is why he could say, "The prince of this world cometh and hath [findeth] nothing in me."[5]

Eastern Gurus and the Dweller

In the Eastern traditions, we find the dweller-on-the-threshold in other guises—such as the ferocious temper of

Jetsün, a yogi-to-be in the eleventh and twelfth centuries. We know him now as Milarepa, universally revered by Tibetans as a great Buddhist saint who became fully enlightened.

However, as Jetsün, son of Mila-Sherab-Gyaltsen, Milarepa had a great deal to learn. The task of teaching this chela fell to Marpa, his chosen guru. And the lessons were long and hard.

Chela is a term meaning "student or disciple of a religious teacher." It is derived from the Hindi *cela,* which is taken from the Sanskrit *ceta,* meaning "slave." In the Eastern tradition of chelaship, a path of self-mastery and enlightenment, one desiring to learn the mysteries of universal law applies to an advanced yogi, known as the guru, to teach him. He serves that teacher until he is found worthy to receive the higher teachings.

The guru-chela relationship is a binding one made by choice on both sides. The guru gives teaching and testing by way of the chela's service to him. Ultimately, the goal is for the chela to pass his trials with the guru and thereby earn access to the mysteries. By doing so, the chela proves his worthiness to receive the teaching and the keys to union with his Real Self.

In order to become a chela worthy of a guru, Jetsün had to learn that humility is the way of attainment. Thus, his pride had to be broken. His guru, Marpa, had to resort to extreme methods for Jetsün to learn this lesson and to balance the karma of his angry dweller actions.

Jetsün endured many hardships in his chelaship training, including unlearning the false teachings of dark ones who taught him how to manipulate energy. He had to overcome his momentum in the practice of black magic and balance the karma of havoc he wreaked on his relatives and neighbors.

The inspirational story of Milarepa's life and path has come down to us in a biography written by one of his disciples.[6] As we reflect on the major tests Milarepa faced, let's ask ourselves, How would I have handled that situation? We learn a lot about ourselves as we imagine facing the tests of the saints. We can also take advantage of the opportunity to maximize our strengths, shore up the weaknesses and pass our own tests!

Of course, Milarepa was a rather intense fellow and his path of chelaship a dramatic short-cut—the most expedient way he could redeem serious mistakes. Fortunately, most of us are graced with somewhat less intensity and a more gentle path of redemption.

The Testing and Vengeance of Jetsün

In the first discourse covering his childhood, Milarepa explains how his family came into dire circumstances after the death of his father. Knowing he was dying, the father entrusted the care of his widow, children and property to Jetsün's paternal aunt and uncle until Jetsün should come of age. Then he was to marry Zesay (to whom he had been betrothed at birth) and take over the care of the property.

Thus, the father's property was divided between the aunt and uncle. Jetsün and his mother went to work as field laborers for the uncle in the summer and as spinners and carders of wool for the aunt in the winter. No longer were they treated as family; instead, they were compelled to work without respite.

(What would your reaction have been? Make a note of it.)

When Jetsün was in his fifteenth year, his mother called the relatives together and requested the marriage of Jetsün and Zesay and the restoration of the property to Jetsün's care, in accordance with the wishes of her late husband. However, the aunt and uncle scoffed at the request and flat-out refused to honor the father's deathbed request.

From that time on, the bereaved family chose to live and work on a small field the mother owned. Jetsün was sent to a lama to be educated, and his sister worked in the field and did small tasks for other people. The maternal relatives tried to help as best they could, and the mother and sister made do with meager food and ragged clothing.

(Ask yourself, How would I feel if that had happened to me?)

How Jetsün got into the black arts is another story: He accompanied the lama who was his spiritual teacher at that time to a feast and got drunk. In a prideful desire to show off his talent for song, he was singing loudly (and drunkenly) as he neared the house of his mother. Shocked, she rushed out of the house, threw ashes on him, struck him and fainted—which brought him to his senses.[7]

After his mother revived, Jetsün asked what he could do for her and promised to do whatever she asked. The mother, in her pain and grief, bade him learn the black arts so that he could kill their enemies, the uncle and aunt. Faithful to his promise and his mother's desperate request, Jetsün did as she asked. Thus he entered the left-handed path, the path of black magic.

(What would you do if your mother out of total desperation asked you to do something wrong?)

He apprenticed himself to a black magician and studied with him for a year. With the sorcerer's help, he wreaked vengeance on his aunt and uncle: During his cousin's wedding feast, he used sorcery to tear down the home of his uncle. As Jetsün describes it:

> A maidservant, formerly ours, but now our uncle's, came out of the house to fetch some water. As she passed the fenced-in yard where a large number of ponies had been enclosed . . . the whole place seemed to be filled with scorpions, spiders, snakes, frogs, and lizards; and, in the midst of them all, one monstrous scorpion was driving its claws into the principal pillar of the house, tugging at it and pulling it outwards.
>
> She was terrified at the sight, and barely had time to get away when several colts and mares, which had been tethered together below the house, became excited and raised a great commotion. Some of the colts, getting loose, rushed upon the mares. The whole lot were flung into the utmost confusion, the colts neighing and the mares kicking, until one of them knocked against the main pillar with such terrific force that it broke and fell, and the whole house came down with a tremendous crash.[8]

Thus Jetsün took revenge on the relatives who had deprived him and his mother and sister of their rightful inheritance. His vengeful deed killed the bride and thirty-five other people, including the uncle's sons.

(Ask yourself, Have I ever deliberately taken revenge on someone who purposely hurt me?)

Jetsün's Remorse and Pursuit of the Holy Dharma

Ultimately Jetsün felt such deep remorse for his destructive magic that he could not sleep. He longed to adopt a religious life but couldn't bring himself to ask his sorcerer-teacher's permission.

(When you feel shame and remorse, how do you handle it?)

At the same time, the sorcerer experienced the death of one of his followers, a good layman. This reawakened him to the misery of earthly existence and the bad karma he was making through practicing and teaching black magic. He shared this change of heart with Jetsün and asked him to learn and practice the holy dharma*—not only for Jetsün's sake but also for himself. He even offered to supply Jetsün with the necessary material support.

Overjoyed, Jetsün asked for and was immediately granted permission to pursue the religious life. He then consulted a famous lama who advised him to go to a monastery to seek out Marpa the Translator, the worthiest of all men. "Between thee and him there is a *karmic* connexion, which cometh from past lives," said the lama. "To him thou must go."[9]

Milarepa was deeply stirred by the lama's advice: "On hearing the name, Marpa the Translator, my mind was filled with an inexpressible feeling of delight, and a thrill went through my whole body, setting in motion every hair, while tears started from mine eyes, so strong was the feeling of faith aroused within me."[10]

(Ask yourself, When do I feel such deep emotion or spiritual delight?)

Immediately Jetsün sought out Marpa, who, after a prophetic dream indicating that he would be receiving a new chela, encountered Jetsün walking along the road near the field he was plowing. He agreed to teach Jetsün, and he put him through many difficult trials over many years.

At first Marpa told Jetsün to do sorcery, including hailstorms and killings. When he returned after doing so and asked Marpa to give him the saving Truths (teachings for enlightenment), Marpa spurned him and rebuked him for

---

**dharma* (Sanskrit, literally "carrying," "holding," "that which holds one's true nature"): an Eastern term referring to the universal doctrine, the teachings of the Buddha, the Great Law.

doing evil deeds. This was, of course, a test and a spiritual thrashing. It was the beginning of a long period of adversity calculated to test Jetsün's depth of determination and help him balance his bad karma. Jetsün was often disconcerted and confused, but he tried to be obedient.

(What would your reaction to the chastisement have been?)

Over the course of several years, Marpa proceeded to have Jetsün build a series of complicated houses from whatever materials he could find. As soon as a house was built, Marpa would order him to demolish it and restore the materials to wherever he had procured them. Sometimes Marpa would deny ever having given the order to build such a house.

All of this put Jetsün into a frenzy of building and despairing. And he developed terrible sores on his back. When he went to Marpa's wife for help, she tried to intercede on his behalf. She even suggested that he pretend he was going away because he had not learned the Truths. When Marpa found this out, he proceeded to give Jetsün the beating of his life.

Jetsün almost decided to go and seek another guru but then realized that unless he obtained emancipation in this lifetime, the evil deeds he had committed would be enough to commit him to hell. So he resolved to try his best to endure his initiatic trials. He also determined to be tireless in his search for the saving Truth, by which he could secure his victory.

Mrs. Prophet explained to her students:

> In the Eastern tradition, the chela is the "slave" of his master for a good reason—not for the loss of his true identity but for the replacement of the pseudoimage with the Real Image of selfhood. The chela, by submission, day by day is weaving into his consciousness the threads of the garment of his master. The master's garment (as

> the much sought-after robe of the Christ) is synonymous with the master's consciousness.
>
> In return for illumined obedience and self-sacrificing love, the chela receives increments of the master's attainment—of the master's own realization of his Real Self. Through the acceptance of the word of the master as inviolate, the chela has imparted to him the Christ consciousness of his master, which in turn is the means whereby the base elements of the chela's subconscious and the momentums of his untransmuted karma are melted by the fervent heat of the sacred fire in the master's consciousness.
>
> Thus by freely and willingly setting aside the momentums of his human consciousness, the chela discovers that these are soon replaced by his own teacher's mastery, which, when he makes it his own, serves as the magnet to magnetize his own higher consciousness and attainment.[11]

Jetsün went on with his work, stacking stones and gathering clay for the building. Then Marpa's wife suggested that he offer a turquoise of hers as an initiation fee to receive the Truths. He followed her instructions. But Marpa declared that what was hers was already his. He went into a fit of temper and told Jetsün to get out of his sight.

At this point, Jetsün resolved to kill himself, but Marpa's wife gave him solace. The next morning, Marpa summoned him and asked if his refusal to initiate him in the Truths had shaken his faith. Jetsün tearfully said that it was his great evildoing which had debarred him from the ceremony and that he was pierced with remorse. He burst into tears, and Marpa again ordered him to get out.

Once again, Jetsün decided to leave his guru but later changed his mind and returned. He did not know that when

Marpa's wife told him that Jetsün had gone away, Marpa had tearfully called to the great gurus and guardian spirits to bring back his destined chela-to-be. Still, when Marpa learned that Jetsün had returned, he ordered him to go on with his building, which threw Jetsün once again into despair.

(When have you felt that kind of despair? What did you do?)

From the Frying Pan into the Fire

Again Jetsün left the house of his guru. And in sympathy for his plight, Marpa's wife gave him a faked letter and gifts, supposedly from Marpa, that persuaded another lama to take him on.

(Would you have accepted some sympathetic assistance?)

Jetsün walked right out of the frying pan into the fire, so to speak, because the new lama immediately requested Jetsün punish some lawless people by launching a hailstorm on their lands. Jetsün did the sorry deed but bitterly repented the fate that had put this terrible power into his hands.

The lama taught Jetsün specific methods of meditation but to his bewilderment Jetsün received no spiritual acceleration. The lama said it was as if something were standing in the way. Jetsün was alarmed at this because he knew he had been accepted by way of pretense and deception. He realized he should never have left Marpa but didn't have the courage to own up to what he had done.

(Have you ever been in a similar situation? What did you do?)

Shortly after this, Marpa sent a note to the lama requesting him to send some loads of small branches for the ornamental topping of his house. He invited the lama to attend the consecration of his house and the coming-of-age celebration for

Marpa's son. Furthermore, he referred to Jetsün as a wicked person whom the lama should bring back to him.

Jetsün confessed that Marpa had not given his permission and that Marpa's wife had furnished the letter and gifts. The lama then told him that their work could not possibly bring any gain because Jetsün had not gained Marpa's permission.

With Jetsün accompanying him, the lama set off to see Marpa. He sent Jetsün ahead to offer gifts and announce their coming. Jetsün found Marpa sitting in meditation and asked Marpa to receive the lama who had been teaching him. Marpa immediately went into a rage and Jetsün quickly left.

Once again Marpa's wife interceded and personally received the lama. Then Marpa greeted the lama with apparent graciousness until in Jetsün's presence he fiercely rebuked him for conferring Initiation and Truths upon Jetsün. The terrified lama replied that he had done it because a letter with Marpa's seal had requested him to do so.

Marpa severely rebuked Jetsün and pursued his wife with the fiery intent of punishing her. In total despair, Jetsün determined to commit suicide, while Marpa's wife locked herself in the chapel until Marpa's temper cooled. The lama caught Jetsün, comforted him and dissuaded him from suicide by giving him the teaching that there is no greater sin. All of this was related to Marpa after he calmed down and called his wife to him.

(Have you ever reached such a depth of despair that you thought about suicide? How did you get through it?)

The Divine Pity of Marpa the Guru

In divine pity, Marpa sent his wife to invite the lama and Jetsün to come to him where he and his devotees were assembled. He even said that Jetsün was to be the chief guest. They responded to the invitation, Jetsün with an understandable sense of doubt and hesitancy.

To Jetsün's utter amazement Marpa proceeded to explain the divine purpose behind all of his trials and seeming affliction. The eight deep tribulations had cleansed him of his heavier sins, and the many minor chastenings had purified him from minor sins.

Marpa explained that the religious anger of the guru is a means of causing repentance, thereby contributing to the spiritual development of the individual on the receiving end. He concluded by stating that he, Marpa, would now care for his spiritual son Jetsün and give him teachings and initiations that Marpa himself held dear.

Jetsün felt as if he were dreaming and could scarcely express his joy. That night, offerings were laid on the altar, Jetsün was ordained a priest and he was given the Elixer of Spiritual Truths. As the great yogi Milarepa later told his followers, "Thus it was that my *Guru* encouraged, praised, and gladdened me, and that my happy days began."[12]

For those of us walking the path of spiritual tribulation and chastening, it is worthy to note that the Latin roots of the word *tribulation* are *tribulare,* "to thrash," *tribulum,* "threshing floor," and *terere,* "to rub or grind." Even as Milarepa went through his tribulations, so are we brought to the threshing floor of the LORD that our human substance might be ground into submission. Of course, most of us have not committed such evil deeds as Milarepa and therefore do not go through such intense tribulation as he did.

The Latin root of the word *chastening* is *castigare,* "to correct." Milarepa was chastened that his soul might be corrected and redirected. And so it is for each of us. All adversity becomes an opportunity for the soul's spiritual advancement.

Commenting to her students about this remarkable story of testing and initiation, Mrs. Prophet said:

> The Great Law does not require you to take a step for which you are not prepared. You can only take one step at a time. The step you can take is the step that you *should* take. And therefore, if you can see what you can do, you ought to do it because it brings you nearer to the heart of the Christ Self, who is your real and living Guru. More than that the Law does not expect.[13]

In the midst of adversity and the results of his own folly, Milarepa kept taking that next step. Sometimes he passed a test; sometimes he failed. Yet through thick and thin his soul continued to seek the Truth. Thus was he ultimately able to fulfill his divine destiny. And so it can be for each one of us.

The "Y" in the Road to Victory

There comes a time when every serious seeker on the spiritual path who has gained the full awareness of the goal of union with the Divine is faced with what is known as the Y in the Path. This is the point of testing where we choose either to glorify God or to glorify the lesser ego. We either surrender the dweller and become one with our Christ Self (Buddha Self, Higher Self) or we identify with and become one with the dweller. We can't have it both ways—good and evil do not reside together. One or the other ultimately wins out.

Mrs. Prophet has described what can happen if an individual does not transmute the not-self:

> Confusing the lower self for the Greater Self through his own self-created spiritual blindness, he enthrones the dweller-on-the-threshold in the place of his Holy Christ Self. His personality, his psyche, his stream of

consciousness all flow into the not-self.

Instead of saying, "I and my Father are One,"[14] he declares, "I and my ego are one," and it is so.... Behold Rudyard Kipling's "man who would be king"[15] who meets his fate in the abyss of the astral plane. Though he thinks he is in control, the nonentity [the egotistical not-self] eventuates in nonexistence....

You see, the one who embodies that dweller—being self-willed, and inordinately imposing his will on others, having passed the point of the Y—is actually incarnating that momentum of evil which is the equivalent of the light he had when he departed from the temple and fell from grace.

In other words, he has inverted his original dispensation of light to generate evil. Moreover, he has deified that evil and himself as its progenitor.

Now, evil, in itself, is misqualified energy.... It is a veil of illusion—an energy veil, or *e-veil,* enshrouding the Deity and all his marvelous works. Illusion, or *maya,* as the Hindus call it, then appears more real than Reality itself. In fact, men's illusions become their gods, and evil is deified....

This is why John the Baptist and Jesus Christ as well as the prophets and the avatars of all ages have come to the earth.... They come because they want to give a reprieve to the blessed children of God who are tormented by these fallen ones and yet have not the ability—the externalized Christ consciousness—to move against them.[16]

Each of us has the opportunity to make the right choice when we come to that point of the Y. If we follow the saints and sages who have preceded us, we will choose to surrender the will of our human self. We will challenge the carnal mind and dweller-on-the-threshold that would tell us to do otherwise.

We will pursue our soul's union with our Higher Self. We will pray for guidance from the ascended masters. We will choose the high road in every circumstance. And when we make a mistake, we will dust ourselves off, determine to do better and keep on going. Ultimately, by effort and by grace, we will attain eternal reunion with the Divine.

6

The Quest for Enlightenment

Lead me from the unreal to the real!
Lead me from darkness to light!
Lead me from death to immortality!

—BRIHADARANYAKA UPANISHAD

Our soul contacts God as Spirit in many ways. We may have mystical visions or dreams of days of old when adepts in the mystery schools taught us the secrets of enlightenment. We may experience a sense of inspiration, idealism and transcendence as we contact our Higher Mind. We may have tremendous passionate experiences in our feeling world when we are inundated with divine love. And we may be invigorated, uplifted and totally centered —"in the zone," as athletes say—when exerting ourselves for a cause we hold dear.

All of these experiences are reminders of the path of enlightenment. They are a glimpse of the higher energies of the etheric world touching into the physical. They are soul memories of a time when we walked the path of enlightenment in mystery schools of old, and they give us a forward thrust toward reunion with God.

Camelot: The Once and Forever Mystery School

Every soul who has ever dreamed a dream of the Holy Grail or said yes! to the hopes of King Arthur and Queen Guenevere and the knights and ladies of the flame—everyone who has ever dreamed that dream is a part of "Camelot." The best of that once and forever mystery school is a dream that inspires all of us to pursue the path of enlightenment today.

Many stories have been told about Camelot and many movies and stage plays have been created and performed. Yet many miss the essential essence of the tale.

As Elizabeth Clare Prophet told her students in a ceremony of reenacting the dream of Camelot:

> We have had a shining glimpse of that oneness, and it comes to us as the memory of the Ancient of Days, who long ago drew us into the oneness of the flame and called us to "Camelot." Our coming together again and again over the centuries, always dreaming of Shamballa and the Grail cup, is fulfilled as we relive together that once and shining moment that was Camelot and that will one day again be Camelot.
>
> In tracing the history of Camelot, such as it is written, we find this continuity—the continuity of the mystery school, of Christ and his apostles, of Buddha and the teaching and the sangha, of Maitreya, and of the children of Israel who made the trek to the promised land.
>
> Camelot was that promised land, the promised land where brotherhood and community would balance the inner fires of the soul for that creativity, that experience under the aegis of the Father and the Mother, the Son and the Holy Spirit.
>
> All mystery schools are formed after the pattern of the thirteen, and so we find that our own community has been based upon Christ and his apostles. It is to this

matrix that we gather again, and we recall in the great gathering of those who have elected to do the will of God that even in medieval Europe the guilds were mystery schools.

The cathedrals that were built reflected the mysteries of an inner law of the soul in their architecture, in their design, yet it was far beyond the comprehension of medieval man. The artisans were skilled in raising the consciousness of those who entered the cathedrals by building around them that inner geometry that is God (the "*g*eometry *o*f *D*ivinity").

Many of the secrets of the Temple of Solomon and of the Great Pyramid are evidenced in the teachings of the mystery schools. Pythagoras taught music as mathematics in the mystery school at Crotona. And the romances of King Arthur and his Knights of the Round Table are the reports of the mystery schools of the Brotherhood.

According to legend, the Round Table was made by Merlin through his alchemy and given to Uther, father of Arthur. The Round Table commemorated the table of Jesus, around which the apostles sat at the Last Supper. The table itself was said to have spiritual powers and could enlarge itself as the number of virtuous knights increased. After passing through other hands, Arthur received the table as a dowry on the occasion of his marriage to his queen, the Lady Guenevere....

On the occasion of the marriage, the table was blessed by the Archbishop of Canterbury. Merlin then bade the knights to rise and give homage to their king. The focus of king and the role of king is held by the one who is to hold the *k*ey to the *in*carnation of God [k-in-g] for that cycle and for that mystery school.

And so, after having given homage to the king, when they arose, there appeared upon the table in letters of gold the name of each knight—save two. One of these places Merlin called the "Siege Perilous"—the seat perilous. No one should occupy it but the most virtuous of knights, the one to achieve the Holy Grail. Anyone else attempting it would be destroyed. The Siege Perilous was filled at last by Sir Galahad at the conclusion of the mission of this mystery school.

At the center of the Round Table there was carved a rose. The rose was the symbol that they were of one brotherhood, of one quest, the quest for the mystery of the teachings of the Christ and the mystery of the flame of Christ. And so that mark has appeared again and again as the symbol of the unfoldment of the heart flame. There were places for twenty-four knights arranged in twelve pairs and then the double throne for the king and the mysterious unknown knight who would be worthy to sit in the perilous seat.

The rites of the Round Table descended from the celebration of the Pentecost by Joseph of Arimathea at Glastonbury, where he had come following the crucifixion and resurrection of Jesus. It was therefore ordained by King Arthur that his knights should renew their oaths each year at the high feast of Pentecost.

The knight initiates of the Brotherhood of the Quest performed special religious ceremonies, upheld the vision of the kingdom—that precious community of the Holy Spirit—and lived by a strict moral code, much like a religious order.

The jousting and competition of the knights at tournaments was the measuring of the levels of the inner soul attainment on this initiatic ladder. And it was training for the mastery of the soul in the God-control of the energies of the sacred centers of life.

The knights of the quest were dedicated to the defense of the feminine ray. Their ideal was the Cosmic

> Virgin, whom they would defend in every woman and every lady of the court. They upheld the sanctity of marriage as the Holy Family, commemorating the life of Christ, Mary and Joseph. They stood for the preservation of truth and of justice throughout the realm. And they guarded the knowledge of the inner truths of the Brotherhood and of the community....
>
> So this evening we bear the record of the great mystery, the inner mystery of this "Essene" community, and the karma and the dharma of all who have been a part of Camelot in every age.[1]

Mystical Teachings: Our Spiritual Heritage

You may be wondering what happened to the inner truths, the mystical teachings that were the foundation of Camelot and the other mystery schools. They are a part of our spiritual heritage. They have been passed down through the esoteric traditions founded by the Great White* Brotherhood—the spiritual order of Western saints and Eastern adepts who have transcended the cycles of karma and rebirth and ascended into a higher reality.

The Brotherhood also includes certain unascended disciples of the ascended masters. And all members of this sacred order work with earnest seekers of every race, religion and walk of life to assist humanity.

Mark Prophet, disciple of the ascended master El Morya, explains that the Brotherhood teaches the higher truths to those who seek the upward path of spiritual self-mastery:

> The mystery schools often find that one of the best ways they can actually contact man is through the initiatic experience, which means that man codifies the teachings.

*The word *white* in Great White Brotherhood refers not to race but to the aura of brilliant white light, the halo that surrounds these immortals.

And they say, "We're going to give you ten teachings, ten expressions of God. And when you've completed these ten teachings, you understand them and you obey them, then we'll give you ten powers."

And then mankind move a little forward and they say, "Now we're going to give you seven teachings. When you complete these seven teachings and you apply them, then we'll give you seven powers. And we will tie your growth—your spiritual growth—to the powers we will give you."

And so, step-by-step, the mystery schools take man up to the pinnacle of achievement. The mystery schools are run by people under divine direction, and occasionally in the world somebody has very faithfully represented them to humanity.

And then all at once the old man dies, you know, and the son comes along and he says, "My, that's a pretty good thing Dad's got," and he forgets all about the Brotherhood. He decides that he's going to carry on, he's going to give these powers, and he's going to charge X number of dollars for them. What does the Brotherhood say? The Brotherhood says: Freely ye have received and freely you will give....

We express today the same original teachings that were given to us first. But we do not give everybody all of our teachings in one evening or one hour, nor do we attempt to do it in a year. It is a lifetime work, and we give as much as we can and as much as people are ready for on a given occasion. And they take as much of it as they can apply in their own world.

We do not make promises and then not fulfill them. If we promise someone something, it is fulfilled, providing they keep their part of the bargain. And the bargain is actually with the Law, and God is law manifest. And

> that's the only way you can bargain with God....
>
> You can't fool him, can't turn around, decide, "Well, I'll do this if you do that." It doesn't work. But what does work is the cosmic law that our teachings are based on.[2]

Thus, the mystery schools are communities of people who devote themselves to codifying and living the higher teachings that reflect cosmic law. They have included the sangha of the Buddha, Pythagoras's mystery school at Crotona, the community of the Essenes, Camelot and the Knights of the Round Table, and organizations today that teach the inner truths, such as the Rosicrucians, the Theosophists, the I AM Activity and The Summit Lighthouse.

People who have walked the mystical path include saints, sages and yogis of all the world's religions, people not so different from you and me. What we have in common is the development of our intuitive faculties and higher consciousness through a steady and unwavering communion with God.

Contemplation, prayer and meditation are rewarding avenues for all of us who seek to remember who we really are and may become. When we quiet the busy outer mind, we are receptive to the inner guidance of our Higher Self and the angels. As we attune to the divine through our intuitive faculties, we come to know inwardly what we have never studied academically.

When we cultivate a contemplative lifestyle in today's world, we develop an inner conversation with God even as we outwardly fulfill our job, family and social responsibilities. This spiritual connection helps us make better decisions at the same time that we gain an understanding of the inner mysteries of soul and Spirit. Thus we pursue a path of spiritual practicality by which we pass our tests and gradually transcend this earthly plane of existence—ultimately to reunite with our Father-Mother God.

This understanding brings us to the story of Parsifal (or Perceval),* the classic story of a devotee who, in the innocence of his soul, walked the mystical path on earth and won his spiritual victory. Like Arthur and the Knights of the Round Table, he has left us a spiritual legacy. In the 1880s Richard Wagner popularized this sacred drama in his opera *Parsifal,* based on the narrative poem *Parzival* by Wolfram von Eschenbach.

Although the legend of Parsifal goes back a thousand years or more, the problems for the soul haven't changed that much. Always, those seeking the higher good for their soul must outwit the trap of evil. And the continuing battle of good and evil is startlingly evident today in worldwide terrorist activity, illegal drug trafficking and the ongoing threat of nuclear war.

Every time we surf the Net or turn on the TV to relax, we are bombarded with images of people committing violence, mayhem and destruction—not unlike the rampaging Queen of Hearts in the topsy-turvy world of Alice in Wonderland. Our consciousness is wounded and battered by the continuing barrage of negative, volatile energy—and so is our soul.

How do we retain our balance and our soul's sense of innocence in these difficult times? We can intensify our connection with God and live our spiritual values. And Parsifal's innocence and valor in facing evil can be a guidepost for our soul and spirit.

The Quest for the Holy Grail

Parsifal, a knight hero of the Arthurian legends, was distinguished by his quality of childlike innocence, which

*Both names, Parsifal and Perceval, reference the Arthurian knight; the spelling of the name depends on the source of the translation.

protected him and set him apart from other knights. As the simple hero, the guileless one or "pure fool," Parsifal is victorious in his search for the Holy Grail.

Through a series of adventures and temptations, Parsifal learns the meaning of chivalry and its connections with the true mysteries of Jesus Christ. As a youth, after his father is killed by an evil one, Parsifal's mother takes him into the depths of a forest where he meets Launcelot du Lac and other Knights of the Round Table. And thus begins his yearning to fulfill the quest for the Holy Grail.

In a series of brave exploits, Parsifal overcomes attacks by evil knights and resists the seduction of subtle wickedness. He is tempted by Klingsor and Kundry—masculine and feminine representatives of the dark side—who attempt to trap him through threats, sympathy and illusion. But he passes his tests and thus passes through the valley of maya, or illusion.

Parsifal completes a perilous journey to an enchanted castle, where he finds his true bride and recovers the Grail chalice. And by knowing to ask the correct question, he earns the initiatic transfer of divine light.

Through the story of Parsifal, we understand that the quest for the Holy Grail is the search for union with the hidden man of the heart, our own Christ Self. As the pure fool for God, Parsifal becomes one with the Grail, the Christ. We, too, can walk that path. We, too, can let go of our expectations and receive our Christ Self with the guilelessness of the little child.

In Wagner's opera, we see Parsifal as a probationer on the path to higher consciousness. He is striving to attain to the fullness of the Christ consciousness. He passes through many temptations and testings in his quest for the Grail.

In teaching her students, Elizabeth Clare Prophet compared Parsifal's experiences with those of Jesus Christ and described the mystery of the Holy Grail as a state of oneness with God, a spiritual consciousness to which each of us can aspire:

> Jesus Christ went into the wilderness to be tempted of the devil forty days. One would not think that the Lord Jesus Christ required temptation. We all require temptation. It is important that we meet temptation with the full understanding of the science of the Holy Grail.
>
> The question, What is the Holy Grail? is an inappropriate question. Parsifal asked the question correctly. He asked his teacher, "*Who* is the Holy Grail?"
>
> This is the great mystery. We speak of the body and blood of Christ as the energy of Alpha and Omega, the person of the Father-Mother God. . . . In the plane of Spirit, the hosts of the LORD are clothed upon with bodies celestial, as the apostle Paul teaches us. They are not simply vapory spirits without form. They have and occupy form and their bodies are entirely in the plane of Spirit.
>
> We think of the etheric body, but the etheric body is yet a part of the matter plane. It is a body that we presently wear and which we use when our souls periodically leave the physical temple in our journeys to the etheric retreats, especially during sleep.
>
> All of the ascended masters have spiritual bodies, entirely of the Spirit plane. They may use them or not use them. They may choose to use the form or the formless.
>
> Alpha and Omega, when we are speaking of them in the sense of personification, would occupy form. As letters of the Greek alphabet, Alpha and Omega signify two energies, plus and minus, masculine and feminine, that weave the cosmic caduceus on which hangs the entire Spirit-Matter creation.
>
> When the energy of Alpha and Omega descends into matter, it is not useful as the redemptive "body and blood" until it becomes personalized through the Word

incarnate. So we find in the mystery of the Holy Grail that the term *Holy Grail* itself means the personification, or the Word incarnate.

The meaning of the Word incarnate is that the Son of God embodies in the physical, in the matter universe, and contains within himself the balance of the energy of Alpha and Omega, masculine and feminine, and also the balance of the person of the Father-Mother God. When the Father-Mother God are fused into one person in incarnation, we call that person the Christ, the Son of God.

So when Parsifal asks his teacher, "*Who* is the Holy Grail?" he is asking the most significant question that the student aspiring to probationer, aspiring to disciple, must ask: Who is the Guru? Who is the embodied Lamb? Who is the present chalice for the descent of the body and blood of the Alpha-Omega?

We speak of the body and blood rather than the Alpha-Omega energy because by the pronouncement of the words *body and blood* we know that it must come from a man embodied in flesh, flesh and blood, and that that flesh and blood is no longer that which was formed of the earth earthy, but it has become the quickening energy of Alpha and Omega incarnate.

So we find that Parsifal, the pure fool, is no fool; he knows he must find the embodied Word. So the Holy Grail, cup as it is, symbol as it is, is the incarnate Word, Jesus Christ, who contains the Alpha-Omega currents. That person Parsifal seeks because he knows in the hour of temptation, the only safe passage through temptation is the tie to the Guru.[3]

A Sorcerer's Black Magic

In the second act of Wagner's opera we see Klingsor's magic castle deep in the dimmest caverns of the earth. This wicked one prepares to trap Parsifal, the "fool," in the psychic web of his sorcery. And Parsifal must pass the test of discerning good from evil if he is to win his victory—even as we are called to do today.

Klingsor knows the dual meaning of the "fool." He knows that Parsifal is the holy innocent and that his innocence is his protection. So he belittles Parsifal when he calls him a fool, carefully calculating his words to throw the aspiring one off guard. Klingsor wants Parsifal to accept his identity as fool in the worldly sense of feeling ignorant and incapable because he does not have Klingsor's mastery of the occult power of black magic.

Klingsor also possesses the sacred spear that punctured the side of Jesus on the cross, and traces of the blood of Christ that remain on the spear give it spiritual power. Klingsor gained possession of the spear from Amfortas, chief knight of the Round Table, when Amfortas attempted to destroy Klingsor in his magic garden.

To his deep regret, Amfortas succumbed to the temptations of human sympathy and sensuality and was subsequently wounded by the very spear that he carried. Thus, the spear went to the side of evil, and the black magician Klingsor gained the power of the Christ through the blood on the spear.

Klingsor calls forth his feminine counterpart, Kundry, out of the blackness of the pit to help him trap Parsifal. Under the spell of Klingsor, she is as the devil's bride and is the temptress of the knights of the Grail. However, Kundry does enough good things so that her role is confused and one is tempted to feel sorry for her.

At first she refuses to help Klingsor, but he reminds her of his unbridled power. He believes if he can defeat Parsifal, he will gain custody of the Grail. He is also fully aware of the prophecy that someone will appear through whose efforts Amfortas will be healed and the circle of the knights closed.

Klingsor curses the knights, the guardians of the Grail. And he projects an evil decree at Parsifal that he is too young and stupid, that he will fall into Klingsor's power and be stripped of his purity. Yet Parsifal remains unmoved by the black magician's accusations that he is an incompetent fool.

Then Klingsor creates the temptation of lust. He and his castle sink into the earth, and a magic garden of pleasure rises into Parsifal's view. Beautiful flower maidens appear, who are at one moment flowers and in the next, maidens. They are clad in enticing veils of pastel hues.

They sing, "We play for love's reward. Come, come, fair lad, let me bloom for you. If you cannot love and cherish us we wither and die." They surround Parsifal seeking to embrace him, but he rejects their erotic advances.

"How cold is he," they declare. "Leave be," cries Parsifal. "You'll not trap me, false flowers; you cannot snare my heart."

Ask yourself, Have I ever been tempted by eroticism masquerading as love? If I gave in to it and later regretted it, what is the lesson I need to learn? What will I do the next time around?

Make a note of it for future reference! There are people who make sexual advances simply for the erotic pleasure, yet we may be fooled into thinking the person really loves us. And we look back at those moments in our lives with deep regret.

Mrs. Prophet compared the temptation of Parsifal to that of Buddha under the Bo tree where Mara, the tempter, sent his three voluptuous daughters to seduce Gautama:

> Just before Gautama Buddha rises into nirvana in his meditation under the Bo tree he must pass the initiation

> of temptation—whether or not to give this enormous light stored in his chakras through six years of asceticism in the forest to these dancing, pleading maidens who come with all of this gravitational pull attempting to drive down the energy and create this enormous magnetism in the lower chakras. . . .
>
> Gautama Buddha told his disciples that the temptation of sex was the greatest energy that he had faced. He acknowledged its power and he confessed to them that it was his greatest initiation. . . .
>
> When we look at him today and when we read about his temptation, we think that it was just nothing at all—it was like shooing away a few flies and then into this nirvanic meditation. But he confides in us so that we will not make of him a God but realize he was human and wore a human body as we wear.
>
> So he does resist and he keeps the light within his base chakra, and by that base chakra he goes into meditation and the Mother flame begins to rise. It comes to the station of the seat of the soul, the very next chakra, and as a fountain of light it carries the soul right up through the succeeding chakras for the seven days of initiation.[4]

Manipulation of the energies of the base chakra has become a game on earth today—and the undoing of many sons and daughters of God. Yet the power of God is able to raise that light in those who are committed to pursuing the path of purification and redemption. God's forgiveness is without limit when we earnestly desire to redeem our misdeeds, whatever they may be.

Parsifal goes through additional initiations and ultimately wins the victory over evil through his purity of heart and soul. Moved by the inner fire of the Divine, he confronts and denounces the dark side. He proves himself an instrument of God.

The Victory of the Holy Innocent

In the conclusion of Wagner's opera, Parsifal returns to the Knights of the Round Table, bearing the purified spear that once wounded Amfortas but will now be the instrument of his healing. And again Parsifal encounters Kundry. She has embraced the path of penitence and service. In a spirit of holy compassion, he forgives her misdeeds toward him, leaving her judgment to the LORD God.

Now the knights bring Amfortas by litter to the altar of the Holy Grail. And Parsifal enters, saying:

One weapon suffices—
The wound is healed only by spear
That caused it.

You are whole, purified and atoned!
For I now perform your office.
Blessed be your suffering
Which gave the timid fool
The highest power of pity,
The might of purest knowledge!

This holy Spear,
I bring it back to you!

Oh, what a miracle of utter bliss!
From this which healed your wound,
Holy Blood I see flowing forth
In longing for its kindred source,
That flows there in the Grail's depth.
No more shall it be closed:
Reveal the Grail—open the shrine!

Parsifal ascends the steps of the high altar and takes the resplendent Holy Grail from its shrine. From a ray of light in the chapel dome swoops a white dove, symbol of the Holy Spirit, which hovers over Parsifal's head. Angelic voices from on high and knights of the Grail sing:

> Highest Holy Wonder!
> The Redeemer redeemeth!

Parsifal's teacher Gurnemanz and the chief knight, Amfortas, kneel before Parsifal as he passes the Holy Grail in blessing over the worshiping knights.

In the finale of the opera, we see the healing and resurrection of Amfortas and the resurrection of the knights, who have aged since they were deprived of Communion. And we also see the redemption of Kundry, who with new-found faith sees the glory of the Grail and then falls to the ground, lifeless. She cannot contain the body and blood of Christ, for the light consumes all darkness and she has much darkness to redeem.

As the guileless one, Parsifal's true identity as the "pure fool"—the holy innocent—wins the victory. It is his quality of innocence that kept him from being enmeshed with evil in the form of the enticing flower maidens. And the power of his purity and spiritual resolve defeated the denizens of the lower world—Klingsor and Kundry.

From Parsifal's journey we understand that when we seek union with our Higher Self and hold firmly to purity of motive, thought, word and deed, we intuitively live our higher values. We, too, become as holy innocents serving the light of the Grail.

By walking the path of Parsifal in our daily life, we claim the mystical chalice of our inner being, thereby allowing our soul to remember the mysteries of God. Even though we make mistakes along the way, if we persevere in healing our wounded spirit, outwitting the dweller, and anticipating and passing our tests, we gradually clear the way for our soul to reunite with our Higher Self. With heart and soul in steady communion with God, we, too, can fulfill the divine imperative to become the Grail—the Christed One.

"Hymn of the Pearl"

The "Hymn of the Pearl" (also called "Hymn of the Soul") is a poetic story from Gnostic scriptures about the journey of the soul, "the King's son," who descends to the earthly plane of existence to fulfill a divine mission. This story is also instructive to our soul.

As Elizabeth Clare Prophet explains, "The King's son is thought to be symbolic of the saviour or messenger who is sent on a mission to save the 'Pearl.' But in donning the garments of the world to which he has descended, he meets the same fate as those he has come to save. Thus the story of the prince's adventures becomes the story of every soul."[5]

One commentator believes that the "Hymn of the Pearl" was derived from the same Iranian religious myth that also underlies the Perceval (Parsifal) legend. Perceval's quest of the Grail would thus be another version of the prince's quest of the Pearl.[6]

There is support for this parallel in that the name Perceval derives from Persian roots (for instance, *Perce-val* would mean "the pure pearl.")

We can see how the pearl symbolizes the soul—pearls have a beautiful translucent quality. As we seek to understand the soul's journey to the earth plane to expand knowledge and higher faculties (as it is presented in the "Hymn of the Pearl"), let us also be thinking of our own soul's pearl-like translucence and earthly journey.

This magnificent, allegorical poem describes how, in his

journey into the veils of matter, the King's son becomes immersed in ignorance and forgetfulness. Ultimately, he has only a dim yearning for the higher world from whence he came. Each of us also yearns to remember our spiritual origin and to know what it will take to pass our earthly tests and return to the realm of Spirit.

As Mrs. Prophet points out:

> There is a great mystery to your life—that it is a known path, that others before you and others after you have walked it and will walk it, that some have graduated and have ascended as saints unto God, as ascended masters, and others will do so because *you* determine to conquer and win.
>
> Life does not leave us in a state of chaos of going to and fro trying to discover the mystery of being—in relationships or in our psychology or in past-life readings, and so forth. We know that there is an outer self evolving but the soul has been forever in the heart of God.[7]

As the story progresses, we see the King's son gradually losing his way in the lower world and his human mind magnifying self-serving desires, passions and pride. Yet he is sufficiently evolved within to receive help and teaching from an advanced soul, an "Elder Brother," between incarnations on earth.

This instruction between lives occurs in the etheric retreats or in "devachan." G. A. Gaskell, author of *Gnostic Scriptures Interpreted,* describes devachan as a higher mental plane to which the soul may withdraw between lifetimes. And Elizabeth Clare Prophet explains this plane of existence as one in which we are steeped in satisfying our worldly dreams and fancies until, ultimately, we yearn only for the higher etheric world from whence we came.

Mrs. Prophet instructs us not to condemn ourselves for our human desires but gradually to transcend them:

> When we can understand the levels of our being, our desires, our wants, and sometimes the thoughts we entertain in the light of an evolution and a descent that must bring us to that impelling moment of answering the call to come up higher, we do not condemn ourselves....
>
> We realize that the spiritual ascent is a process ordained of God, that God understands that we will come in contact with all things in this world, learn our lessons, pass some of our tests and not necessarily all, overcome some temptations and not necessarily others.
>
> The fruit of this experience is our own self-mastery and a greater love in us that intensifies as we are liberated from the lower self. Therefore, not in a world of sin and condemnation, hellfire and brimstone, but in a world of heaven and earth where we are making our way toward a higher reality—this is where we desire to see ourselves.
>
> The apostle Thomas is supposed to have sung this poem, the "Hymn of the Pearl," as a song of comfort to his fellow prisoners in an Indian prison. You remember the apostle Thomas went to India to spread the gospel of Jesus. Truly it is a comfort as we are in the prison house of matter....
>
> The pearl represents our lost soul, which must be retrieved, and also the *gnosis,* or the true knowledge of the Higher Self, which the soul must gain on its journey in order to be saved.[8]

Heaven to Earth—Earth to Heaven

As we examine key stanzas from the "Hymn of the Pearl,"[9] we will see how the archetypal story of the King's son relates to our own quest for enlightenment. (Stanzas that are commentary on the poem are enclosed in parentheses.)

THE HOME ON THE HEIGHTS

When a quite little child, I was dwelling
In the House of my Father's Kingdom,
And in the wealth and the glories
Of my Up-bringers I was delighting,
From the East, our Home, my Parents
Forth-sent me with journey-provision.

(...I went forth of my parents—the Divine Will
and Wisdom, which had clothed me in the
vestures of heaven.)

We are reminded of our origin in the heaven-world and how we came forth from divine parents, our Father-Mother God. The commentary goes on to describe how the prince's higher vehicle of consciousness remains in the heaven-world even as he descends into the lower planes of existence:

THE VESTURES OF HEAVEN LAID BY

(And as I descended unto the lower planes, my
Parents bereft me for awhile of my rich garments.
They took from my consciousness the buddhic vesture
which corresponded to that which was
The vehicle of the higher life.)

We also have a higher body, what the commentary calls "the buddhic vesture," as our vehicle in higher realms. And the physical body is our earthly vehicle.

The poem and commentary explain the pact with the Father-Mother God—if the King's son "goest down into Egypt," the material world, he must return with the "pearl," which represents the mystical union of the soul and Higher Self. Only through this union can he be heir to the kingdom of God. Accepting the challenge, the King's son begins his earthly quest:

THE DESCENT TO THE LOWER NATURE

(I quitted the point on high, from whence I began my
journeying, and went down;
But ever present with me were two intuitive
counsellors, Intuition and Hope, or Intelligence
and Will;
For the way was unknown to me, and full of
illusions to try me, my evolution being guided from Above.)

In the stanzas that follow, the poet speaks of how the King's son comes down into Egypt (the world of temptation and lust for material things) and how in this lower realm he must wrest the pearl (of higher consciousness) from the serpent (the carnal mind). The commentary describes this as the fall into materialism, ignorance and evil and how the earthly senses gradually replace higher intuition and hope.

The King's son has a journey of many embodiments and much testing before he finally wins his victory. And we realize that the journey and testing of the King's son is also the odyssey of our soul. We have gone through many lifetimes and similar dramas, which continue to the present day. Yet we have recourse to the wisdom of those who have gone before us.

THE ADVENT OF A TEACHER FROM WITHIN

(He was an Elder Brother, one who had attained
liberation from the fetters of sense,
And was a Teacher, gentle and benignant, able to
assist those in need of aid.
For he could extend the hand of help towards a pupil,
and inspire one like myself.)

Mrs. Prophet explains that the Elder Brother is an ascended master in the etheric octave—the soul's contact between incarnations. Thus, between earthly embodiments, the King's son is counseled by the Elder Brother to fulfill his quest to recover the pearl of the Higher Self and return to the realms of Spirit.

As the poem continues, in "The Reincarnation of the Ego," the poet describes how the Elder Brother warns the King's son against taking on the worldly consciousness. The commentary explains that he is being cautioned against the "wiles of the lower mind" and "illusions of the sense nature."

Yet the King's son, in forgetfulness, partakes of those wiles and illusions. Becoming a slave to the nourishment of this world, he becomes absorbed in the senses and inverted ideals. And he forgets his divine heritage and his mission to recover the pearl.

In the stanza that follows, the poet tells how the divine parents reach out to rescue their son. He will no longer be without guidance in the earthly realm of "doubt and speculation," as the commentary describes it. Their appeal comes to him, swift as an eagle flying, as the Holy Spirit bearing divine truth to his soul.

Thus, the divine parents send forth "The Spiritual Message from Within," which rouses the King's son from his sleep of forgetfulness and brings to his remembrance the higher kingdom. He is reminded of the root cause of his enslavement—clinging to the desires of the senses and disregarding the intuition of the Spirit.

He is called to remember his inner wisdom and the promise of union with his Higher Self (Christ Self or Buddha Self). As the commentary describes it, "When the Higher Self and thee—the lower Self—are united, then thou art with Us in heaven."

"I Am an Emanation from the Absolute"

In the poet's description of "The Reception of the Message," the message strikes a chord deep in the heart, and the

King's son awakens from his deep sleep of forgetfulness. With joy, he remembers his divine sonship and swiftly begins to seek reunion with his divine parents, the Divine Will and Wisdom (the Father-Mother God).

He remembers and renews his quest to recover the pearl. He lulls the serpent mind to sleep by chanting the names of Father, Mother and Brother (his Higher Self). Thus he outwits the influence of the carnal mind and turns his face homeward to God.

The poet describes the process of the King's son withdrawing from the lower emotions and the vain meanderings of the lower mind. He shuns the left-handed path and sets himself firmly in purified consciousness and true humility for his return journey to the heaven-world. With vision and perseverance, he pursues the reunion of his soul with his Higher Self.

Ultimately, the King's son regains his spiritual vestments and presents the pearl (his purified and redeemed consciousness) to his divine parents. He ends the long earthly journey and receives the blessed gift of immortality. And, as recorded by the commentator, he affirms his true nature with gladness and rejoicing: "I am an emanation from the Absolute!"[10]

As we meditate upon the journey of the King's son from heaven to earth and back again, we contemplate our own soul's journey and destiny. We, too, are destined to recover the "pure pearl" and return to the heaven-world, the vestments of our soul transformed into a crystal chalice reflecting God's rainbow light.

Take a few moments now to review the tests of the King's son:

1. Exercising right use of will in adverse circumstances
2. Accessing wisdom and discernment in the face of confusion and illusion

3. Surrendering the lust for material things
4. Outwitting ignorance and mental density
5. Resisting the temptations of evil
6. Overcoming the burden of lethargy and despair
7. Maintaining a higher vision and spiritual attunement in the midst of worldly affairs

Ask yourself, Which ones might have been my Achilles' heel?

You might also ask yourself these thought-provoking questions: When I set a goal for myself, do I pursue it one-pointedly? If not, why not? What kinds of situations distract me from pursuing my higher hopes and dreams?

Do I seek company indiscriminately when I am lonely? How can I keep from being distracted by other people's opinions or behavior? What spiritual strengths can I develop to take their place? What kinds of activities nurture and uplift my soul and spirit?

Write down your intuitive response to these questions and keep your notes as a reminder of how you can move forward in fulfilling your dreams—and your soul's divine destiny.

The "Hymn of the Pearl" can be as a guiding light, as each one, man or woman, sheds the lower nature and puts on the garment of higher consciousness. Our loving Father-Mother God have sent avatars and angels to show us the way of redemption and resurrection. Our Higher Self is only a prayer away. And all of heaven, in joy and expectancy, await our return Home!

PART THREE

Love Is the Alchemical Key

7

Dilemmas of Soul and Spirit

They that wait upon the Lord shall renew their strength;
they shall mount up with wings as eagles;
they shall run, and not be weary;
and they shall walk, and not faint.

—ISAIAH 40:31

Sometimes clients say to me, "These are modern times and I don't see how I can walk the path the saints have walked in the past. My family wouldn't understand and my friends would think I was crazy. Do you think Parsifal could make it in today's world?"

I believe that if Parsifal embodied today he would be true to himself as the holy innocent because that is who he is. The particular period of history isn't the deciding factor—it is our state of consciousness that determines our destiny.

We have all lived through many lifetimes, and we have been positioned in different cultures and circumstances. We win the game of life when we uphold the values of our Higher Self in our motives, thoughts, words and deeds. This is the way we balance our karma, accelerate on the spiritual path and claim our victory. And by doing so, we transcend time and space. When we achieve that victory, our soul and spirit rejoice and affirm with complete understanding, "I AM everywhere in the consciousness of God!"

Many of the saints have been persecuted; many good people are misunderstood. The important point is being true to our self—our Higher Self. And if we aren't sure what that means in a particular situation, we can follow the golden rule: "Do unto others as you would have them do unto you."[1]

Some highly successful people have chosen to live their lives that way. For example, James Cash Penney lived by the golden rule and gave that name, Golden Rule, to his first store. And, as we all know, J. C. Penney's stores are major retail outlets in every major city across the United States today.

This successful merchant was the son of a Baptist minister, who taught him to live by the highest moral standards. And J. C. Penney went on to make his mark in the financial world without compromising his morality. Following his rise to the top in the retail market, he shifted gears and devoted his energy and money to philanthropy. And he kept his faith even when he lost his $40 million fortune.[2] Thus his moral fiber sustained him, and his influence continues to shape the company he founded.

Will Rogers is another famous person who lived by the golden rule, although he might not have labeled it that way. Will was an actor and humorist, perhaps best remembered for his cheerful remark, "I never met a man I didn't like." That statement was much more about Will's consciousness than the people he met. He had a big heart, an open mind and a philosophy of giving to life instead of taking or hoarding. Will's approach to life is one we would do well to emulate.

Let's take a look at a saint of recent times who transcended persecution and calumny by devotion and spiritual fervor—and never let life's reverses slow him down. Who is that man? Padre Pio, a twentieth-century Capuchin monk of Italy, whose entire life was a living example of the golden rule. As we review his life and trials, let us view them as lessons and principles that we can apply in our own lives.

Padre Pio, Exemplar of the Twentieth Century

Padre Pio was born Francesco Forgione on May 25, 1887, in Pietrelcina, at that time one of the poorest and most backward areas of southern Italy. His parents were devout people who raised their children to be holy and to emulate the saints. And Francesco enjoyed being alone and praying, often to his namesake and patron saint, Francis of Assisi.

At the tender age of five, Francesco dedicated his life to God, he loved God so much. And when his friends would say something negative about God, he couldn't stand it; he would run away and hide.

When Francesco was eight years old, he witnessed a miracle. He was visiting a church with his father when a distraught woman brought her deformed and retarded son to the altar before a statue of the martyred bishop Saint Pellegrino. The boy could neither walk nor talk, and the mother begged the saint to heal her son, but nothing happened.

The mother completely lost control, cursed the saint and threw the child at the statue. As his body hit the statue, he bounced off and crashed to the floor. Then to everyone's amazement, the boy stood up and ran to his mother crying, "Mother, Mother!" This miracle made a lasting impression on young Francesco.

At the age of fifteen, Francesco entered a Franciscan Capuchin monastery. As he was meditating on the spiritual life on New Year's Day, his physical senses were momentarily suspended and in a vision he suddenly saw himself in battle with a fearful giant.

With the help of a celestial being, he defeated that formidable opponent. Two days later, his soul was "suddenly flooded with supernatural light" as he understood that his life as a religious would be a prolonged combat with that giant.

During his novitiate, Francesco was an example to all in his passionate devotion to God and deference to his superiors. However, he suffered poor physical health, including raging fevers, severe stomach upsets and intestinal distress.

Elizabeth Clare Prophet teaches that through these difficult physical experiences Padre Pio was being prepared for his lifelong service to God. Thus, his body was put through the rigors of physical cleansing that he might be prepared to bear a tremendous amount of planetary karma—the sins of the world. She explained that the fevers were the burning up of toxins and astral substance.[3]

In 1907, Francesco pronounced his final vows and three years later he was ordained into the priesthood. He received the stigmata* visibly for a short time but begged God to take them away. A year later he offered himself to God as a sacrifice for the salvation of souls.

Padre Pio was drafted during World War I and served in the Medical Corps but was too sickly to continue. He was later transferred, at the age of twenty-three, to the friary of

*The stigmata are the wounds of the Passion of Christ reproduced on the body. They may be invisible, wherein pain is experienced without any physical signs, or visible, wherein open wounds or scars are seen on the hands, feet, near the heart, on the head, shoulders or back. These wounds may bleed continuously or periodically, usually on Fridays or during Lent. Saint Francis, to whom Padre Pio was devoted, was the first saint known to have received the stigmata.

Our Lady of Grace in San Giovanni Rotondo, where he resided for over fifty years. He began his service as spiritual director of a seminary that was annexed to the monastery—a school for boys considering entering the religious life. Padre Pio enthusiastically accepted his assignment and served as confessor, principal and teacher to the boys.

Eleven years after his final vows Padre Pio again received the stigmata, the wounds of the crucified Christ, in his hands, feet and side. These wounds began to appear on August 5, 1918, when a heavenly being hurled a sharp, fiery blade at him resulting in a wound in his side. On September 20, the same divine being radiated beams of light with shafts of flame that wounded him in the hands and feet. These stigmata remained for fifty years and became a subject of controversy among certain of the holy fathers.

Padre Pio's mass was often two hours long, and during the consecration he would experience the passion of Christ and feel intense suffering in his hands, feet and entire body. Many people who came to celebrate the mass with Padre Pio were transformed.

However, in 1920, several prestigious priests and theologians denounced him to the Vatican as a fraud. Some even reported that the stigmata were due to hysteria. (You might remember that this was the era of Sigmund Freud, who diagnosed a number of his patients as having hysteria, a form of neurosis where anxiety is converted into physical symptoms.)

All of this controversy was a tremendous burden to Padre Pio. He spent many hours in prayer asking God to help him get through this time of trial. But the earthly spiritual authorities would not rest.

In 1922, the Holy Office (today known as the Congregation for the Doctrine of the Faith) became so concerned about the crowds and publicity that they began to limit access to Padre Pio. They ordered his mass to take place in a private chapel early in the morning, and he could no longer bless crowds from the window. He was absolutely forbidden to show anyone his stigmata.

Padre Benedetto, Padre Pio's spiritual director, was ordered to have no contact with him. And Padre Pio was forbidden to respond to letters from his spiritual children. The Holy Office even tried to transfer him to a friary at Ancona —some distance away. That move didn't succeed, but the bottom line was that the faithful were not to treat Padre Pio as a saint, nor were they to venerate his reputed supernatural gifts.

However, the plan backfired: more than ever, people sought to visit Padre Pio. And there were continuing reports of conversions, healings and prophecies. During this time, Padre Pio applied to serve as a missionary in India (which might have solved the problem for the Holy Office), but he was refused.

Three years later, in 1925, the Holy Office ordered Padre Pio not to talk to visitors in the sacristy, guestroom or corridor after mass. And he was not to allow anyone to kiss his hand in the traditional sign of respect. In 1931, Padre Pio was ordered by the Holy See to stop all activities except his private celebration of the mass. This official ban on contact with his spiritual children was hard to bear, even for one as disciplined as Padre Pio. Yet he bore it with grace and obedience.

Consider Padre Pio's spiritual and physical burdens and ask yourself, How did he sustain his soul and spirit through all these hardships and restrictions? Then think of the trials in your own life and ask yourself, What is it that sustains me?

Two years later, in 1933, Pope Pius XI ordered the Holy

Office to reverse its ban on Padre Pio's public celebration of mass. And his priestly functions were progressively restored. First the confessions of men were allowed and then of women. He continued to serve his Lord and the people God brought to him.

In 1956, Padre Pio founded a hospital, the Home for the Relief of Suffering. This man of God understood what it means to suffer, and his life was a sacrifice to alleviate the pain of the world. He lived and breathed the golden rule.

On September 23, 1968, the beloved padre died at the age of 81, softly murmuring the names of Jesus and Mary. And the stigmata were completely healed before he died. He had completed his walk in the footprints of his Lord with humility and grace.

Padre Pio continues to fulfill his holy service from higher octaves. Like Saint Thérèse, the "Little Flower," who asked to spend her heaven on earth helping people, he attends those who pray for his intercession. He was beatified by Pope John Paul II on May 2, 1999, and canonized as a saint of the Catholic Church on June 16, 2002. He is revered by people everywhere for his fiery dedication to God's work, for his loving compassion to those who suffer, and for his life of heroic virtue.

Take a few moments to reflect on the life of this devoted servant of God. Ask yourself, What virtue of Padre Pio would I want to emulate? Make yourself a promise to cultivate that quality. And write it down where you'll see it daily. Try it on for size!

Saint Francis: The Divine Poverello

The Franciscan Order, to which Padre Pio was devoted, was founded by Saint Francis, his namesake. The life and teachings of Saint Francis were an inspiration to Padre Pio and continue to inspire many of us today.

As prologue to understanding the humble life of Saint Francis, consider the cogent words of William Shakespeare in *King Henry the Sixth,* a play written in 1591 but apropos of the materialistic bent of the modern world:

> My crown is in my heart, not on my head;
> Not decked with diamonds and Indian stones,
> Nor to be seen: my crown is called content;
> A crown it is that seldom kings enjoy.[4]

And the sentiment is echoed by the simple words of poet Robert Greene in "Farewell to Folly," also penned in 1591:

> Sweet are the thoughts that savor of content;
> The quiet mind is richer than a crown.[5]

Francis Bernardone was born in Assisi, Italy, in 1181. His father was a wealthy merchant in the cloth-trading business and expected Francis to join him in his business. However, Francis had an instinctive compassion for the poor that didn't match his affluent way of life.

After fighting in a war, spending a year in prison and suffering a long illness, Francis was moved by an inspiring vision and conversation with God. God asked, "Francis, who can do more for you, a lord or his servant, a rich man or a beggar?" When he replied that a rich man could do more, he was asked, "Then why are you abandoning the Lord to devote yourself to a servant? Why are you choosing a beggar instead of God who is infinitely rich?"

Francis immediately withdrew from his father's trade and followed his calling from God. And his father promptly disinherited him. Francis went away penniless to live a life poorer than those he would serve. When we understand the spirit of Francis, we realize he was a man who loved God more than the things of this world.

At the beginning of his mission, Francis had a vision in which God spoke to him through an ancient crucifix in the forsaken wayside chapel of San Damiano. God's words were: "Go, Francis, and repair my house. You see it is all falling down." Francis took this instruction literally and sold his horse and some bales of cloth to get money to repair the church.

He also moved in with the priest at San Damiano, which so infuriated his father that he dragged him home and put him in chains. In her husband's absence, Francis's mother set him free, but his father brought him before the bishop of Assisi. Francis promptly stripped himself of his clothes, giving them back to his father in a spirit of complete renunciation of worldly possessions.

Thus he sought to strip himself of earthly attachments and to embrace poverty in a spirit of joy. At the same time, he remained deeply compassionate toward the humble people he served. Francis spent time nursing victims of leprosy in Gubbio and then returned to Assisi, assuming a hermit's mode of dress and way of life. He immediately set to work repairing the chapels of San Damiano, San Pietro and Portiuncula.

Ask yourself, What principles do I embrace with a joyful spirit? What earthly reverses am I willing to take? What physical service do I offer to my God and my fellow man? How do I show compassion to people I meet along the way?

Francis's renunciation of a worldly life and dedication to serving the poor was an important step on his spiritual journey. And we can liken his one-man repair of the chapels to

Milarepa's building and tearing-down tests. We can also ask ourselves how those tests apply to our own life: What do I need to tear down and rebuild—physically, emotionally, mentally, spiritually?

Francis took a further step after attending a mass where the priest read a scripture from the Gospel of Matthew in which Jesus exhorts a rich man to possess nothing.[6] This fervent young man threw away the last remnants of his worldly goods—his shoes, cloak, pilgrim staff, and empty wallet. In the simplicity of a barefoot preacher, Francis pursued his chosen vocation of poverty and devotion to humanity in the spirit of Christ.

In 1209, Francis wrote a brief Rule for the Brothers who began to serve with him. This document guided their life and work in the imitation of Christ. Subsequently, Francis and eleven companions went to Rome seeking an audience with the pope. Pope Innocent III gave his approval to Francis's Rule and granted the group permission to preach repentance everywhere.

Francis and the Brothers, now called the Friars Minor, were characterized by their love for Christ in all, a profound spirit of brotherliness, an abiding love for poverty, their deep humility, devotion to prayer and work, and a wholehearted submission to obedience.

Through complete dedication to God's service, Francis lived his life for the spiritual benefit of others, continually preaching the gospel—not only to people but also to the birds and other creatures. He loved all life. And God guided his speech through revelations and supported his words with many miracles.

The Brothers were given the little chapel of Saint Mary of the Angels (the Portiuncula) as the place where they would serve God's people. Close to the chapel they built a few small huts of wattle, straw and mud as simple places of contemplation. This settlement became the cradle of the Franciscan Order and the center of the life of Francis.

Ask yourself, How can I apply in the twenty-first century the essence of what Saint Francis taught in the thirteenth century?

The Founding of the Poor Clares

The Franciscan Order began to include women due to the efforts of a devotee of Francis, a young woman also from Assisi, whom we know as Saint Clare. Clare was eighteen when she heard Francis preach in the cathedral and was so impressed that she resolved to live as Francis did, after the manner of the Gospel. Francis approved her resolution, but because of her family's opposition, Clare had to leave her home in secret.

The night of Palm Sunday, 1212, she left home with an elderly relative and went to the little chapel of the Portiuncula. Here Saint Francis and the friars met her with lighted candles and led her to Our Lady's altar. Her hair was shorn as a symbol of her renunciation of worldly concerns. And she exchanged her fine clothes for a habit of rough sackcloth. Then they took her for safety to the Benedictine convent of Saint Paul, where she was affectionately welcomed.

Her family found out and determined to rescue her. She resisted valiantly. When her relatives tried to drag her out of the chapel, she hung on to the altar. She declared that Christ had called her to his service, she would have no other spouse, and the more they continued their persecution the more steadfast she would become. The family finally gave up. And Francis moved Clare to the nunnery of Sant' Angelo in

Panzo, where her younger sister Agnes, a child of fourteen, soon joined her.

Sometime later, Francis placed the two young women in a humble abode adjacent to his beloved church of Saint Damian on the outskirts of Assisi. In 1215, Francis appointed Clare superior and gave her his Rule to live by. By this time, Clare's mother and several other women had joined her—sixteen women altogether.

They all felt the strong appeal of poverty and sackcloth and gave up titles and estates to become humble disciples with Clare. And within a few years, similar convents were founded in a number of cities in Italy and in parts of France and Germany.

The Poor Clares, as they came to be known, practiced physical austerities. They went barefoot, slept on the ground, abstained from meat and spoke only when absolutely necessary. They considered silence desirable to keep the mind steadily fixed on God and to avoid the sins of the tongue.

Clare occupied her office as abbess for forty-one years. She was a loving mother to the nuns, rising at night to look after their comfort or the needs of the sick. She had a cheerful disposition, and like Saint Francis, constantly praised God for having made the world so beautiful.

Think about the life of this loving nun, and ask yourself, What are my hopes and dreams? Do I pursue them in the face of opposition or setbacks? If not, why not? What inner strengths do I need to cultivate to fulfill my destiny?

The Final Testing of Saint Francis and Clare

In 1219, Francis went on to join the Crusaders at the siege of Damietta in Egypt, where, at the risk of his life, he preached to the Sultan. He returned to Italy and underwent a severe spiritual trial when some of his friars sought to change his fundamental Rule to a more moderate approach. He obtained appointment from Cardinal Hugolin to be the Protector of the Order and also received inner assurance that Christ would always remain the principal head of the Franciscan Order. Only then did he resign as the Order's administrator.

In September of 1224, while praying in his cell on Mount Alverna, Francis experienced the mystical joy of holding the Babe of Bethlehem in his arms, which was followed by the imprinting of the stigmata. This came about after a fast of forty days and nights, during which he had a vision of a crucified seraph.

As the vision disappeared his heart was ablaze with eagerness and upon his body was impressed a miraculous likeness of Christ's wounds in his hands and feet. His right side was marked with a bright scar, which often bled.

He continued to preach, day after day, getting little or no rest, and developed a severe infirmity of the eyes. Riding on a donkey, he made a preaching tour in Umbria and the Marches and the following year visited Clare at San Damiano. By then, almost blind, he underwent various treatments for his eyes, which produced no improvement. And when he went to Siena for further treatment he became seriously ill.

He insisted on being carried to the Portiuncula, where he called the Brothers to him and blessed them. He asked to be dressed in a hair shirt and to be sprinkled with ashes since his body was soon to become dust and ashes. Francis's soul was released from his body on October 3, 1226, and he was canonized as Saint Francis on July 16, 1228.

Clare followed in his footprints: her order flourished and spread to other parts of Italy and to France and Germany.

She became so revered that her advice was sought and accepted by popes, cardinals and bishops. And she was credited with many miracles, including saving Assisi from Frederick II's soldiers in 1241 by her prayers. Next to Saint Francis, Clare was most responsible for the growth and spread of the Franciscans. She died at Assisi on August 11, 1253, and was canonized as Saint Clare two years later, in 1255.

We can look at the lives of Clare and Francis as symbolizing the spiritual journey of our soul and spirit. We are moved by our soul when we yearn for union with God, and we recognize our spirit in our zest for life. When we uplift both soul and spirit, we are as one with our Higher Self. In that oneness, our soul is peaceful and our spirit fiery in service to God and man.

Ask yourself, What does my soul desire to absorb from Saint Clare? What does my spirit need to learn from Saint Francis? How can I embody these virtues for the victory of my soul and spirit?

Prayer of Saint Francis

Here is a beautiful prayer, attributed to Saint Francis, that can help us to synchronize our consciousness with this great saint:

> Lord,
> Make me an instrument of thy peace.
> Where there is hatred let me sow love;
> Where there is injury, pardon;
> Where there is doubt, faith;
> Where there is despair, hope;
> Where there is darkness, light; and
> Where there is sadness, joy.

O Divine Master,
Grant that I may not so much
Seek to be consoled as to console;
To be understood as to understand;
To be loved as to love.
For it is in giving that we receive,
It is in pardoning that we are pardoned, and
It is in dying that we are born to eternal life.[7]

A Spiritual Journey for Everyday People

Now let's take a look at the spiritual journey of people like you and me, everyday people who love God, do their best and hope that will be enough.

I have clients who say, "I don't really know what to work on, but I have a feeling of uneasiness and I'm not sure what that's all about." When we get into an in-depth discussion, we often discover that it is not the outer person who feels uneasy; rather, it is some level of the soul or spirit.

I remember Jim, who felt constantly tortured by doubts and fears. Sometimes they would be so extreme that he couldn't clear his mind enough to function on the job. Yet he couldn't put his finger on any particular problem in his life.

Jim was married with two children. He and his wife both worked, and they had an amicable relationship. Finances were reasonably okay, and there hadn't been any major accidents, illnesses or deaths in the family. Nothing he could think of accounted for his fearful state, so I began to probe.

I knew Jim was dedicated to his spiritual path, and I asked him if there were any problems in that area. Jim thought for a few minutes and then shook his head as he responded, "I don't think so. My wife and I don't exactly see eye-to-eye about spiritual matters, but we don't fight about it or anything.

I guess I wish Anne were a little less definite in her opinions, but she has a right to disagree with me—as she is always pointing out."

"Let's look at that, Jim," I responded. "What happens inside of you when the two of you disagree on spiritual matters?"

Jim said, somewhat hesitantly, "Well, I start out feeling all churned up, and by the time we're through, I feel kind of empty, and sad."

I encouraged him: "Tell me about feeling sad and empty and when you have felt that way in your life before."

He was silent for a few minutes, and then said, "What's coming to mind is a time when I was a kid and trying to figure out God. I remember I asked my dad if he knew God, and he laughed. So I didn't ask him again. And then he told my mom and they made a big joke out of it. As you can guess, they didn't go to church or anything, and I suppose they didn't know what to say. But it really upset me. Maybe it's my soul that's sad."

"Why don't you ask your soul about it?" I responded.

"Okay." Jim closed his eyes for a few minutes and then began to tear up. "My soul thinks everyone has given up on me, and she doesn't know what to do."

"Tell your soul that you love her and you will help her," I suggested.

Jim opened his eyes and asked me, quizzically, "How am I going to do that?"

"You are going to let her tell you what she needs. Okay?" I responded.

"Okay," he replied, and was silent for several minutes. I knew that Jim didn't like to dialogue out loud so I simply waited.

When he described his inner dialogue, it was with a tone of sadness. "She wants to know for sure that I'm not going to give up my spiritual work just because Anne doesn't agree with it. She told me she's scared I will because that's what I did when I was a kid. And, actually, she's right. After my parents made a joke out of God, I just turned my spiritual faucet off, so to speak. And I didn't do anything about it until I was out of college."

"When did you get back on a spiritual path?" I asked.

He sighed. "That was almost an accident in itself because I was too put off to go looking for it. But I met this girl who was studying Christian mysticism and wasn't shy talking about it. In fact, that turned out to be another bad experience because when I didn't take her seriously, she got all upset. I didn't mean to upset her, but I didn't know how to relate to what she was telling me. I should have kept my mouth shut. Anyway, she told me to get lost."

"You certainly have had a lot of tests around your spiritual path, haven't you?" I responded. "How did you get into the teachings you are following now?"

Jim brightened up. "That was actually the result of a lot of praying. After that girl dumped me, I realized that I had gotten pretty far away from who I was as a kid when I felt God's presence but didn't understand what to do about it. So I decided not to talk to anyone else but to start talking to God as if he were right in the room with me. At first it was kind of hard, but then I began to feel a kind of tingling all over, and I remembered that is how I would feel as a child. So I asked God, what is this tingling? And then I had a really neat experience.

"I had my eyes closed, and all of a sudden it was like I was in the middle of a beautiful field of light—that's the only way I can describe it. And I felt completely safe and like all of me was back together again. I didn't want it ever to stop. Of course, it did stop after a time, but I never forgot it. So then I started looking for someone who taught about the white light, and that's how I found the teachings of the ascended masters."

"That sounds like a marvelous experience," I commented.

With a smile and nod, he said, "Yes, it was. And remembering it brings back some of the good feeling."

"Okay," I said. "Now talk to your soul again, and ask her what she needs from you right now."

He did so and shared the experience with me. "She says, if we just stay in touch with the light, we'll be okay, and she won't be sad anymore."

"How do you feel right now?" I asked.

He pondered. "It's a mix of feelings. When I think of the light and my soul, I feel really good. But when I think about trying to get my wife to share it, I feel kind of discouraged because she isn't into mystical experiences. And it's kind of ironic because the girl who was so put off with me would have really appreciated what I'm experiencing these days."

"Do you love your wife?" I asked.

"Yes, I do. And she loves me. But we don't see eye-to-eye on religion," he responded.

"Does she have a spiritual path?" I asked.

He replied, "Yes, she's into studying the world's religions. But she doesn't have the inner experience with the light. And I think it kind of scares her when I talk about it."

"Do you have to experience God in the same way in order to appreciate each other's spirituality?" I asked.

Jim was thoughtful for a few minutes, and then said,

"Maybe that's the problem we've been having. I want her to experience the light and she wants me to study the world's religions. Then we end up arguing with each other, and there we go again. Maybe if we just made an agreement that it's all about God anyway and let each other have our own path, we could get through this."

"That sounds like a good idea. Why don't you share what you just told me with Anne?" I replied. "Just talk about it and see what happens. And however she responds, I suggest you remain thoughtful and loving."

Jim did just that and also shared with Anne what had happened in his therapy session. They made an appointment with me to talk about what they both thought was a breakthrough. Jim realized that when he was honest and thoughtful in sharing his inner experience, Anne was receptive. She simply wanted him to honor her path, too. And when he told her about his childhood experience with his parents, they both realized that Jim was afraid she would make fun of him like his parents had.

On Anne's part, she was enthusiastic about exploring the world's religions. This was the first time in her life that she had been excited about spirituality, and she didn't want to be put down because she didn't "see the light" the way Jim did. In the end, they agreed to pray together, stay together and respect each other's spiritual journey.

This couple's experience is a lesson in how the soul can feel put down and the spirit dampened when we feel misunderstood, particularly when it involves our spiritual journey and someone close to us. Yet many times it can be worked out if we have the courage to address it honestly.

Jim and Anne learned that it was safe to open their hearts to each other and that childhood hurts can be healed by love and compassion. They also realized that by sharing their spiritual journey with grace and nonjudgment, they could meet the challenge of their differences. Each one's search for God, in his and her own way, became a common ground.

Many times we are hurt or disheartened out of some kind of misunderstanding with someone we love. A prescription I often give is, "Give each other the benefit of the doubt." Each of us has secret hurts that are difficult to talk about, yet keeping them secret weighs heavy on our soul and spirit. So I encourage people to give friends and loved ones an opportunity to understand where they are coming from.

The comforting bottom line is that no matter how friends or family respond, we can always share our hurts with God, who is the Great Healer of our heart, soul and spirit.

8

Curing the Angst of the Soul

Go to your bosom;
Knock there, and ask your heart what it doth know.

—WILLIAM SHAKESPEARE
Measure for Measure

Our soul's most painful dilemma is feeling separated from God. Caught in the veils of maya, she yearns for the bliss of Reality. As we heed that inner yearning, we catch a glimpse of our original purity. We begin to remember who we really are and to welcome the sun of God-reality that shines through the veils.

In the sunlight of clear vision, our consciousness is uplifted. We gain insight into our higher nature and the energy tangles that need to be straightened out before we come Home.

When we are "awake!" as the Buddha put it, we can shine the light on aspects of darkness, within or without. We can free ourselves from the debris of old records, mistaken ideas, unruly emotions and physical misdeeds.

In contrast, when we are "asleep," we live in a shadow world where we no longer remember who we really are because we have identified with unreality. We become preoccupied with shadowy motives, thoughts and feelings. The light of God seems unreal and far distant from our human experience.

We have outer examples of this inner dilemma: remember an eclipse of the sun and imagine it lasting forever. Chilling thought, right? Or think of the long winters in the northernmost parts of the planet, for example, Alaska or Siberia. How would you feel?

During winter months everywhere, a number of people develop what has been called the SAD (Seasonal Affective Disorder) syndrome.[1] This malady results from a lack of sunshine over a lengthy period of time, and the symptoms are depression or gloom. In fact, the syndrome has been nicknamed "the winter blues."

Although artificial sunlight has been found to help people physically, the spiritual dilemma remains unresolved. The sun, besides warming the body and lifting the spirits, is also a daily reminder of a higher plane of existence where divine light and warmth prevail. Thus, in the sunshine the soul feels uplifted and the spirit energized. When the sun is clouded over, we feel somehow bereft.

In much the same way, when our karma deals us a serious setback in our livelihood or a relationship we value, our mood darkens and our sense of connection to God may fade. We become edgy and reactive.

We feel a bit unsure of ourselves and tend to revolve mistakes we have made. At the same time, our soul feels anxious and our spirit depressed. Thus, we flip back and forth between anxiety and depression, two sides of major emotional distress. Inwardly, we feel as if we're riding an emotional roller coaster.

Outwitting Anxiety and Depression

Anxiety and depression are basic emotions that many of us encounter, especially during turbulent times. As W. Walter Menninger, M.D., wrote in 1995, "Anxiety is a basic, ubiquitous emotional experience. Its discomforting, unsettling feelings provoke the individual to seek relief, either by mastery or by avoidance and escape from the anxiety-provoking situation.... A history of quiet desperation and limited hope for relief is not uncommon."[2]

This statement is even truer today than it was when Dr. Menninger wrote it, before the advent of worldwide terrorist strikes and the economic crises on Wall Street.

Ask yourself, What kinds of situations provoke anxiety in me? How do I access my higher consciousness when I am overwhelmed with anxiety, confusion and depression? Reflect on your answer in the light of instruction from the ascended master Saint Germain:

> Anxiety is the great warp of life. It warps perspective without producing any perceptible benefit whatsoever....
>
> Anxiety is a symptom of insecurity; it stems from man's incorrect concept of himself and from his lack of perspective. Many people feel unfulfilled, unloved, unwanted, and they are not sure of just what they should be doing with their lives. Their uncertainties under adverse conditions are easily turned into mental and emotional states of depression bordering on extreme self-deprecation....
>
> Unless the deterrent forces which are imbedded in the psyche of man are brought under the power of divine grace and emptied of their content (i.e., of the misqualified energies which sustain their forms), they will

peer as haunting specters waiting to devour the offspring of all benign activities and to literally turn man's light into darkness. . . .

Anxiety stems from a lack of faith in the ultimate purposes of life. The hard experiences that have come to many in childhood and in later years, creating stresses and strains and producing the fruit of bitterness, have prevented their development of that refined spirit which would enable them to shed their anxieties. . . .

Through alchemy, the shedding of your anxieties can be accomplished, but first you must build a mountain of faith to counteract the negative thoughts of the world which are primarily responsible for man's failures.

How is this so? Each time individuals have a failure and lament it, each time they have a problem and sorrow over it rather than commit it unto the Father, each time individuals resent their problems and see them not as the return of karma or as a test but as an act of Deity whom they defy, they are building up in their own worlds frustration, resentment, anxiety, and confusion. And these momentums draw to their own doorsteps the negative conditions of the outside world. . . .

A secondary enemy to anxiety . . . is confusion. This, too, can and should be healed by the fires of the Christ mind. For we know that the Christ mind is calm yet capable of focusing the fiery energies of the Creator to overthrow evil both in the self and in society. . . .

Anxiety must go. It must be replaced by faith and solemn confidence in the outworking of the divine plan. This certain knowing, I say, is a happy state! When you begin to understand fully what I mean, you will see that the developing of this confidence in the Real is one of the greatest ways in which all deterrents to successful alchemy can be vanquished. In fact, all deterrents to abundant

> living can be knocked down as you cease to fight "as one that beateth the air,"[3] as Saint Paul once said.
>
> You were born to win, and I say this to counter the lie that man was "born to lose." And if you will make this statement, "I AM born to win!" as an act of supreme faith, it will overcome the world's consciousness of failure....
>
> Understand the duality of life and realize that anxieties must go. But in order for this to take place, you must make the conscious determination that it shall be done.[4]

Are you ready to make that determination? If so, I suggest you do it right now. Ask your Higher Self to strengthen your faith in God and yourself. Affirm out loud your desire to fulfill your higher purpose and to act accordingly. Let go of the anxiety, confusion, depression or self-doubt that have been as an emotional cloud between your soul and the Sun of your I AM Presence.

As you release the grip of self-defeating thoughts and feelings, it is easier to affirm your faith in God, to develop clarity of purpose and to form a habit of looking at the sunny side of life. As this positive thrust becomes a daily practice, you feel increasingly more comfortable with yourself. And you no longer turn small setbacks into calamities. Instead, you find a way to go through or around the obstacles and move on. Once you firmly identify with who you *really* are, you overcome the moodiness that comes from identifying with the not-self.

All of us tend to identify with the attitudes of people we associate with, for good or ill. Thus the Buddha taught right mindfulness, whereby our higher values are strengthened. And when we reclaim our identity as the son or daughter of God we really are, we see a shift in our relationships. Our true friends remain but those connected with our "unreal self" often drop away.

Thus we understand that we relate to each other by way of the energies we unconsciously project back and forth. Through the "movie projector" of the mind we focus our motives, thoughts and feelings upon the screen of the other person. The result is that we see that person through a veil of our projections. And they do the same. Is it any wonder that we find ourselves caught in unreality?

What is the answer to this dilemma? First, we pray for and develop self-knowing—knowing who we are in all dimensions of consciousness. Second, we ask our Higher Self to help us clean the mirror of consciousness and focus on seeing clearly. Third, we reclaim our projections; for example, we take responsibility for our own attitudes and actions instead of blaming the situation on other people. Fourth, we monitor our motives and thoughts, feelings and behavior—not just when we are alone but also when interacting with other people.

We become as commander-in-chief over straggly elements of the not-self and drill them until they march in precision with our Real Self.

The Bully and the Wimp

I remember a young woman, Melinda, who had not-self elements that definitely needed reforming. She came in presumably to work on herself but immediately shifted to venting her hatred for her cousin. As she put it, he was just "a no-good wimp." According to Melinda, every time they got together at a family gathering, Buddy would complain about the way she was treating him and she would get in trouble. As she described it, "He comes unglued the minute he sees me. And then he ruins everything."

"What happens?" I asked. "Give me an example."

She reflected a minute. "Sometimes he has a point. I provoke him for no real reason. I just plain don't like him."

"Why not?" I queried.

"Like I said, he's wimpy and he gets me in trouble!" she said. "All I have to do is look at him and he falls apart. And then I kind of take a perverse delight in doing things I know freak him out."

"How come?" I asked.

She looked slightly chagrined. "I don't know. Mostly because he acts like such a jerk—kind of like I used to be before I determined to get over it. Sometimes he does it just to get my goat."

"How do you know?" I asked.

She responded, "I can tell. And every time I test it out, he proves it."

"Tell me how you test it out and how he proves it," I requested.

"Okay," she said, "like last summer. It's a really hot day. I'm watering the yard and he comes around the corner. So I kind of playfully squirt him with the hose, and it's not like he's got on good clothes or anything. Does he think it's funny? No. He starts whining that I hate him and always pick on him. I get disgusted, turn my back on him and keep on watering. Then he yells he hates me, goes off sulking like a little kid and tells the family I'm bullying him. Then I get in trouble. He made a federal case out of it!"

"What were you feeling when this was going on, before you got disgusted?" I asked.

"Well, I don't like him but I was sort of kidding around until he started whining," she responded.

"Let's try something here," I suggested. "Pretend you're him. How would you have reacted?"

Melinda smirked when she said, "I'd probably have tried to beat him up!"

"You really don't like him, do you?" I commented.

"You're right about that!" she answered definitively.

I wondered out loud, "If you dislike Buddy so much, were you really being playful when you turned the hose on him? And what did you mean when you said you used to be a wimp?"

She was silent for a minute and then responded, "Maybe I was being a little bit mean as well as playful. And I did used to get upset when kids would pick on me. I'd go crying to my mom, and she'd say, 'You have to fight your own battles.' So I learned to do that. I got over being a wimp."

I was silent while she contemplated her own words.

"So you're thinking I'm calling him a wimp because I was a wimp, right?" she asked.

"What do you think?" I replied.

Melinda sighed. "You know, he didn't used to be such a wimp. He started reacting that way around the time I decided I wasn't going to be wimpy anymore. Maybe that's one reason it makes me so mad. It's like seeing a mirror of the old me, and I suppose now you're going to say I'm projecting my own stuff on him when I call him a wimp, right?"

"Keep on going. You're doing fine," I said.

"Okay, I guess that's why he makes me mad. I think there's a part of me that still feels kind of cowed around other people, and I don't like that part of me at all. I really hate it when I see it in someone else!" she said emphatically.

"So this is more about you than about Buddy?" I suggested gently.

Melinda sighed again. "Okay, okay. You're right. I have to admit he doesn't act as dumb around other people. It's mostly with me, especially when I rub him the wrong way."

We continued to talk it through, and Melinda began to feel less disgusted with Buddy and more upset with herself. When she took a good look at the situation, she realized that Buddy was telling her the truth. She had been dumping on him the same way other people had dumped on her, even though she knew how painful it was.

Once Melinda became aware of what she had been doing, she decided to cut it out. At first, she focused on being neutral around Buddy and refraining from bullying him. Eventually, he asked her, "How come you aren't picking on me anymore?" By then, she was ready to explain what had happened to her and how he was like a mirror of her own stuff.

Buddy was strongly affected by Melinda's honesty and her change in behavior. He did some serious thinking on his own part and started trying to be real instead of playing outraged victim. And he realized that under the surface "wimp" behavior, he had a bully of his own. Mostly he bullied himself about what a weakling he was. But when Melinda was mean to him, as he finally told her, he had actually fantasized beating her up—"the worm turns" kind of thing. And that had really scared him.

Melinda and Buddy started being civil to each other once they realized they had something in common. And they developed a code for signaling each other when one of them slipped into "wimp" or "bully."

Psychologically, we would say they both reclaimed their projections: Melinda was projecting "wimp" on Buddy; he was projecting "bully" on her. And each had played their part to the hilt. Both of these young people ultimately took an honest look at what they were doing because inwardly, at the level of their soul and spirit, they wanted to be real instead of "wimp" or "bully."

When we reclaim our projections and identify with who we really are, we can disclaim unreality. Instead of staying stuck in self-condemnation or blaming other people, we can do a turnaround. We can choose a positive stance that expresses who we really are.

As we focus on giving other people the benefit of the doubt, we usually get along with each other a lot better. Whatever happens, we know we're going to be okay because we're straight with ourselves. And that brings me to a quick prescription for addressing any problematic situation.

Quick Prescription

1. Center in your heart and ask God, What can I do to resolve this situation? What positive step can I take? Once you get an answer, take that step.

2. If the answer is, "All you can do is pray," do that. Ask God to handle the situation the best way possible. And surrender the outcome of the situation to him.

3. The answer may be, "This isn't your problem." In this case, ask God to help you detach from the situation. Do a simple prayer for whoever is concerned and let the situation go—mentally, emotionally and physically.

4. Father-Mother God and the angels always respond to your prayers. Trust that the will of God is good, and be at peace with yourself.

In other words, talk to God, do what you can and unhook from whatever you can't change. Just let it go and give it to God. This process can save a lot of wear and tear on your mind and emotions.

Depression and the Dweller

On a spiritual level, depression is an emotional manifestation of the soul's entrapment by the dweller. When the soul is overwhelmed or shamed, depression creeps in. If anger or rebellion take root, depression gains a stronger foothold. And the soul feels helpless and hopeless in the midst of the deadly game the dweller is playing.

Kuthumi gives a graphic description of this dilemma of the soul:

> Depression is that state of the twilight zone where the individual has neither slain the dweller nor entered fully into the heart of Christ. It is the most dangerous situation of the soul in this octave of the matter universe. . . .
>
> Some of you have recurrent dreams of walking over very insecure bridges, over deep chasms or through narrow passageways, or of being confined in a box. You may wake up in a cold sweat, you may experience terror in the night.
>
> And thus, a lesson is coming through from your Higher Mental Body [Higher Self] that tells you that you have placed yourself in a condition that is dangerous, that you must pass through it, you must make a move, you cannot go back and you cannot stand still: you must move forward.[5]

Thus depression is the "never-never land" of the soul who has yet to slay the dweller-on-the-threshold and embrace the

Christ Self. This malady is a manifestation of the despair of soul and spirit stuck in a morass of wrong choices. And the solution is to turn one's face to the light of the Christ and keep moving toward the light, no matter what! But to a depressed person, this may seem like the most difficult action in the world.

Studies in Overcoming Depression

I remember a friend many years ago, Casey, who was so seriously depressed that she had trouble getting out of the bed in the morning. Yet she had children to care for, so she knew she had to get up. And all of this was before the days of medication for depression (which I consider to be a grace that God has extended through science).

Casey's solution was simple. She made it a point to "kick myself out of bed," as she put it. And then she immediately made the bed to keep herself from getting back in. Then, step-by-step, she took care of the duties before her: feeding the baby, dressing the toddler and making the grocery list.

Once she got moving she was able to get through the day. And she would make herself sit in the sun for a few minutes whether she felt like it or not. She always felt better once she did that; it was getting started that was hard. And this was the case for every aspect of her life at that time.

As Casey told me, "It was just one foot in front of the other, like a wooden soldier, until I got moving. Once I overcame that tremendous lethargy, I could make it. And fortunately, I had two little ones who prodded me by their needs. I wonder how people do it who don't have someone who needs them?"

This story had a happy ending. Casey never had the benefit of medication but she created a habit that outwitted the depression. She simply didn't give in to it. After several years she no longer gave it a lot of thought.

Of course, sometimes depression has a physical cause. And for that reason it is important to see a doctor and get a proper diagnosis. But many times depression is more a problem of the soul, who may be in rebellion to her karmic predicament or in despair about making it home to God.

Another of my clients, Judith, discovered that her depression was rebellion against her karma and anger at God. As we were working through disturbing dreams,[6] she remembered turning her back on God many lifetimes ago. And she had become embroiled with other people who were equally rebellious.

In that past lifetime Judith had embraced the eat-drink-and-be-merry-for-tomorrow-we-die philosophy of the fallen angels. She had squandered her energy in many ways, including prostitution, which at that time in her culture was punishable by death. And eventually she was stoned to death.

As Judith relived the trauma of that lifetime she felt absolute hopelessness. But at the end, when she was being stoned, her soul cried out to God for another opportunity. And her desperate appeal was answered. She was given the same test in another embodiment, and this time she turned her back on the dark side. That was the turning point for her soul.

In her present life Judith is an accomplished woman who is devoted to her spiritual path. She married and bore children and has lived a life of service to others. And the only reason she came for therapy was to resolve this old record that had surfaced through her dream work.

As she told me, "Now I understand the urges I have had in this life. They were old habits coming up for transmutation. I am truly grateful for God's redemptive path. If I can make it, anyone can make it!"

Thus we see the power of determination. I firmly believe that God helps those who help themselves. That isn't to say that we don't need help from one another or that we should ignore the cries of those who are caught in the toils of the dweller. But it is spiritual truth that the soul must cry out to God for help, be truly repentant, and walk the path of redeeming her karma. This is the way we forge our spiritual victory.

Gnosis and Self-Knowing

Throughout the ages there have been people who focused on self-knowledge as a way of overcoming their karmic predicament and achieving enlightenment. The Gnostics were one of the better-known groups who separated out from religious tradition to follow their own spiritual path. They suffered the wrath of the early church fathers, who believed they were a threat to the mission of Christianity and therefore destroyed all records they could find of Gnostic teachings. However, the Gnostic tradition of knowing the self has made its impact upon the mystical traditions.

As you remember, this quest for self-knowledge is the mystical story of the King's son in the "Hymn of the Pearl." Although for a time he gets lost in maya and forgets his divine heritage and his quest, the message from his divine parents awakens him to who he really is. And that self-knowledge, "I am an emanation from the Absolute," is the goad that quickens his determination to recover the pearl, the true knowing of his Higher Self. We are also the sons and daughters of God—and through awakening to oneness with our Real Self, we, too, can fulfill our quest and propel ourselves Homeward.

Elizabeth Clare Prophet teaches that self-knowledge is

essential to the soul seeking reunion with God. In order to achieve that union, the seeker must not only know and claim the qualities of the Real Self but also overcome the perversions of the human consciousness and the "electronic belt."

Mrs. Prophet explains that this belt of negative energy is positioned in the aura around the lower portion of our body. It extends from the waist to beneath the feet and contains the records of our impure motives and actions as they have piled up over many lifetimes. The electronic belt can be likened to a kettledrum of impurities, which can be clearly seen by clairvoyants. And we are influenced by those impurities until they are cleaned up.

Mantras and decrees to the violet flame are an excellent way to cleanse the electronic belt.* As we invoke the purifying violet light and direct it into the electronic belt, the negative energies are purified and transformed. Then we make certain not to re-create them all over again. And that means that we strive for purity of consciousness.

We ask ourselves, What would my Higher Self think of this attitude, idea, verbal expression or physical action? Our Higher Self prompts us intuitively, and we typically get an uncomfortable gut feeling or solar-plexus churning when we're on the wrong track. The more we check in with our Higher Self the better we get at making right decisions. This is an aspect of the path of self-knowledge.

Mrs. Prophet gave the following teaching on Gnostic texts to help her students expand their self-knowledge and self-mastery:

> The Gnostics emphasized *gnosis*—esoteric knowledge or knowledge of one's true self—as opposed to the orthodox emphasis on *faith*. For the Gnostic, gnosis

*See prayers, mantras and decrees to the violet flame, pp. 47, 310–11.

brings redemption, not from sin but from ignorance. We could say that ignorance is the only sin and the only cause of suffering, coupled with the failure to undo that ignorance.

In the Book of Thomas the Contender, Jesus is quoted as saying, "Whoever has not known himself has known nothing, but he who has known himself has at the same time already achieved knowledge about the depths of all things."[7]

And in the Gospel of Thomas, Jesus says, "If you bring forth what is within you, what you bring forth will save you." He is speaking of the causal body* and the great light of Christ. "If you do not bring forth what is within you, what you do not bring forth will destroy you."[8] He is speaking of the electronic belt and the subconscious [and unconscious].

If you don't know that you have a demon of anger that periodically erupts to destroy your loved ones and yourself, if you will not face that the cause is within you, if you will not stop blaming others for your getting out of hand and being obnoxious, that thing will destroy you. And no one else can deliver you from it, only you yourself.

And so, you must bring out of the subconscious what lurks there. It trips you in moments of unawareness. You stumble over it and it is always involved in some circumstance, some outer happening, some relationship. And you point the finger and blame it on someone else.

What you don't bring forth in self-knowledge of the lower nature inside of you, hereditary problems, prob-

*The causal body: the interpenetrating spheres of light surrounding each one's I AM Presence at spiritual levels. The causal body contains the records of our virtuous acts through our many incarnations. See illustration p. 312.

lems of psychology with your parents—if you don't look at these things, they can destroy your soul on the Path. Believe me, I have seen it.

And if you don't bring forth the power of your I AM Presence, you will not have the power to overcome what is coming out of the lower nature.

Like it or not, karma is descending upon you every day. Like it or not, the dweller-on-the-threshold of your carnal mind will appear to challenge your Christhood. Now, if you know who he is and what he is ahead of time, you will not fail your tests.

So you can begin to observe, without self-condemnation or the sense of being a sinner, what are the lesser untransmuted things that are there to get in your way and what is the real virtue and power of God that you've already externalized in previous lives. These you must now bring forth because they are your armor, your weapons, your defense. These are the virtues and good deeds stored in your causal body.

Mrs. Prophet emphasized the similarity of Gnosticism to Buddhism:

The Gnostic term *gnosis* is parallel to the Buddhist concept of *bodhi,* which is enlightenment or supreme knowledge. "This state," explains professor Peter Slater, "is the condition of our release from a seemingly endless spiral of fears, cravings, immature attachments and distorted perceptions of who we really are and where our true happiness lies."[9]

Thus, enlightenment is freedom, freedom from what Gautama preached were the causes of suffering: desire or attachment to the world, to the self, the lower self, so as to make oneself liable to suffering. We have become attached to our lesser desires because we have thought

> they were our self and we have not come to realize they are not the Real Self. And you cannot avoid that issue in your life if you are to move forward....
>
> When you know a portion of reality and you see a friend who is accepting illusion as reality, it burdens your heart. You try to help that one, and when they cannot be helped because they cannot perceive beyond the illusion, you pity their plight and you think that such individuals are, above all people, most miserable. And therefore you come to the place of Buddha and Christ to solve the problem of how to deliver people from their illusions when they do not even desire to be delivered from those illusions.[10]

Mrs. Prophet advised her students to pay heed to the Gnostic belief that people caught in illusion neglect their most precious reality—the knowledge of the soul's divine destiny. She explained that true self-knowledge is knowledge of God because the real self and the Divine are one and the same.

She went on to say:

> When you know that the self and the Divine are identical, you have gnosis, you have become it.
>
> Both Gnosticism and Buddhism share the common theme of the attainment of Christhood or Buddhahood by the disciple. Mahayana Buddhism teaches that all sentient beings have the Buddha nature, or the potential to become a Buddha.
>
> One Buddhist text says: "Because the Buddha-cognition is contained in the mass of beings, / Because it is immaculate and non-dual by nature, / Because those who belong to the Buddha's lineage go towards it as their reward, / Therefore all animate beings have the germ of Buddhahood in them. / The Body of the perfect Buddha irradiates everything, / Its Suchness is undiffer-

entiated, / And the road to Buddhahood is open to all. / At all times have all living beings the Germ of Buddhahood in them."[11]...

In the Gospel of Philip, one of the Nag Hammadi texts, we read: "You saw the spirit, you became spirit. You saw Christ, you became Christ. You saw [the Father, you] shall become Father.... You see yourself, and what you see you shall [become]."[12]...

One Gnostic teacher by the name of Monoimus, said, "Look for [God] by taking yourself as the starting point. Learn who it is within you who makes everything his own and says, 'My God, my mind, my thought, my soul, my body.' Learn the sources of sorrow, joy, love, hate....If you carefully investigate these matters you will find him in yourself."[13]

I would explain to you that you also find God in your hatred because you discover that hatred is the misqualification of God as love. You move from the antithesis back to the thesis. When you examine your karma and you experience the suffering of it, you discover God in the right way you should have done things in the beginning. So by the positives and the negatives, all roads lead back to God as long as you observe all things without the sense of anger against God for making you or your life in the circumstance in which you are.

If you are to look to God within, you must look to that God within as the co-creator, the manifestation of him as co-creator. And that you, in a lesser God-awareness, created all those things that now bind you and surround you. So you observe God as the law of karma, as the law in your being, and when you work with it, you can conquer the lesser self and see the fullness of God as he really is....

Throughout the Gnostic gospels there runs the same

> theme of the Master urging his disciples on to self-discovery. The Gospel of Thomas records that Jesus' disciples said to him, "Show us the place where you are, since it is necessary for us to seek it."
>
> Instead of directing them to "a place," Jesus answers: "Whoever has ears, let him hear. There is light within a man of light, and it lights up the whole world. If he does not shine, he is darkness."[14]

We hear this teaching echoed in the Gospel of John, in which Jesus states: "I am the light of the world: he that followeth me shall not walk in darkness, but shall have the light of life."[15]

And in the Sermon on the Mount, Jesus says: "Ye are the light of the world. . . . Let your light so shine before men, that they may see your good works, and glorify your Father which is in heaven."[16]

The ultimate cure for the angst of the soul is claiming the divine light within and achieving gnosis, knowing our true nature as sons and daughters of God, divine beings clothed in flesh. So it was with the Christ and the Buddha. So it is with us today.

9

The Living Flame of Love

The best and most beautiful things in the world cannot be seen or even touched... but are felt in the heart.

—HELEN KELLER

All of us desire to love and to be loved. Yet we do not always fully comprehend love as a quality of the developed heart rather than as sentimentalism. Those who would express true love draw on their heart's strength to be unmoved in adverse circumstances. They understand that the essence of love is divine pity, which does not falter in the presence of human failings.

Devotees of the living flame of love stoke that fire whenever they encounter the malady of anti-love. They live love as gentle compassion for the human condition. And the compassion of the developed heart is enduring, wise and kind in all circumstances. Even tough love is actually a kindness to the soul and spirit because it realigns them with the Higher Self. All of us can benefit by becoming devotees of the living flame of love.

Now this does not mean we will instantly become paragons of virtue who never give in to human failings.

What it does mean, however, is that we will strive to behave lovingly when life is difficult or people we encounter are out of sorts. We will remember to draw on the inner power of the heart when our human self would prefer to retreat into helplessness. We will seek to understand instead of indulging in emotional reactivity. And we will offer kindness as the balm of Gilead to soothe the wounded soul.

The Buddha suggested that we look upon all people as our children. I interpret this teaching to mean recognizing the divine child of the heart. In a similar vein, Jesus spoke directly to the holy innocent in everyone: "Verily, I say unto you, Whosoever shall not receive the kingdom of God as a little child, he shall not enter therein."[1] Thus we are called by the Great Ones to nurture the Buddha and the Christ aborning within us.

Nurturing the divine child within is a spiritual practice that softens the heart and purifies the soul. It means to be mindful of higher precepts—to be benevolent and truthful, generous and respectful. As we relate to people as God's children, we cultivate loving-kindness and a compassion for the soul and the human condition we all share.

Compassion does not mean sympathy—a human pitying of self or others. Compassion is a heartfelt understanding, a caring that binds up the wounds of soul and spirit. In contrast to sympathy, compassion uplifts and strengthens both the giver and the receiver.

"Getting a Leg Up"

One of my clients, Gina, had a serious issue with sympathy; mostly she sympathized with herself. Whenever anything went wrong in her life, she would weep and wail and blame someone else for her troubles. And then she would collapse into helplessness. She saw herself as a victim of life's circumstances and other people's lack of consideration for her plight.

When I didn't sympathize with her victim self, Gina would become hostile and demanding. So I began to point that out to her. And she didn't like it one bit! Yet she had a spiritual side that did understand what I was trying to do. And every now and then her better self would come through.

One day Gina said to me, "I really can't stand this victim side of myself but I keep giving in to it."

"What would you rather do?" I asked.

"Well, I'd rather have my life going the way I want it to, but I don't suppose that's what you mean," she replied, in a bit of a huff.

I was silent, waiting for her to indicate she was open to feedback. There was a long pause.

Gina finally said, "Okay, what do I do with this victim consciousness?"

"Give it up," I answered.

That remark almost set her off again but she caught herself. "How would you suggest I do that?" she asked, somewhat caustically but not as huffy as before.

"Why don't you try being compassionate toward yourself?" I suggested. "Compassion is what I think you really need, not the sympathy that you keep pulling for."

Now Gina was curious. "What's the difference?"

"Sympathy is when you align yourself with your wounded stuff and get stuck in it. Compassion is when you stay one step removed and give yourself a lift out of the bog," I responded.

"How do I know which is which?" she asked, with genuine interest.

"Sympathy is commiserating with your misery. It makes you feel worse and turns other people off," I responded. "Compassion is finding a way to cheer yourself up and patting yourself on the back for doing it."

"Oh," she said. "What if I can't figure that out?"

"I have complete faith that you can," I responded.

Gina closed her eyes and reflected for a few minutes. Then she began to laugh. "You really won't give in to my dweller, will you?"

"Would you want me to?" I queried.

"No, not really," Gina replied. "Maybe what I need to do is make a list of the positive ways I can cheer myself up. And then reward myself each time I succeed. Does that make sense?"

"Yes, I think it's a good idea," I answered. "Why don't you try it for a week and let me know how it works. Do you want to make the list now?"

"I guess I'd better before I change my mind," she said, with a faint grumble in her voice.

Gina made the list, asking for input here and there, and gave it an honest try. When she came in a week later she looked a bit frazzled but on the upswing.

"This is a lot of work!" was her first comment.

"What's been happening?" I responded.

"Well, first of all I decided I needed to do my laundry—and I didn't realize how much I had let pile up. But I want you to know I got it done!" she reported.

"Congratulations!" I said with a smile. "That was a good first move. And then what happened?"

"Well, I kind of slipped back into feeling sorry for myself because I overdid it a bit. The laundry had piled up for over a month, and I was really tired by the time I got it done,"

Gina said with a sigh but hurriedly added, "but I caught myself! And I started congratulating myself for getting it done. I couldn't believe how much better that made me feel."

"That's great!" I responded. And I meant it because I realized what a major effort it had taken for Gina to do that laundry.

Gina was smiling now. "Thank you! I was kind of proud of myself."

We both realized that Gina had done an about-face in her personal world. And what she needed now was to build a momentum on taking care of herself. So each week she would decide on a project she thought she could complete and do it. I must say I was rather amazed because she had almost convinced me of her helplessness. It was a good lesson for both of us!

Gina was learning to love herself in a very down-to-earth way. Each time she came in with a project accomplished, she felt better about herself, and we talked about that.

At one point, she mused, "I am really beginning to understand what loving myself is all about. It's not about sympathizing with me because of how hard everything is; it's about giving myself a leg up, a boost to get on top of things, and feeling good about that."

Gina was learning compassion for her own human condition. And she was gradually exchanging self-pity for a sense of self-worth. As she told me in her final session, "I am so grateful that you didn't sympathize with my 'pity-pot' attitude. I needed to hear the truth and get a push in the right direction. I'm feeling much better about myself. And I intend to keep it up."

The Dalai Lama is quoted as saying, "If you want others

to be happy, practice compassion. If *you* want to be happy, practice compassion."[2] All of the great spiritual teachers have given us the same message. Let's take it to heart!

If we take the concept a step further, being an instrument of God's love means surrendering wrong motives and redeeming the habits of anti-love that reside within us. For example, instead of pointing the finger at other people, we take accountability for ourselves. Rather than grumbling about a difficult situation, we choose constructive action. And we give up the habit of sulking when things don't go our way—instead, we forgive and move on.

Ask yourself, What would I want to let go of? And what would I want to trade it in for?

I remember an old technique I used in workshops many years ago where we had a "swap shop." You could buy any virtue you wanted at the swap shop, but you had to trade in the vice you had put in its place. I remember we had a lot of fun with it, and people got the point!

As we choose to regroup our inner forces through positive focus, we open ourselves to our inner wisdom. We mobilize a sense of equanimity and self-mastery. Then we can take constructive and compassionate action.

Guided Imagery Exercise

Try this imagery exercise to help you get started:

1. Think of a real-life situation where you would like to be your best self.
2. Focus on your breathing and the beating of your heart. Stay with it for a minute or two.
3. Bring to mind an inspiring situation while you continue to be aware of your breath and heartbeat. You

might remember a moment of joy, a person you admire, a favorite activity or an enlivening or soothing experience in nature.

4. Envision yourself maintaining that upswing in mood in that "best self" situation. Play it out in your mind.

5. Try it out in a real-life situation.

As we commit ourselves to a positive turnaround, we begin to feel a spark of joy. And when we actually pull it off in our daily life, we feel that spark burst into a living flame of love—love for God, for ourselves and for those around us no matter how they happen to be behaving.

The Maha Chohan, ascended master representative of the Holy Spirit, teaches: "The disciplining of the emotions must be found in interaction with others. There is no more certain way to gain mastery of the emotions than to have to mingle with people from all walks of life and to always prefer to impart the flame of love and of charity toward those who do not have the flame of harmony."[3]

Stoking the Fires of Love

How do we restore harmony when we encounter inharmonious situations? One of the best ways is to stoke the fires of love in our own heart. We do that by giving prayers or affirmations to balance, expand and intensify the light of God within us. Then we direct that divine light into our relationships as well as personal and world conditions.

My favorite affirmation for this purpose is "I AM the Light of the Heart:"*

---

*When we say "I AM the light of the heart," we mean "God in me is the light of the heart."

I AM the light of the heart
Shining in the darkness of being
And changing all into the golden treasury
Of the mind of Christ.

I AM projecting my love
Out into the world
To erase all errors
And to break down all barriers.

I AM the power of infinite love,
Amplifying itself
Until it is victorious,
World without end![4]

As we center in our heart and give this affirmation a number of times, the sacred fire within us increases in intensity and begins to transmute the misqualified energy of wrong motives and thoughts and the disturbing feelings that accompany them. We may even feel a sense of physical heat around the heart area when this transmutation is going on.

As the sacred fire of the heart intensifies, it penetrates every aspect of our being. We may sense the fires of divine love gradually building and causing a boiling of the waters of anti-love. At that moment we have a choice.

If we let the waters of anti-love boil over, we are likely to do something we'll regret. However, if we stop that anti-love from boiling over, an amazing alchemy takes place that is similar to turning up the heat under a teakettle: the water bubbles, becomes steam and eventually evaporates. In much the same way, the fires of divine love bring the emotional waters of anti-love to a boil. When not acted on, they evaporate.

Thus we can free ourselves of all that is anti-love within us. When we intensify divine love and identify with it, we dispel anti-love, and our soul and spirit and body are at peace.

This is the way every aspect of darkness and the negative karma we carry can be transformed into light—by transmutation through God's perfect love. And that light is the light of God that inspires our soul and the souls we encounter to seek higher consciousness.

When our whole being is filled with light, our physical senses become imbued with the higher vibrations of our Real Self, and we are transformed by it. We become vessels through which our spiritual faculties and Christ consciousness bless life.

Forge Your Victory in Love

In October 1973, during the first conference of The Summit Lighthouse I had ever attended, Elizabeth Clare Prophet delivered a fiery dictation from Chamuel and Charity, the archangels of love. These divine beings urged God's people to turn the tide of human affairs:

> How great is the devotion of the angelic hosts toward mankind in this hour of change, of transition. It is a time of the turning of the tide—the turning of the tide of the human consciousness by an action of love that is borne within the soul, a love that . . . prefers the God-self above the human self.
>
> To be born in that love is to be reborn. And therefore the new birth of freedom is at hand as mighty tides of love turn the entire course and the tide of human thinking, human feeling. . . . This is a mighty wave which sons and daughters of love must ride to its culmination, to its fulfillment in the heart of the Great Central Sun.* . . .

*The Great Central Sun is the center of cosmos; the point of integration of the Spirit-Matter cosmos; the point of origin of all physical-spiritual creation.

In our retreat there is an altar and a flame that is dedicated to the flow of life from the heart of God, the I AM Presence, to the heart of the Christ, the Christ Self of all mankind, and thence to the heart of man.

This is an age when mankind must learn to protect the heart as the center of being, the center of life. The sensitivity of the heart is beyond comprehension. Thought and feeling waves register upon the hearts of mankind. It would be well, then, if you would reinforce the protection of the heart daily.*...

This is also the era of the coming of the Holy Spirit, the Comforter, whose open door is the heart chakra. The Holy Spirit appears in man as the flame upon the altar of the heart, and thus man's being becomes the temple of the living God....

Precious children of the light, hearts must be nourished physically, emotionally, mentally and etherically. ...You must also nourish the heart flame by the action of love, by the action of intensifying the feelings of love, releasing a torrent of divine love through the heart at eventide, when the pink flame is seen in the sunset. It is a reminder that evening is provided for blessed communication with the heart center of God, of Christ, of man....

Now here is the mystery of love. As man kneels before the altar of God, pouring love and gratitude to God, there is a release of energy through the heart center, a mighty flow of love that acts to flush out darkness....

To release the love ray from the heart in the evening gives you the momentum of the protection of love, for it is simple to understand that as the mighty torrent of

---

*We can reinforce that protection through our prayers, affirmations and decrees, e.g., "I AM the Light of the Heart," on p. 200, "Alchemical Formulas for Spiritual Transformation," pp. 305–11, and the other decrees and fiats throughout this book.

love is released through the heart center, nothing can penetrate. Nothing can go against the tide of that love. . . .

Thus, to adore God is one of the surest protections that man can have for the safety and the endurance of the heart chakra. This, then, is the best way to use feeling. Feeling energy, like all energy, accumulates in the chakras and in the feeling body, and if you do not periodically, hourly, qualify that energy with the feeling of God, you will find that that energy will begin to accumulate and to clog the feeling body.

Then what happens? The dark ones . . . that require your light to propagate and to perpetuate—these ones will take note of this buildup of energy, and then they will try to trick you into releasing it as discord, as inharmony, as irritation. And if the energy buildup is great enough, it can be released as anger, as hatred. . . .

These conditions come only from neglect, the neglect of the adoration of God. If you continually pour your love to God, the energies of your feeling body will be continually qualified with love and continually ascend back to the throne of God, carried by angel messengers, by cherubim of fire, by angels of our bands. . . .

As they carry your love (God's love requalified by your love), they afford to you that protection of the sacred spheres of the Great White Brotherhood. And the *antahkarana** of life, the web of love and reason, of logic and truth, of power and will, is fortified. And so you, too, are fortified.

This dictation from Chamuel and Charity was both a blessing of love and a warning of circumstances unfolding

*The net of light spanning Spirit and Matter, connecting and sensitizing the whole of creation within itself and to the heart of God.

at that time and coming to a head now, thirty years later. They gave spiritual instruction concerning the Middle East crisis, advice that is as apt today as it was when the dictation was delivered:

> The crisis in the Middle East is essentially a crisis of the heart chakras of mankind. You must understand that the war between these two factions* is actually a war against the heart of all mankind.
>
> *You* are under attack, but you do not realize it. All mankind are under attack, but they do not realize it. For those energies that are expended in hatred, in the desire for war, in the desire to kill—this is the motivation of darkness to slay the very heart of the Mother, to plunge the dagger into the heart of the son and of the daughter.
>
> While these energies rage, you must put on the protection, not only upon yourselves but also around the heart chalices of the children of light everywhere upon the planetary body. For there is a danger that the impressions, the jagged impressions of war and hatred should be left upon the hearts of children as an improper record—a record that may one day provide the opening for the entrance into their consciousness of the wedges of darkness when they, too, will come to the place where they must fight the good fight for the right in the personal battle of [good and evil].
>
> Let love be without dissimulation.[5] Let love be the action of the Law. God rests in motion. Let your motion be his energy perpetually giving forth the energies of love. . . .
>
> The temptation of the carnal mind is to pervert love into possessiveness, desire, selfishness and carnality. As we release our love, it is encased in a sheaf of blue fire that all who receive that love should use that love in

*In October 1973, Israel was at war with Egypt and Jordan.

> purity, desiring only to see God and to be God. Thus to the pure in heart our energy flows. . . .
>
> Let love be the fulfilling of the Law in this age. Let love be the endurance of the faithful who receive the testing of the Law with rejoicing, with gratitude, who enjoy the challenge . . . as an opportunity to prove the strength of the Law, the strength of the heart, the strength of the soul. . . .
>
> So let the sons and daughters of God be counted as victors of love in this century. . . . Let love expand and flow![6]

Love is the key that opens the door to higher consciousness and bestows the grace of heaven on earth in every age. If we would offer the elixir of love to those we meet, we will console those who mourn, those who are burdened, those who must walk alone trusting in the grace of God. This is the spirit that stirred our hearts during and after the 9/11 attack on the United States and inspired courage in those who gave their all.

In the Aquarian age we are called to trust in the mysteries of divine love. We are meant to follow the higher urges of our heart. And we are intended to extend mercy to ourselves and to those we meet along the path of life.

This means we must defeat the energies of anti-love in ourselves. So we remind ourselves of the old adage "no pain, no gain." Instead of anesthetizing ourselves to avoid the pain of our karma, we welcome that karma as a lesson of love and anti-love. We take advantage of karmic circumstances to see ourselves more clearly and to meet the challenge to be divine love in action.

If we ask our Higher Self to meet us at the crossroads of our karma, we will be guided through the lessons we need to learn. And if we must go through pain and injury, let our heart be softened, layers of pride consumed and our soul strengthened for the victory. God teaches us love in many ways, and we learn best when we open our hearts in gratitude for each lesson. And that brings us to perhaps the most difficult lesson of all—forgiveness.

Bind the Dweller! Forgive the Soul

When we find it hard to forgive others for wrongs they have committed against us, it helps to remember that it is the soul we are forgiving, not the dweller-on-the-threshold. When we make fierce calls for the binding of that dweller, we actually extend compassion to the soul. And the angels answer our calls in accordance with God's will. When any individual is ready to "have done" with the dweller, divine help is given. That help is only a prayer away.

A person may be impure and have all sorts of imperfections, but the soul still has the potential to realize God. Therefore, no matter how badly someone has treated us, we can call upon the law of forgiveness for that one. Wouldn't we want someone to do the same for us?

We can also call to Archangel Michael and Mighty Astrea* to liberate that one from negative habits and past records that are causing him or her to make wrong decisions. We can ask that the soul be cut free by the angels and taken to the retreats of the Brotherhood to be tutored and repolarized to the light. And we can make the same request for ourselves.

We can pray for the soul to do a turnaround, to be converted by the Holy Spirit and to come into the service of God. And then we turn over the soul and the entire matter to

*See pp. 48, 49, 307.

divine justice and the will of God. When our inner work is done, we can know that, in God's own time and way, justice will be meted out and the soul will be assisted and given opportunity.

When someone has wronged us and we call for the binding of the dweller-on-the-threshold but forgive the soul, both divine justice and mercy are satisfied. And we can be cut free from any sense of injustice or anger that would tie us to that person. Wouldn't we want the same done for us?

You might be thinking, what about our enemies? Sometimes our enemies can be our greatest teachers, for they mirror back to us the untransmuted elements of our own consciousness. The lesson comes not only from the enemy's behavior but also from our reaction to it. Thus, curiously enough, we can praise the enemy for the lesson! Try saying something like this when you're confronted by wickedness and find yourself reacting:

> Praise to the enemy! My thanks to you, enemies and persecutors, within and without. You have been my teachers, and I shall remember your lessons.
>
> Through wind and storm and angry waves of the astral sea, I shall not be moved, neither to the right nor to the left, neither up nor down by circumstances, by whatever negatives you hurl at me.
>
> From your warring I have learned the value of guarding the peace. From your cruelty I have learned kindness. From your hatred, I have learned love. Praise be to the enemy![7]

There are moments in our lives when we receive true and profound forgiveness from someone we respect. And we realize that forgiveness is a key to love, that forgiveness is perhaps the greatest gift we can receive—knowing that someone loves us enough to forgive a wrong we have committed.

Perhaps an even greater challenge is forgiving ourselves and letting go of the memory of our wrongdoing. From many years of working with people in therapy I have come to realize that this is perhaps the most difficult task of all.

I have seen over and over again how problems get magnified when guilt and remorse remain unresolved. Therefore, we need to study our own psyche and how we might make amends. We can benefit from expanding the heart, as Chamuel and Charity talked about earlier, and offering love and forgiveness to ourselves and others.

The ascended master Jesus Christ teaches: "The best way to forgive others is first to forgive oneself for all errors and then to expand this forgiveness infinitely to all. Be sure to cover every circumstance; make no exceptions. If God be a flaming fire and all of his offspring divine sparks, why should not one spark forgive another, no matter how much the sacred fire may have been misused?"[8]

As we offer compassion to our soul and commune with our Higher Self, we increasingly separate out from the negative programming we may have given ourselves or received from others. We grow in grace and are better able to forgive ourselves and to extend love and forgiveness to others.

As Elizabeth Clare Prophet says, if we are not at peace with ourselves, we are not at peace with God. How do we open the door to inner peace? Try these two keys: mercy and forgiveness.

Exercise in Mercy and Forgiveness

Think of an experience in your life when you felt wounded to the core by someone else—a friend, colleague, family member, mentor or whoever else might come to mind. Ask yourself, Am I ready to let this go? And if not, ask yourself, Why not? Then take some time to contemplate whether you are being helped or hurt by holding onto that memory.

When you feel ready to let it go, walk yourself through the following exercise in mercy and forgiveness:

1. Offer a prayer to your Higher Self to help you let go of this wound to your soul and spirit.
2. Dialogue with your soul about what happened until you gain an understanding of why you feel so wounded.
3. Respond to your soul's pain with compassion and caring. And ask, How can I help you right now?
4. Give your soul the help she requests and continue to dialogue until you feel some resolution.
5. If you get stuck or don't know how to respond, put your arms around yourself and tell your soul you love her.
6. Offer a prayer to your Higher Self to intercede, and try again. Ask your soul, What can I do for you right now?
7. Respond to your soul's request with loving-kindness and a firm resolve that you will help heal the pain.
8. Continue to dialogue and offer comfort and understanding until your soul feels encouraged.
9. Ask yourself, What is my lesson from this hurtful drama?
10. Share the answer you get with your soul, and get her input as well.

11. Decide on a practical follow-through so that your soul will continue to feel your love and support.

12. Thank your soul for sharing, and set a time when you will talk again.

Move On with the Holy Spirit

Once you have offered mercy and forgiveness to yourself, it is time to move on. As you do so, observe this guidance from the Maha Chohan, ascended master representative of the Holy Spirit:

> Understand, then, that the moments in time and space are cubicles for the resolution of consciousness and not much else. They are a stopover as you descend into lower densities to reconcile your accounts, pay your debts, leave some thrust of momentum of light and journey on. . . .
>
> It is time that some of you tended to the weeds in your garden and pulled them out by the roots. Yes, beloved, you can change old habits if you want to, but there must be the will.
>
> When there is the will and when there is the fusion of your soul with my flaming reality, then you have teamwork. . . . Then I may take you under the wings of the Holy Spirit and bring you to that point where one day you yourself feel that you are of supreme usefulness to the millions of the earth by prayer, by dynamic decrees, by deep groanings of the spirit[9] as you come into conformity with the mind of God and of the Holy Christ Self. . . .
>
> The disciplining of the mind can be found in the practice of meditation. The disciplining of the emotions must be found in interaction with others. There is no

more certain way to gain mastery of the emotions than to have to mingle with people from all walks of life and to always prefer to impart the flame of love and of charity toward those who do not have the flame of harmony.

The choice is always there—to be pulled into the morasses, the cesspools, vortices, quicksands of negativity or to shun them. And always remember the words of your Lord: "What is that to thee? Follow thou me."[10]

In other words, forget it. Let it go. Do not become further engaged as you see your energies escalating and, with the escalation, the loss of your God-control.

There is no more important achievement for those who desire the Holy Spirit and its gifts, even one at a time, than to be able to offer to others perpetual love, perpetual comfort, perpetual sweetness, perpetual helpfulness, compassion and charity.[11]... As Mother Teresa has said, "Give until it hurts."...

Nothing is too hard for the Lord. Yes, you can learn to let go.... And you can let go of all who have wronged you, and you can learn to forgive their wrongdoing. ...Showers of mercy soften hardness of heart, nonforgiveness.... Be humble enough to receive God's forgiveness, to be strong enough to go and sin no more, to be loving enough to forgive your brother as God has forgiven you....

Hasten the day, beloved! Make thy peace with thy God and do not be moved. Accept correction, no matter how it is given or by whom. Learn your lessons from friends and enemies,... from life's experiences. And, above all, learn the lessons your own karma is there to teach you every day....

Think of what empowerment will be your option when you shall have cleared those records and when these mighty vessels of consciousness are emptied to be filled forevermore only by divine love. When you shall have achieved that, beloved, you will know that your ascension is a realistic goal.[12]

PART FOUR

Ascent to Eternal Selfhood

10

Karma and Reincarnation

Forget not that I shall come back to you.
A little while, and my longing shall gather
dust and foam for another body.
A little while, a moment of rest upon the wind,
and another woman shall bear me.

—KAHLIL GIBRAN
The Prophet

The spiritual teachings of the mystery schools and of the saints, sages and enlightened ones who have gone before us on the path to the ascension are the legacy we need for our own soul's victory. We can learn from the victories and defeats of our elder brothers and sisters on the spiritual path. Some have not been recorded or passed down through the oral tradition, but some have, and they are worthy of our understanding. As we shall see in this chapter, the life of Phylos the Thibetan is such a story. It is a living teaching about karma and reincarnation.

The case for reincarnation has been visited and revisited by many erudite philosophers and theologians, including such well-known international figures as French philosopher and author Francois Voltaire and German philosopher Arthur Schopenhauer. And the American statesman Benjamin Franklin made it clear in his own humorous way that he believed in reincarnation.

As Elizabeth Clare Prophet wrote in her groundbreaking book *Reincarnation: The Missing Link in Christianity:*

> When he was twenty-two, Ben Franklin drafted an epitaph for himself predicting that he would reincarnate. He compared his body to the worn-out cover of a book with "its contents torn out." He predicted that the contents would "not be lost" but would "appear once more in a new and more elegant edition revised and corrected by the Author."[1]

Well-known literary figures are among the ranks of Western thinkers who have accepted or thought seriously about reincarnation. They include essayist Ralph Waldo Emerson, poet Henry Wadsworth Longfellow, British novelists Aldous Huxley and Rudyard Kipling, and Irish poet W. B. Yeats. And Edgar Cayce, the famous American healer, known as the sleeping prophet, made reference to past lives many times in his readings.

Mrs. Prophet's unique contribution has been her understanding of how karma, reincarnation and psychology interconnect. She taught her students about it through a spiritual analysis of the earthly journey of Phylos the Thibetan (or Tibetan), written down in *A Dweller on Two Planets, or The Dividing of the Way.*[2] This amazing book is written in the first person because Phylos dictated it to his amanuensis, Frederick S. Oliver.

Phylos's personal reason for dictating his story is explained in his own words: "I have sought to explain the great mystery of life, illustrating it with part of my own life history, extracts which cover years reaching into many thousands.... As the world is helped, so has my work been; I hope I have returned help for help."[3]

A Historical and Spiritual Perspective

Mrs. Prophet put Phylos's remarkable story into historical and spiritual perspective:

> The book was begun in 1883 or 1884 when Frederick Oliver was about eighteen years old. It was completed in 1886 and first published in 1899. The subject is the story of Phylos's life in his embodiment as Zailm Numinos on the ancient continent of Atlantis, the greatest nation on earth at that time.
>
> The book also covers Phylos's embodiment in the nineteenth century as an American by the name of Walter Pierson. It shows how he reaped the karma he had made twelve thousand years before on Atlantis.... *A Dweller on Two Planets* gives to us an understanding of karma as well as grace, the grace of our Lord and Saviour Jesus Christ, which gives us the opportunity to live and serve again to balance karma.
>
> In the Old Testament we had a dispensation of the Law and very few individuals in that period of history retained the fusion to the Holy Christ Self. Therefore they did not have the mediator, and Jesus Christ had not yet come as the Son of God to fulfill the promise of God to draw all men back to him through that Son.
>
> So the Old Testament, under the law of Moses, gives us the example of the harshness of the Law descending. Moses himself would act as mediator before the people. And when God said he would punish them and would bring great calamities to come upon them, Moses would

reason with him and urge him to mitigate his wrath against his people. Sometimes Moses was successful and sometimes he was not.

With the coming of Jesus Christ, the mediator is in embodiment through Jesus. He came for the specific purpose to reignite the threefold flame [our divine spark] and to make sons of God of us, of whoever would believe on his name and receive him.

We have that same opportunity today. In the last two thousand years, because of the dispensation of Jesus Christ, there has been a tremendous opportunity for souls to reestablish their fusion with the Holy Christ Self through Jesus. . . . The reigniting of the threefold flame is a part of that process for those who have lost that flame. . . .

The pendulum of orthodox Christianity has swung in many cases to a far position of saying that only grace is necessary. Other Christians say that Jesus did it all on the cross. . . . Still others believe that grace is a part of it, that faith is necessary, but they also say that faith without works is dead. . . .

What we find is that no matter what the gradations of belief, the basic orthodox Christian tenet today is that you do not have to balance your karma because Jesus paid the price.

My feeling about Phylos's book is that it makes quite clear that grace is present and that we are bound to follow the teachings of the Old and New Testament, to know that grace and to know that union with God through the heart of Jesus Christ. But that does not exempt us from our karma. Our karma must be paid.

And what this book shows is that most often (as we also find in Hindu teachings) the cycles of returning karma do not return in the same life as the karma is made. This often explains to us why so much injustice goes uncorrected and the evildoer may continue in his evil ways for a lifetime and to all appearances will not be stopped in any measure.

This is a puzzlement to us, except when we understand the law of reincarnation along with karma. Reincarnation says that these cycles come full circle in their time as the fruit that ripens on the tree. And when that karma is ripe, then we are there to reap it. And therefore we never know from day to day why we are reaping calamities or situations. We don't seem to necessarily connect them with any recent right or wrong that we may have done. This is because of the wide orb of the cycles returning.

This text, then, gives us an eyewitness view of ancient Atlantis, where all of us were embodied. We were there. Many of you were there in the golden ages. Many of you were in the decline. Many of you were there in the hour of cataclysm of the sinking of Atlantis, which, according to some commentators, happened in stages beginning about twelve thousand years ago to eleven thousand five hundred.

So we are all dealing with those records today, and we are dealing now with a final embodiment. . . . And we can understand in the light of what we must fulfill in this final embodiment what kind of karma we may have had not only on Atlantis but in the interim.[4]

Karma Is a Fact of Life

Mrs. Prophet went on to discuss the purpose of bearing karma. She reminded her students that karma is a fact of life, yet the days may be shortened for the elect:

Our belief in karma is that we do not believe that every last jot and tittle of every act and deed that we have ever committed against life must necessarily be balanced before we experience the resurrection and the ascension. First of all, we may make our ascension having balanced 51 percent of our karma.

In addition to that, we should understand that God does not deal our karma to us as punishment. Karma is a manifestation of an impersonal law as well as a personal law. There is the law of justice and there is the law of mercy. . . .

Karma is our teacher. We must learn the lessons of how and why we misused the energy of life. We receive our karma because we are, in the final analysis, responsible for all of our actions, words and deeds, for the causes that we have set in motion.

If therefore we have a certain karma that is grievous to be borne that may require several lifetimes to balance, and if we embody and live a life of service combined with the violet flame, then by giving mantras and decrees and totally committing ourselves to the service of life and giving all that we are, God may take this exemplary sign of our daily deeds and shorten the days of our travail.[5]

And God has said he would do this for the sake of the elect [those who elect the Homeward path], that he will receive a certain set of deeds, a certain series of long sufferings under a certain burden, with virtue and great holiness accompanying it, and say, "You have borne enough. You have satisfied the Law. And by the grace of Jesus Christ you may come up higher because you have proven that you will not make this mistake again."

So in that sense of the word, the 100 percent of karma may not be the full 100 percent of every last situation that we have ever been under. That is a Hindu concept and it is largely true. But there is grace and there is intercession. There is mercy as well as justice.[6]

The Interweaving of Psychology and Karma

Phylos's life as Zailm is a story of a lightbearer's karmic predicament and how it interweaves with his psychology. And he makes it very clear that each of us is accountable for our karmic dilemma.

As Mrs. Prophet notes:

> Psychology is intricately woven with karma. What we see in our psychology that we can trace to our roots in this life is also traceable to previous lifetimes. Fortunately Zailm has told us about previous lifetimes before the embodiment on Atlantis that is the subject of this book. And fortunately he has told us about his final embodiment in the nineteenth century.
>
> So we have many keys to how his karma is interwoven with his psychology. One begets the other. And it is truly a circle that determines how, why, where and who we reincarnate as....
>
> Phylos, then, makes abundantly clear that we have accountability for karma. He also shows how grace is the intercessory light of the Christ. And it does not absolve us from the responsibility and the accountability of our karma....
>
> Causes we have set in motion, both plus and minus, are our accountability. He shows us the inexorable nature of karma, the exactness of it and how it does pursue us until we resolve it. But then, so does our psychology pursue us until we resolve it. So we almost see them as twins—psychology and karma.[7]

How then does grace through the intercessory light of the Christ enter in? Grace has been given through the teachings and example of Christ Jesus. And grace is given when the light of the Christ prompts us by awakening our conscience.

When that light shines bright in our heart, mind and soul, we realize we have karma to balance and a divine destiny to fulfill.

Mrs. Prophet explains why the burden of karma has intensified all over the world today:

> Every single person on planet earth, not one of us excepted, has received an increment of karma, not only an increment of karma that is heavier than we have borne in thousands of years, but specifically Atlantean karma, and specifically that karma which Jesus has borne for us.
>
> Jesus has borne our karma for us for two thousand years and is now giving it back to everyone upon earth because it's the age when we should be in our maturity as sons and daughters of God. And it is the age when we, then, have a sudden jolt and we come to the realization that we are no longer being carried....
>
> At subconscious and unconscious levels, every one of us has to work with a dweller-on-the-threshold who has had a heyday during the period of Jesus carrying that karma. Now the soul must bear it, and now there is a great weight. We need to deal with that in ourselves and we have to come to terms with unconscious, unseen, unfelt anger....
>
> Upon arising this morning my first counseling session was with someone who was telling me a story about himself and in whom I perceived there was deep-seated and profound anger against God. And I can tell you that, as an archetypal unconscious force, the anger against Father, Son, Holy Spirit and Divine Mother is seldom absent from anyone, to a lesser or greater degree.
>
> People get angry at God for their karma, for their lot in life, for God not doing this, not doing that, not doing the next thing for them. This produces on the surface perhaps a melancholy, a passivity, a dishonesty with

> oneself, an irritability, an immobilization of one's forces where one cannot get on with life, one cannot change, one cannot get going because of unresolved problems with God the Father and God the Mother....
>
> We need to take a long, hard look at whether or not our forces are engaged for the victory, whether we have all of our energy focused, or whether our anger against God results in our being perpetually ill, perpetually inactive, unable, for one reason or another, to lock in to true service, to a true work, to a true calling in life and to give ourselves totally to it. When we cannot pour ourselves totally into our life's calling, it is because of the hang-ups that we have.[8]

As a minister and psychologist, I have come into contact with many people who carry deep anger, resentment and rebellion against their karmic predicament. Consequently, when they encounter difficult, frustrating situations, they lose control and the inner volcano of anger erupts.

Although such an individual may indeed be furious about an aggravating circumstance or another person's actions, a deeper drama is occurring. The angry dweller is disclaiming any responsibility and essentially shaking its fist at God saying, "I don't want to carry my karma. I will not carry it!"

In reality, this is the perfect moment to bind that dweller* and to accept the opportunity for our soul to learn a karmic lesson.

A Psychological Study: Zailm of Atlantis

What we actually know about Zailm is from Phylos's testimony, which we can readily believe. He writes about himself, giving enough clues for us to understand in depth the psychology of his soul.

*See pp. 308–9.

Phylos's story speaks to all of us today. As we consider his lifetimes and karmic lessons, let's ask ourselves, What would I have done? What similar situation have I faced in my life? How did I handle it? What is the spiritual lesson? Have I learned it? If not, why not? Such self-analysis is highly beneficial to our psychological healing and spiritual progress.

Mrs. Prophet summarizes the karmic circumstances and major characters in Phylos's life on Atlantis, a life in which he encounters many difficult challenges to his inner path of adeptship:

> In the very beginning of the book we are introduced to Zailm, who is a mountaineer's son, poor and fatherless. At the age of sixteen he makes an arduous pilgrimage to the summit of the highest mountain on Atlantis.
>
> Zailm is making the dangerous trek in order to pray to Incal. Incal is the one true God of the Atlanteans, represented by the Sun. Zailm is seeking assistance in fulfilling his goals in life: to achieve success, fame, and power and to become one of the foremost citizens of Atlantis.
>
> In answer to his prayers, Zailm discovers a lode of gold as he wends his way down the mountain. He collects the gold and uses the income to pay for his education. Zailm then leaves his mountain home and moves with his mother to Caiphul (the capital of Atlantis), where he enrolls in the college of science. There he comes to the attention of the emperor and finds favor with those in the highest ranks of government.
>
> After four years in Caiphul, the emperor's chief adviser, Prince Menax, adopts Zailm as his son. Menax tells Zailm that his wife and only son have died and that Zailm reminds him of his son. Menax also has a daughter by the name of Anzimee, whom Zailm is in love with.
>
> Another main character in the story is Lolix, a beau-

> tiful but heartless woman. She is the daughter of the head of the Chaldean armies. Chaldea is a warlike nation that attempted to attack the land of Suern, which is present-day India. By advanced occult powers, the leader of Suern, the Rai Ernon, caused the drowning of the Chaldean soldiers before they could even attack. Subsequently, Lolix, who had witnessed this event, was exiled to Atlantis.[9]

A Karmic Predicament

Phylos sets the stage for understanding Zailm's karmic predicament in his chapter entitled "A Maternal Desertion." He makes clear how tenderly Zailm loves his mother. The mere thought of her and the hardships she has endured brings tears to his eyes. He is dedicated to caring for her.

Thus when Zailm is adopted as the son of Prince Menax, he hastens to tell his mother the good news and to advise her that they will be moving to the palace. To his shock and despair, his mother tells him that she cannot go to the palace, that she has no desire to do so. She shatters his dreams by declaring that since he has come on such good fortune he no longer needs her.

His mother further informs him that she is going back to the mountains with her new husband, a lover she had before she married Zailm's father. Without Zailm's knowledge they had been wed that very morning. She adds insult to injury by telling her devoted son that she never loved his father, that it had been an arranged marriage, and that she feels for Zailm, the fruit of that union, only the same love she has for friends, nothing deeper.

Zailm so loves and idolizes his mother that he is overcome by her revelations and heartless rejection. He falls to the floor, unconscious. When he regains consciousness, it is not his mother at his bedside but Prince Menax. He tells

Zailm that he has been very ill with brain fever for two weeks and came close to death.

His mother, true to the words that pierced his heart and soul, had not remained to care for him. She had said Menax's private physician would do as well or better and immediately left with her new husband for their home in the mountains.

Zailm went on with his life but continued to have a deep pain in his heart. At one point he received a message from his mother to come and see her. But when he got there he could tell she had only done it as a courtesy gesture, that she would rather he hadn't come at all. This was the last time he ever saw his mother. As he says, "She acted wisely in not going to the palace, constituted as she was; it is a painful subject; let it be dropped."[10]

Mrs. Prophet comments:

> The dropping of the subject was the dropping of that pain to the subconscious and the unconscious levels. That, of course, is the place to which many pains and heartaches have been dropped by ourselves because they are too painful to keep in the conscious mind. We cannot get on with our lives if we are to recount them to ourselves daily.
>
> And so, by and by, when we have the strength, the development, new lifetimes, we move on and we come to the place where these things may come up again, in new situations in life when we are able and prepared to deal with them.
>
> Nevertheless, the pain and the sorrow and the heartache do influence our thoughts and feelings and our actions for the rest of our lives unless we enter therapy and use the violet flame. The violet flame is the great factor of transmutation that softens these records and allows us to attain resolution.

> Many times the scars are so deep that along with the violet flame we need to review our psychology and the causes and cores in our consciousness that come up in daily interchanges where we see ourselves doing things and saying things that we wish we had never said or done and do not understand why we do them.
>
> When we look at Zailm, we find that everything else we hear about him takes off from this moment of extreme agony. And you can see what agony it was when he is unconscious for weeks in a state of continuous nightmare.
>
> This is a turning point in Zailm's life and psychology. He is forced to confront the fact that the mother he has idolized has deserted him for a lover and, in fact, never loved him at all. His mother's abandonment creates a need for resolution—both outwardly with the women in his life and inwardly with his own feminine nature. This need for resolution becomes the motivating force in his life. Even though it is unknown to him, that motivating force is moving him at subconscious and unconscious levels.[11]

We can well understand how Zailm's vision of himself as a man is now turned upside down. We can imagine his despairing thoughts: "What's wrong with me? What kind of a man is rejected by his own mother?" Even his joy in being adopted by Prince Menax is marred by the sudden reversal in his mother's affections.

For Zailm, it is as if his burgeoning success as a man and the appearance of his longed-for father figure have caused his mother to desert him. And he collapses in despair. Fortunately he has the "good father" in Prince Menax to help him through this bereavement.[12]

In his father's absence, Zailm at a young age takes on the role of provider for his mother. He is preoccupied with caring for her up to the time he is asked by Prince Menax to move into the palace. By assuming the role of provider, Zailm seeks to affirm his identity and place in the family by filling the father's position.

When his mother spurns him as faithful son and provider, Zailm is stunned and disheartened. And when she deposes him in favor of a lover, he is overcome with despair. It is no wonder that he falls to the floor unconscious and nearly dies from the fever of his tortured mind.

Karma: The Absence of Father

Zailm having to grow up without a father in this Atlantean life was the result of karma from an earlier lifetime. As we will see, he had misused his masculine energy in barbaric ways. His karmic lesson this time around is to develop the higher qualities of manhood by going straight to God the Father.

Thus his arduous climb up the mountain, described at the beginning of his tale, is both real and symbolic. Since Zailm has not had the example of father in his life, he goes in search of the highest example of the Father principle. And his steady climbing of the snow-covered mountain through two days and nights is his yang, or masculine, thrust of energy.

Mrs. Prophet explains the significance of his climb:

> He wants to greet his Father alone on this mountain and have a heart-to-heart talk with him. He prays to him. He talks to him. It is a profoundly meaningful experience. He is dedicating his life and asking his assistance. He offers himself to the Supreme Father; he seeks Incal's aid in supporting his mother and Incal's approval and guidance in setting the course of his career.
>
> His climbing the mountain can also be seen as one of the rites of passage into his manhood. The mountain, the

sun, and the tremendous power of the elements that are present in this episode are all symbolic of the masculine dimension of life that he seeks to internalize. He is looking for the epitome of his manhood and he has gone to the right place. It is a very healthy action because he has no one to go to that he may call "father."

Psychologically, Zailm's goals of success, fame and power are an expression of his need to resolve his fatherless state. He seeks to be successful to compensate for an absence of father. He aspires to a lofty position of service to the state. The state itself represents the father.

One can see the same correlation from an astrological point of view. In astrology the tenth house rules the father as well as career and status. The Sun rules the father and the masculine principle. And Zailm climbed the mountain to be there at sunrise to greet Incal.

His close, loving relationship to his mother is intensified because he is without his father. At an unconscious level he may have sensed his mother's lack of genuine love for him, felt guilty about it and tried even harder to win her love.[13]

Trapped in the Oedipus Complex

Zailm is caught in the grips of the Oedipus complex, where the son unconsciously desires to overthrow the father in order to possess the mother.* According to classical psychoanalytic theory, the boy resolves this inner conflict by surrendering his mother to his father. He then identifies with the father, which sets the stage for his unfolding manhood.

Mrs. Prophet describes how this dynamic influences Zailm's behavior:

---

*The Oedipus complex derives from the Greek myth in which Oedipus unknowingly kills his father and marries his mother.

> He is still attached to his mother throughout his young adulthood. He brings his mother with him when he goes to college in Caiphul. During his college years Zailm reads to his mother in the evenings and worries about leaving her alone at night because, as he once told Prince Menax, "She hath an infirmity of nervousness that cannot well withstand my absence at night."[14] He wants his mother to be dependent on him.
>
> His unresolved Oedipus complex is apparent when he and his mother first visit the royal palace in Caiphul. A guide approaches them to take them to the emperor and says, "Come, I will conduct thyself and mother." Zailm thinks to himself, "Mother! How does the fellow know that one so fair and so young looking is my mother? She might be my sister, or even my wife, for aught he knows to the contrary."
>
> "The supposed presumption of the man nettled me, for I was proud not only of my mother's youthful appearance, but also of my own fondly fancied mature looks; I had not infrequently been told that I looked seven or eight years older than I really was."[15]
>
> Thus Zailm thinks of his mother not only as mother but as wife, which is the Oedipal dream of the young boy. For Zailm, that dream has come true and he is playing out the role of husband and father.[16]

As we have seen, when the husband-father role is stripped from him, Zailm falls apart. Yet this karmic predicament didn't begin in that lifetime. It traces back to more ancient times.

Prelude to Zailm's Atlantean Troubles

Mrs. Prophet explains how Phylos's previous lifetime as a barbaric master set the stage for his life on Atlantis:

The roots of Zailm's problems go back to his embodiment on Lemuria as a barbaric master. Zailm's feminine split [split of the good and bad feminine within him] may have originated on Lemuria when his evil priestess-mother, representing the "bad feminine," demanded that he kill the "good feminine," who is Anzimee, embodied in that lifetime as a slave girl. Phylos doesn't turn on his evil mother, nor does he kill the slave girl. Instead, he kills himself and avoids the confrontation and the resolution.

The conflict between the two representations of his inner feminine is brought forth in succeeding embodiments. In his next life, the barbaric master must now be the slave. He is deprived of nurturance, ill fed and ill treated until his dying day.

In the following lifetime he is successful but suffers from insatiable hunger. This could represent his longing for the nurturance of the good mother. He then develops stomach cancer, which kills the insatiable hunger. The cancer could be seen as an expression of self-hatred or the karma for his barbaric behavior in his previous life, or both. . . .

Again, he avoids resolution and withdraws into the life of a hermit. Thus the stage is set for his next lifetime as Zailm, where he must face a dramatic explosion of these inner dynamics.[17]

The Karma of Black Magic

In the unfolding drama of Phylos's embodiment as Zailm, after his mother's departure and his move to the palace, he continues to love Anzimee but they relate to one another as brother and sister. They travel together to the country of Suern, where Zailm is sent as a high deputy of

Poseid (Atlantis) on state business. He is quick to notice the laziness of the Suerni people, who sit around magically precipitating food yet with a perpetual expression of anger on their faces.

Zailm also sees that the people do not love their ruler, Rai Ernon. They are respectful to him only because they fear his power. And the Rai explains to Zailm that these wayward people have no interest beyond satisfying their physical needs. They are angry with the Rai because he exacts obedience to the higher laws of God and penalizes them for their black magic.

Zailm and Anzimee's arrival coincides with the fateful withdrawal of Rai Ernon, who has striven in vain to teach the Suerni respect for the laws of God. The pathos of the Rai is captured in his cry, "Oh, Suernis, Suernis! I have given up my life for thee! . . . I will no more restrain thee. My people, oh, my people! Ungrateful! I forgive thee, for thou canst not know how I love thee! I go."[18] And in that moment he leaves his body, never more to return to the Suerni.

Zailm, as the envoy from Poseid, immediately asserts the authority of Poseid over the Suerni and deposes the scornful who have been in positions of rulership. In agony over whether he has behaved appropriately, Zailm attends the funeral and the casting of the Rai's body into the Maxin Light.[19] Subsequently he and Anzimee complete their travels and return to Caiphul.

Upon their return, much to Zailm's surprise, Rai Gwauxln, ruler of Poseid, honors him by appointing him Suzerain (governor) of the Suernis. Zailm asks permission to decline the office because he is still a student. The Rai gives him four years to complete his studies, and then he is to assume his duties in Suern. Zailm accepts and signs the appointment papers.

In the weeks to come, Anzimee and Zailm take a vacation journey throughout the kingdom of Atlantis (which takes them to parts of North and South America). And one incident reveals a weakness in Zailm's character that will one day cost him his life.

As they are returning to Caiphul, they decide to shift from flying through the air to journeying underwater in the ocean. (Their vailx was constructed for both aerial and submarine activity.) Zailm enters the ocean too fast and the impact is strong enough to throw the passengers momentarily off balance.

Prince Menax, aware of this incident from a distance, immediately informs Zailm he should not have acted so unwisely. He adds, "I fear that thou hast a vein of reckless daring in thy nature which will some day bring thee misfortune.... Be cautious, Zailm, be cautious!"[20]

The Fruit of Forbidden Love

Upon returning to Caiphul, Zailm falls prey to the advances of Lolix, the foreign princess who desires to marry him. He is afraid to tell her of his love for Anzimee so he tells a lie—that Poseid law forbids marriage with those of alien birth. Through deception and lust, he embarks on a secret affair with Lolix, which will ultimately lead to her madness and demise and his undoing and untimely death. Here is the fateful story of Zailm's reckless daring, which he has been warned about:

Zailm suffers pangs of conscience, particularly because he intends to leave Lolix and marry Anzimee once his studies are complete. However, he continues his duplicity, spending time with Anzimee and Lolix separately. And Lolix, who loves him dearly, keeps the secret even when she realizes he has lied to her about the Poseid law concerning marriage. They even have a baby, whom he persuades Lolix to give up by secret adoption.

When he feels the time is right, Zailm asks Anzimee to be his wife. And she accepts. Zailm is so self-deluded that he believes Lolix will not betray him by exposing their secret affair, even though she and Anzimee have become close friends. When he meets with Lolix to tell her that he and Anzimee are to be married, Lolix is overcome with despair but conducts herself with dignity. Only now does conscience smite Zailm. He realizes what a fool he has been, but he continues his folly of deception with Anzimee.

When the banns of their coming marriage are announced in the temple by the High Priest Mainin, Lolix appeals to Rai Gwauxln to deny the banns because she has loved and wooed Zailm. Even now she does not betray Zailm's part in the matter, and the Rai does not grant her request. Thus the formal procedure continues. When Zailm states his wish to be married, instead of "I do," he says, "Even so, Incal not preventing."[21]

At that precise moment Lolix rushes back in and declares, "Incal will prevent!"[22] In a fit of madness she stabs Zailm in the arm and leaps to the place where the Maxin cube is positioned. Mainin hurriedly completes the ceremony, after which Rai Gwauxln sorrowfully forgives Zailm's sins—as far as human law is concerned. He then severely rebukes Mainin for doing an "accursed deed," which we only understand when Zailm approaches Lolix. To his horror, he discovers that she has turned to stone. This is the accursed deed done by Mainin, the evil priest.

From that moment Zailm wanders aimlessly about, grief

and remorse weighing upon his soul. He tries to escape by slipping away in his private vailx, but he cannot outrun his torturous thoughts. His anguish is such that he experiences horrifying visions, including an out-of-body encounter with Lolix, who is praying for him. To their horror, he and Lolix are visited by their murdered baby—thus had Lolix resolved the unwanted child. Zailm weeps over the dead child, his first real penitence, and begs Incal for mercy.

In a vision of the Christ, that mercy is granted and the babe taken into the arms of the Christ. But Zailm is told that he must balance his karma and repay his debts to those he has wronged. Then Zailm is suddenly back in his body. He sleeps, is feverish and slips into a coma. Ultimately, he awakens, weakened but restored.

Zailm returns to Caiphul and is allowed by Rai Gwauxln to cast the stone statue of Lolix into the Maxin Light. He confesses to Anzimee the entire miserable story of his affair with Lolix and his attempts to escape his tortured memories. He asks forgiveness, which she sadly grants.

A number of months remain before Zailm and Anzimee are to be married. Zailm decides to travel two thousand miles away to mine gold for Poseid—and to avoid any temptation to behave inappropriately with Anzimee. Psychologically, this gold-mining journey connects to his earlier serendipitous discovery of the lode of gold that paid for his education. He unconsciously recreates a victorious moment from his youth to help him through the grief and torment that still lurk beneath his conscious awareness.

In this "no man's land," driven by his usual impulsive curiosity, Zailm explores what looks like the remains of an old stone building. Inside, the building has a certain coldness and gloom that reminds Zailm of a prison. At that moment, we can almost hear the echo of Prince Menax's words ringing in our ears: "Be cautious, Zailm, be cautious!" But he is oblivious.

As he goes to leave the building, he impulsively tests his strength by swinging the heavy stone door on its hinges, and it slams shut. Having overestimated the weight of the door, Zailm loses his balance and strikes his head against the wall. What a lack of caution!

When he recovers consciousness, he realizes he is trapped without food or water. As he attempts to invoke help from Incal, he hears the mocking laugh of the evil priest Mainin. That wicked one has lured Zailm to this death trap. Zailm's torment is increased when Mainin tells him that he has done this not for any ill will toward him, but to torture Anzimee. Mainin hates her because she has exposed him in previous lifetimes. He takes an evil delight in knowing she will suffer from Zailm's fate.

Interlude in Devachan

After his death, Phylos's soul spends time in devachan, a realm of the lower etheric plane where souls are allowed to live out their desires. Here he experiences being with his friends from Poseid, including Anzimee, Menax and Lolix. However he conceives of them, thus they appear.

As he describes it, in his encounters with Anzimee, who is actually still living on earth, he sometimes meets his "conception of her" and "sometimes her higher self."[23] How could this be? I believe Anzimee so longs for him that her soul's higher nature is propelled into devachan.

Ultimately, in this realm between heaven and earth, Phylos loses all desire. And this concludes his time in devachan. He is ready to face his karma on earth. What is the lesson of devachan? A truth that applies to every soul: the fulfillment of desires is not the highest reality. Phylos has a greater destiny, and to fulfill it he must return to earth to balance his karma with Lolix.

Before incarnating again, he is taught higher truths by Mol Lang, a wise teacher who describes the works of God. And he is also granted an experience in the higher world. He is taken to Hesper, a planet of Christlike love,* where he is introduced to Mol Lang's daughter, Phyris, and her brother, Sohma. In truth, Phyris is the Higher Self of Anzimee, who by this time has so evolved that she no longer lives on earth. Yet Phylos's consciousness is not evolved enough to recognize his beloved in her higher body.

Phyris is aware of Phylos's past lives, motives and deeds, which he no longer recalls. And Sohma continues to teach Phylos the higher laws of the realm of Spirit. Although both of them instruct him in the higher realities, Phylos still yearns for the earthly realm. This is the pull of his karma—he must return to earth for his incarnation as Walter Pierson in the nineteenth century. He has been prepared, but will he pass his final exams?

Completion of Karmic Cycles

Back on earth, Walter Pierson is benevolent to a young woman, Elizabeth Harland, who needs help. He loans her money, which she ultimately repays with heartfelt gratitude. He feels drawn to her, realizing he loves her for her beauty and sweet womanhood. He loves her most of all for her effort to triumph over error, from which she emerges, as he puts it, as "pure gold."

Walter asks Elizabeth to marry him, and they live a quiet,

*Hesper, or Hesperus, is the evening star, especially Venus.

peaceful life, raising two daughters together. He continues his esoteric studies, which do not interest his wife. And he begins to yearn for his life on Hesper, which he now realizes was not a fantasy. He cannot get there again but at times is visited by what he calls his "ghost" (his astral body), and this shadowy figure tells him about his experiences on Hesper.

This wraith becomes more and more one with Walter, and he sinks into a peculiar state where at times he seems to relive his experiences on Hesper and the rest of the time he yearns for that high plane that he cannot find on earth. Thus we understand the title of Phylos's book *A Dweller on Two Planets.*

His melancholy state is a detriment to his wife and children. His daughters call him "funny," and Elizabeth is moved to tears when he absently calls her Phyris. Although she does not understand what he is talking about, she feels his withdrawal and the absence of his love. And she sees him becoming thin and pale and more and more removed from an interest in their life together.

When Walter delves deeply into esoteric studies and the rules of the spiritual path, he finally sees how much he is hurting Elizabeth and realizes he can no longer allow his lower nature to rule him. He stops dwelling on his astral experiences, subdues his sorrows and masters his lower nature. He reignites the fire of his devotion to Elizabeth and strives diligently to serve her.

In 1878 Walter and Elizabeth lose their daughters in an epidemic of scarlatina, and Elizabeth is overcome with grief. From that time on, Walter lives his life solely to comfort and serve Elizabeth, who is the reincarnation of the soul of Lolix, whom he so wronged in the ancient days of Atlantis.

He teaches her the law of karma and through his esoteric

knowledge enables her to remember their Atlantean embodiment. As a result, they grow much closer and Elizabeth is impelled to balance her karma through intensifying her efforts to do good works. She diligently follows Christ's teaching: "Be ye doers of the word, and not hearers only."[24]

He and Elizabeth are nearing the end of their lifetime together. Walter's karmic service to Elizabeth is coming to completion. He has become the loving husband and has shared his inner journeys with her. And Elizabeth has come to understand her lessons from the Atlantean lifetime.

They take a last voyage together, he as a mate and she as a passenger, on an American ship. As the ship nears the Bermudas, a terrible storm comes up and the vessel begins to sink. All of the crew climb into lifeboats, leaving the captain, Walter and Elizabeth to their fate. When Walter tries to put Elizabeth into one of the boats, she refuses, preferring to end her life with him. Minutes later, embracing one another, Walter and Elizabeth are engulfed by huge waves as the ship sinks to the bottom of the ocean. Thus they perish.

As the ship is going down, he comforts her, saying, "We will truly meet again, beyond the great deep River, with Him."[25] Fully aware of the past and closer in death than life, Walter and Elizabeth (Zailm and Lolix) move on to a higher destiny.

Phylos explains that certain spiritual tests remained for him to pass. But in their life together, he and Elizabeth had set the foundation. Their karmic journey is over, and Phylos begins a higher service and training. He is tutored and tested until he is ready for divine reunion with Phyris, his twin flame, who has preceded him to the higher realms.

We see that karma may take many lifetimes to come full circle. And in each lifetime we are given opportunities to balance karmic debts to those we have wronged in the past. When we face our karma with courage and nonattachment and serve others without reservation, we put on the garment of higher consciousness.

Through love and devotion to God and reverence for the divine spark in one another, we ultimately reach an attainment, spiritually, where we transcend the pull of earthly desires. We are ready for reentry into the higher realms of Spirit.

Reflections to Ponder

As we reflect on Phylos's karmic journey, we contemplate the truth of the saying "The soul is seldom sold at auction. It is bartered away in a thousand tiny wrong decisions." And we understand how this applies to the journey of our own soul.

Ask yourself, Would I have passed Phylos's tests? Which ones would have been the most difficult for me? What spiritual principles would help me pass those tests? Take a few moments to write down your answers and reflections while Phylos's story is still fresh in your mind.

Now ask, What similar tests do I have in my life today? How can I handle karmic encounters so that my soul makes spiritual progress? What are the major flaws I need to correct? What obstacles do I need to overcome? How will I do that?

I suggest you write down your answers in a journal or diary where they can act as a reminder and a checkpoint for your progress. I also recommend that you set daily, weekly or monthly goals. Review them regularly. Celebrate your victories; learn from defeats. Take time each day to thank God for the opportunity to balance your karma and serve your fellow lightbearers. Reach for the stars and you will discover your divine destiny!

11

The Soul's Connection with the Stars

At times the whole sky was ringed in shooting points
and puckers of light gathering and falling, pulsing, fading,
rhythmical as breathing. All of a piece.
As if the sky were a pattern of nerves
and our thought and memories traveled across it.
As if the sky were one gigantic memory for us all.

—LOUISE ERDRICH
"The World's Greatest Fishermen"

Many have tried to explore our soul's connection with other spheres—through religion, astronomy, astrology, space travel, quantum physics, chaos theory, the study of DNA, unraveling the mysteries of the Great Pyramid, of Noah's ark, ancient alchemists and mystery schools, and of the quest for the Grail. What do they all have in common? They propel us to move beyond human explanation—to reach for the Divine.

The ancients used to say that the sun rules the day and the moon rules the night. They developed concepts about gods and goddesses who were the rulers, such as Apollo, the sun god, and Luna, the moon goddess. And underlying their myths and stories of gods and goddesses there was a higher truth.

The energies of the sun and moon do impact life on earth—for good and for ill. Spiritually and physically, the rays of the sun are the solar energy of God. The sun has an enormous impact on the "day side" of life—on people, animals, and forests and plants that live and flourish upon the earth. And we associate the luminous quality of the sun with the illumination of the mind; thus we speak of luminaries, people who shed light on some subject or enlighten mankind.

Without the sun there would be no life as we know it. And as we have discussed, people's emotions can be powerfully influenced by the presence or absence of sunlight. At the same time, too much sun can cause heat stroke and create barren deserts. What mitigates these situations is water, which corresponds to the emotions.

We know that the energies of the moon are the reflective light of the sun and that these energies exert enormous control over the tides and the water element. And in our own being the water element is associated with the emotional body. Thus we are romantically quickened in the moonlight, and in a negative vein, a full moon is often associated with witchcraft or deviltry.

The moon also reflects the astral plane, a frequency of time and space beyond the physical. The astral plane corresponds with the emotional body as well as the collective unconscious—the part of the unconscious mind that is the repository of archetypal patterns common to all mankind regardless of cultural differences. Because the astral plane has been muddied by impure thought and feeling, the term *astral* is often used in a negative context to refer to that which is impure.

Put the Moon under Your Feet

Remember the old folk saying "Put the moon under your feet"? This means to take control of your emotional, or astral, substance. It's challenging because the water element is powerful, yet we can do it if we catch a reaction early on.

Saint Germain has given spiritual instruction on this topic:

> Most of you know only too well that when your emotions become disturbed over outer conditions, feelings, or concepts, there is a moment when you are yet able to wrest control of your energies from your own emotional body. Subsequently, if these energies are permitted to continue to rage unabated, that moment of control is lost; and then it is easy for people to do, to think, or to say that which they will one day regret.
>
> Conversely, most of you are aware of the great joy and peace that has come to your souls when you have been able to accomplish something for someone else. This happens because deep within yourself there is a loving desire to serve your fellowman. . . .
>
> One of the most skillful ways in which the tired businessman or executive, the frustrated mother or wife, the confused young man or woman, can find integration and wholeness for themselves is to develop the discipline of being able to direct their emotions to do for them exactly what they want. Such discipline will completely change their outlook, for they will then face life with joyous expectancy, not with dissatisfaction.
>
> For example, if it is love for another that you would express, then you must always guard against that love which is selfish, which would exact from the beloved the expectancies of your own mind and heart without ever understanding the givingness of love. In order to love as

> God loves, you must first give freedom to all parts of life, including yourself; and then you must place your trust, as does a nestling bird, in the heart of God, in the heart of goodness and mercy....
>
> The only way to be truly happy is to give oneself totally to the universe and to God, at the same time being aware of and expecting from God the return gift of one's Real Self.
>
> One of the greatest dangers in the religious quest has been brought about as men have given themselves to God thinking that that was *all* they had to do. Not understanding the responsibilities of free will, they then acted the part of the nebulous ninny. Having no will of their own, they would flip and flop back and forth, blown by every wind, obsessed with what we will call the law of uncertainty. "For if the trumpet give an uncertain sound, who shall prepare himself to the battle?"[1]...
>
> We must rise to emotional control; for when God said, "Take dominion over the earth!" he meant individual dominion over one's energies, one's consciousness, and one's four lower bodies.[2]

How do we do this? When we encounter difficult personal situations or world conditions, we exercise firm control of ourselves and of our negative memories, ideas, emotions or physical reactions.[3] Otherwise we find ourselves running off in all directions at their beck and call.

When we allow undisciplined energy to rule us, we typically do something we regret. When we manage our energies wisely, we feel good about ourselves and make better decisions. This kind of self-discipline completely changes our outlook. Instead of fearing the future, we can look forward to meeting life's challenges with an expectancy of a positive outcome.

Once we decide to take command of ourselves, we still need all the help we can get. Let's examine how understanding our soul's relation to the stars can add clarity and guidance for success on the upward journey.

Navigating the Homeward Journey

The positioning of the sun, moon and stars is like a celestial travel guide for the soul's journey on earth. And the study of astrology has guided the steps of ancient peoples and spiritual seekers for thousands of years. The ancients looked to the constellations to understand and guide their daily lives, and to this day the North Star is the point of reference for navigation.

The configuration of the stars at the time of birth is a blueprint for the fortunes and challenges of the soul in each lifetime. Thus, understanding one's astrology can be of great assistance in anticipating what is coming that may set off old patterns or initiate new cycles.

The astrologers of old made use of the sun and stars to guide their way through life, physically and spiritually. The Magi were guided to the place of the birth of the Saviour by the positioning of the stars. And the bright star that lit the night sky when the Saviour was born guided the shepherds to where he lay. Likewise, our soul and spirit have a connection with the sun, the moon and the stars—and thereby with the Creator.

Karen Drye, a talented spiritual astrologer, specializes in exploring the soul's connection with the stars and how it affects our journey on earth.[4] In a revised version of her enlightening research paper "Marsilio Ficino, Astrologer and Physician of the Soul"[5] (which makes up the remainder of this chapter), she offers an in-depth interpretation of the work of this important Renaissance figure, whose writings can help us understand the connection of our soul with our planetary system and the world of Spirit:

Astrology and the Soul by Karen Drye

Historically, the classical methods of using astrology as a tool of prediction were predominant until the early twentieth century. The works of Theosophical astrologer Alan Leo (1860–1917) gradually modernized Western astrology and took it from a purely predictive science to an esoteric, soul-centered practice.[6] As the science of psychology developed, astrology also grew into a useful tool to gain insight into the personality and the soul. In a more profound way, astrology reveals the journey of the soul and her deeper purpose in life.

Today, many psychologists use astrology as a tool to gain insight into and accelerate the understanding of their client's issues. Although Alan Leo was responsible for the shift in Western astrology to an esoteric science of the soul, it can be said that the roots of soul-centered astrology originated with Marsilio Ficino.

Marsilio Ficino, Physician of the Soul

Marsilio Ficino (1433–1499) was a Florentine Christian philosopher, astrologer, priest and physician, and one of the leading figures of the Italian Renaissance. He was known as the physician of the soul and used astrology primarily as a means of helping to heal the soul rather than as a tool of prediction.

He believed, as Plato taught and all believed during the Renaissance, that everything above the moon, including the planets and the stars, was closer to God and to heaven and was therefore divine, perfect and unchanging. The heavenly bodies were, in fact, a part of God's creation, a reflection of God and his perfection. Furthermore, Renaissance man believed in the Hermetic philosophy of the macrocosm-microcosm—as above, so below—and therefore that the planets and stars were a reflection of what was inside of him.

As a Christian astrologer, Ficino taught that by living an aesthetic, religious and philosophic life, and aligning one's energies with the divine nature of the planets and stars, a person could reconnect with his own higher divinity, with God. This aspiration was the purpose of life and one's reason for being. In this light, astrology was considered a divine science, one that was used to bring the soul closer to God.

With the advent of powerful telescopes, we now know that the planets are not perfect in their appearance and orbits. We will see how this knowledge expands upon Ficino's work and takes it to a higher level of understanding of the soul and her earthly journey.

Plato, Hermes Trismegistus and Renaissance Man

To understand Ficino's work in a deeper way, it is necessary to understand Renaissance man and his philosophy as well as Ficino's concepts of the soul. The foundation of Ficino's beliefs can be traced to Hermes Trismegistus's *Corpus Hermeticum* and the writings of Plato.

The Renaissance (1350–1600 A.D.) was the transition period from medieval to more modern times. It began in Italy, predominately in Florence, when Greek scholars arrived with their ancient manuscripts after Constantinople fell to the Turks in 1453.[7] The term *Renaissance* means "rebirth" and for this period in history it means the rebirth or revival of the ancient works of Greece and Rome.

Ficino was head of the Florentine Platonic Academy, founded and supported by the wealthy Italian banking family, the Medici. He was responsible for the Latin translations of the works of Plato and the *Corpus Hermeticum,* which infused medieval society with a new outlook on life.

As a youth, Marsilio had a love of Plato and through his studies came to know and embody the knowledge that Plato taught. It was through this deeper insight of comprehending man as more than a body—penetrating to the soul and understanding the deeper meaning and purpose of man's existence—that Marsilio Ficino pursued astrology.

To Ficino and to Renaissance man in general, the planets and the outer world, the macrocosm, were simply a reflection of what was inside of him, referred to as the microcosm. The well-known phrase "as above, so below" describes this concept and originates from the *Emerald Tablet* of Hermes Trismegistus.

Quoting from Elizabeth Clare Prophet's book *Your Seven Energy Centers*: "The idea that the spiritual world is mirrored in the material world and in our own physical body is an ancient one. 'As is the atom, so is the universe' say the Upanishads. . . . And the famous Hermetic axiom states 'As is the great, so is the small; as it is above, so it is below.' In other words, the pattern of Spirit is indelibly imprinted within the very fabric of our being."[8]

At the time of the Renaissance, people were coming out of the medieval ages where the church was the predominant factor and a powerful force in their lives. Christianity taught that man was inherently a sinner and his only hope of salvation was through the church and the sacraments.

Then, as today, people were not completely satisfied with the explanations given by the church and wanted to explore and know more about their reason for being and the deeper mysteries of life. As we will see, the teachings of Plato and Hermes shed a different light on the inherent nature of man.

With the rebirth of the works of Plato and Hermes, people became inspired with the possibility of man being inherently divine and capable of realizing that divinity. The problem in the Middle Ages, of course, was that it was dangerous to pursue certain philosophies as the threat of punishment from church authorities loomed large.

Among his works, Ficino translated selected writings from the philosophical teachings of Hermes Trismegistus contained in the *Corpus Hermeticum* and published them under the title *Pimander.*[9] While translating a portion of these teachings, Ficino noted similarities between the works of Hermes and the story of creation in the book of Genesis from the Christian Bible.

The Inherent Divinity of Mankind

Frances Yates, author of *Giordano Bruno and the Hermetic Tradition,* points out that in the Mosaic Genesis or Christian version of "the Fall," man is not created as a divine being. Hence Christians believe that there is only one Son of God and man cannot rise to the inner divinity personified by Jesus. In the Hermetic version of the Fall, also known as the Egyptian Genesis,[10] man is a divine being, a son of God, one with the Creator and capable of returning to that original state of divinity.

Yates clarifies these points for us:

"It is true that the Mosaic Genesis, like the Egyptian

Genesis, says that Man was made in the image of God and was given dominion over all creatures, but it is never said in the Mosaic Genesis that this meant that Adam was created as a divine being, having the divine creative power. Not even when Adam walked with God in the Garden of Eden before the Fall is this said of him. When Adam, tempted by Eve and the serpent, wished to eat of the Tree of Knowledge and become like God, this was the sin of disobedience, punished by the exile from the Garden of Eden. But in the Egyptian Genesis the newly created Man, seeing the newly created Seven Governors (the planets) on whom all things depend, wishes to create, to make something like that. . . .

"It is true that he falls, but this fall is in itself an act of his power. . . . It is true that this is a Fall which involves loss, that Man in coming down to Nature and taking on a mortal body puts this mortal body . . . under the dominion of the stars. . . . But man's immortal part remains divine and creative. He consists, not of a human soul and a body, but of a divine, creative, immortal essence and a body."[11]

It should be noted that the reference by Yates to the Seven Governors, the seven inner planets (Sun, Mercury, Venus, Earth, Mars, Jupiter and Saturn)[12] relates to the seven chakras, or spiritual energy centers, within us. These seven planets represent the part of the macrocosm reflected by the seven chakras within us as the microcosm: as above (the macrocosm, the planets in this instance), so below (the microcosm, the chakras). Origen of Alexandria taught the concept of the planets and stars being reflected within us when he said, "Know that you are another world in miniature and have in you Sol and Luna and even the stars."[13]

The belief that man is not a body but rather a soul

and inherently divine was a key concept, not only for Ficino but for Renaissance man in general. In order to further understand Ficino's concept of the soul, we must grasp the logic of his teacher Plato—and Plato's concept of the soul.

Plato: Three Components of the Soul

Plato taught that there are three components of the soul, which simultaneously work together in the dynamics of human life and personality. These three elements of the soul include the rational, the irrational, and passion or spirit.

In *The Republic,* Plato speaks of the rational and irrational aspects of the soul, posing the question:

"Then we may fairly assume that they are two, and that they differ from one another; the one with which a man reasons, we may call the rational principle of the soul, the other, with which he loves and hungers and thirsts and feels the flutterings of any other desire, may be termed the irrational or appetitive, the ally of sundry pleasures and satisfactions? [Plato's answer:] Yes . . . we may fairly assume them to be different."[14]

The rational part of the soul knows what is right and acts in the best interest of the individual. And the irrational or "appetitive," part of the soul seeks pleasure for her own gain. The third aspect of the soul, called spirit, gives life and animates the soul into action through free will. That action is for good or ill, depending on whether the rational or irrational part of the soul is acting.

In the most ideal situation, man self-corrects; he is aware of his irrational nature and still chooses by free will to do the right thing. In contrast, as the soul engages more and more in irrational actions, this task becomes more difficult.

The Dual Nature of the Soul

Yates further describes the Hermetic version of the Fall through mankind's free will when she says, "He [man] can lean down through the armature of the spheres, tear open their [the spheres'] envelopes and come down to show himself to Nature."[15]

When mankind "leaned down," he effectively tore open the seal (armature, or protective sheath) of the chakras and thereby opened up the Pandora's box of irrational, animalistic desires. The pleasure of these inordinate desires[16] is what actually created the lower, irrational aspect of his soul. Man's lower nature is like that of animals, a base-instinct nature—the part of man that causes him to "lean down." This is the same concept and reasoning as to why a man looks up to "heaven," his higher nature, and down to "hell," his lower nature.

Through this process of "the Fall" or by man creating his lower, irrational nature through engaging in animalistic desires (e.g., overdriven passions or addictions), man now has a situation of duality and a dual nature of the soul—the rational and the irrational elements.

Chakras: Gateways between Heaven and Earth

In esoteric teachings, the reference to "spheres" (as in "armature of the spheres") refers to the seven energy centers, or chakras, in man. They are the gateways of the transfer of Spirit to matter, from heaven to earth and from within to without. They are the means by which we express ourselves, our thoughts, our emotions, our words and actions.

Quoting Elizabeth Clare Prophet from *Your Seven Energy Centers*: "In simple terms, you can think of the energy centers [chakras] as receiving and sending stations for the energy that flows to you, through you and out from you moment by moment. Each center is like a step-down transformer that translates this powerful energy from Spirit to a different level of our being, nourishing body, mind and soul.... The seven major energy centers are situated at etheric levels of our being along the spinal column."[17]

Through our free will, the energies of Spirit are qualified, or expressed, through each chakra. For instance, our heart chakra "inspires us with the compassion and generosity to be love in action."[18] The throat chakra gives us the power of communication through the spoken word. For example, we can speak the truth (empowering our rational nature) or use that energy for gossip or criticism (strengthening the irrational nature).

The Nature of "Angel" and Higher Self

In his book *Platonic Theology*, in the chapter entitled "Above angel is God; for just as soul is mobile plurality and angel motionless plurality, so God is motionless unity,"[19] Ficino introduces the concept that the rational nature of the soul is also referred to as angel, commonly spoken of as the Guardian Angel or Higher Self.

Ficino says, "Platonists believe that angel is entirely without motion in essence, power and activity; for it is always the same, its capacity is constant, it understands everything at the same moment [omnipotent], it wills the same things, and, insofar as it can, it does whatever it does instantaneously....

"Soul, because it is in motion, passes from one thing to another. So it contains within itself the one thing and the other. Because it has both, it contains plurality. Soul then is in itself a certain plurality... in motion."[20]

Here Ficino is referring to the soul in a state of duality ("plurality"), moving ("in motion") between her higher and lower nature—between the rational and irrational elements. Being in motion, the soul looks to the left and to the right with desires and therefore wavers in her choices.

Some days the soul chooses to do what is right and good (rational) and some days not (irrational). Thus, as we act rationally we strengthen our higher nature. When we act irrationally, we further create and strengthen our lower nature. As will be shown later, these aspects are clearly depicted in the positive and challenging sides of the astrology chart.

I AM Presence: Our Star of Divinity

Ficino goes on to explain that there is something above the rational nature of the soul. He says, "This is God, the most powerful of all in that He is the simplest of all."[21] This echoes Ficino's earlier statement that "God is motionless unity."

When God is spoken of as "motionless unity," this also refers to the highest essence of ourselves, known as the I AM Presence or Spirit. This is the highest part of our being that has remained pure, in the image and likeness of God. It is motionless in that, like God, it neither moves nor looks to the left or the right with desire. It does not experience the duality of the rational and irrational elements of the soul. Neither does it waver in its desire for goodness and its higher divinity. Hence the I AM Presence, as God, is motionless unity. It is the part of us that is divine, perfect and unchanging.

We were created in the image and likeness of God, born of that Spirit. The I AM Presence is our sun, our star of divinity that we look up to and aspire toward. This is the part of us that is God, the pure Spirit that animates our soul, beats our heart and gives us life. The phrase "I AM THAT I AM" means: I really am the I AM Presence above me, which is God. Therefore I AM *that* I AM.

When the soul separated out and descended into the earth plane, the I AM Presence, our divine, perfect and unchanging essence, remained one with God. This part of our soul has never changed and never will. It will always be there waiting for our return.

When the soul by free will, originally "leaned down," she departed from oneness with Spirit (the I AM Presence). The angel, or rational, part of the soul (Higher Self), remained at the level of Spirit as the mediator, the guiding light to draw the soul back to her original state of perfection. The Higher Self does not waver in purity or goodness. Yet it is plural, or dual, in nature because it is connected to the irrational part of the soul until that lower nature has been transformed.

Ficino, as the physician of the soul, directs the soul dwelling in the earthly realm to aspire to, become like and reunite with Spirit, the I AM Presence, God. He taught, as did Hermes, that the goal of life is to tame the lower nature in preparation for this reunion.

Theoretically, once the soul is purified and the lower nature tamed and transformed, she is then able to reunite with God, the I AM Presence, as Jesus demonstrated. There is no longer a polarity, no longer a duality and no longer an irrational element drawing the soul down from her pure nature. Perhaps this reunion with God is the true meaning of the Christian concept of being "born again" —the soul is restored to her original state of purity.

Furthermore, this transformation of the lower, irrational nature is possibly related to the biblical scripture: "And as it is appointed unto men once to die."[22] In this instance, it would be the lower nature that dies enabling the soul to be born again in Spirit.

Plato: The Quality of Passion or Spirit

Plato discusses his concept of passion or spirit (with a lowercase *s*) in *The Republic*:

"Take the quality of passion or spirit;—it would be ridiculous to imagine that this quality, when found in States [the governing authority], is not derived from the individuals who are supposed to possess it."[23]

In this passage we understand the concept of an inanimate object becoming animate or filled with spirit. For example, a business is an inanimate object or legal entity. What brings it to life is the spirit of the people who work for the business. Through the combined spirit of the employees and owners, each company takes on a spirit of its own. Inanimate entities, such as businesses, are enlivened because of the energy or spirit that infuses them.

In a literal mind-set, Ficino's concept of the planets being ensouled (animated or filled with spirit) or emanating rays that affect us here on earth may sound absurd, almost as if describing a comic character or the fantasy of an inanimate object springing to life. However, upon truly understanding the meaning, it starts to make sense.

Spirit (with a capital *S*) is the animating principle of the soul and its movement creates a certain "spirit." Motion or animation can happen only as a result of the animating principle of Spirit (God). Once something is in motion, it emanates the quality of spirit.

For human life, emotion has been referred to as "energy in motion." And we get the energy for emotion from Spirit. The qualification of emotion through free will (for rational or irrational purposes) creates a quality of spirit relative to that qualification. For example, if you get mad, you will have a spirit of anger around you. This acts like a magnet that attracts more anger to you. Thus, by the law of like attracts like, "what goes around, comes around."

The earth and the planets are in motion as they spin on their axes as a result of that same energy of Spirit. Since planets are in motion they naturally emanate the element of spirit as well. And by the Hermetic axiom "as above, so below," our spirit is reflected to the planets as their spirit is reflected to us.

Ficino speaks of this aspect of spirit in another way:

"Celestial figures by their own motion dispose themselves for acting; for by their harmonious rays and motions penetrating everything, they daily influence our spirit secretly just as overpowering music generally does openly. Besides, you know how easily a mourning figure moves pity in many people, and how much a figure of a lovable person instantly affects and moves the eyes, imagination, spirit, and humors; no less living and efficacious in a celestial figure."[24]

Thus, just as the sun's rays penetrate the earth and give life, so do the planets impart their characteristic rays and influences.

The World Soul: The Seven Planets

Ficino talks about the World Soul, the macrocosmic counterpart of the microcosm of our soul. Again, this is the ancient Hermetic concept that the higher world of heaven and the planetary bodies is mirrored in our material world and in our own physical body. In other words, the pattern of Spirit is indelibly imprinted within the very fabric of our being and in every aspect of life, both animate and inanimate.

Relating to the axiom "as above, so below," the planets would have a spiritual makeup like our individual souls—a rational and irrational element as well as a divine spirit. As the seven chakras are the means of expression of the spirit of our soul, so the Seven Governors (or seven planets) are the means of expression of the spirit of the World Soul.

Healing Practices of Renaissance Man

Renaissance man intuitively understood the importance of surrounding himself with beauty and uplifting images that remind the soul of her divinity. This was reflected, among other ways, in culture, architecture, art and music. Ficino understood this practice as well and used it in conjunction with his knowledge of astrology to help heal the soul.

In Ficino's day, people did not have meditation, psychology and other tools to help resolve their issues. They practiced living an aesthetic and philosophical life, taming their lower appetites and using "natural magic" (i.e., finding elements of God's perfection through nature, geometric forms and sacred images) to raise the soul upward to her higher nature.

When the planets are in positive, harmonious aspects, astrology can be used to enhance their positive impact on people. For instance, Ficino took care to prepare medicines at astrologically auspicious times to strengthen their beneficial effect on his patients.

Ideally, if someone needed a remedy to help the liver, the astrologer would prepare the herbal tincture when Jupiter (which rules the liver) was in favorable aspect. Theoretically, if the Spirit of God through the planet Jupiter were infused into the tincture, that balancing energy would likewise be infused into the person who was seeking healing.

If a soul was burdened, usually a Saturnian quality, Ficino might have chosen to find something with Venusian qualities of joy and kindness to bring the soul back to her natural state of joy, reminding her of her higher origins. Perhaps Ficino would choose an image of a beautiful piece of Venusian art to reflect to the soul her own inherent beauty. Or maybe he would prepare a beautiful piece of jewelry when Venus was in a harmonious aspect to enhance those joyous qualities.

Like Attracts Like

In astrology it is commonly known that each planet has a negative and positive manifestation. For instance, Mars can signify aggressive or violent actions and behaviors (the irrational nature), or Mars can give us courage and a spirit to act for the betterment of ourselves and others (the rational nature).

In much of Ficino's work he chose not to focus on the lower nature of the planets and their malefic influences. During his time, since his reference point was that the planets were perfect, one has to wonder and speculate how he and others must have struggled to understand why the planets had influences that were not divine. What of the irrational nature of the planets? Where does this come from and how does it affect us?

Since we are subject to the rays of the planets, we would naturally draw to us both the rational and irrational energies of the planets. As Ficino said, "This [energy] is absorbed by man in particular through his own spirit which is by its own nature similar to it."[25] This means that whatever we create as the rational or irrational part of our soul through our free will attracts to us the same qualities from the planets—i.e., like attracts like.

So we come to understand that although man's soul contains both rational and irrational parts, as do the planets, there is the capacity through free will for one's soul to choose to either "lean down" or to aspire upward, depending on where one aligns one's thoughts and actions. And as has been popularly stated, the planets incline but do not compel us to take a particular action. We have free will as to what action we take.

If a man chooses by his free will to create destruction by harming another part of life, his action creates a spirit within him relative to that act. He will therefore be subject to the influence of the planet or planets whose lower natures reflect that particular spirit or energy.

Likewise, if a person engages in an act of kindness, when that energy is reflected back to him through the planets, he will be more likely to receive a similar action of kindness.

Chiron: The Wounded Healer

Along the same lines of the concept of the rational and irrational elements of the soul, let us progress for a moment and look at Chiron, discovered in 1977 and classified as both a minor planet and a comet. Since Chiron's discovery there have been additional heavenly bodies discovered in our solar system that are of a similar nature to Chiron. They have been classified as the "Centaurs."[26]

It is important to note that mythologically the Centaurs, who were half man and half animal (horse), were a wild bunch of untamed beasts infamous for their uncontrolled desires and savage behavior. The half-man is symbolic of the rational nature of the soul; the half-horse symbolizes the animal or irrational nature.

Chiron (also known as the wounded healer) was different from the other centaurs. He spent his life learning how to control and heal his lower, animal nature and help others do the same. As Melanie Reinhart says in her book *Chiron and the Healing Journey,* "Chiron became a wise man, prophet, physician, teacher and musician. His ministry included the unruly Centaurs themselves."[27]

In astrology, Chiron rules what we sometimes feel as deep soul pain, the underlying psychic pain that plagues the soul. I believe this is the pain of the split, or separation, of the soul from Spirit (God) into her state of duality, the rational and irrational elements of being. The feeling of wholeness and peace that people seek would be the resolution of that split, achieved, as Ficino described, through the soul's reunion with Spirit.

We see a similarity between the philosophy of Chiron as the wounded healer, learning to heal and transform his lower nature, and that of Hermes Trismegistus and Ficino. All three encouraged taming the appetites and lower nature. In this process, likened to alchemy, the lower nature is purified and transformed to its original state of divine perfection.

In his book *Meditations on the Soul,* Ficino says:

"From what we have said it follows that, as our souls are never fulfilled with earthly food, nor while they gorge on earthly things can they enjoy the heavenly feast, so in this life they strive with all their might to cling to the King of heaven. For the less they are tainted by the bitter tastes of earth, and the more they are refreshed by the sweet waters of heaven, the more eagerly are they drawn toward the spring of sweetness that is above heaven. The nearer we approach the Lord of the world, the further we depart from worldly slavery."[28]

In her purified state, the soul is redeemed and prepared for reunion with Spirit, God. Alternately, if a person chooses to strengthen the irrational nature of his being, the lower nature becomes more empowered and the soul feels greater suffering and increased soul pain. The split between the higher nature and the soul trapped in her lower nature becomes wider and wider. Thus the soul can eventually lose her ability to connect with her higher nature.

The understanding that we are responsible for the creation of this lower, irrational nature is both daunting and empowering. With this knowledge, we realize that our life is in our own hands. We have chosen and created our fate, our reality. And we are empowered to change and transform that part of us that does not serve our higher purpose.

Likewise, we do not have to be the victim of our astrology. By transforming our lower nature we free ourselves from vulnerability to the negative influences of the planets. Then, when the planets do aspect our charts in a negative manner, there is no magnet within us to attract a potentially challenging situation.

Spiritual Astrology

In my astrology work, I use two copies of the astrological chart when doing a consultation. On one copy, I draw the positive, harmonious aspects to represent the rational, Higher Self. On the other, I draw the stressful, challenging aspects to represent the irrational or lower nature.

How people live their lives determines how much they outpicture the positive or negative (challenging) side of their chart. Obviously a notorious character would embody more of the negative side of the chart or lower nature. Likewise a saintly person would embody more of his or her positive attributes.

As Ficino described, the soul is a "plurality... in motion." We are in motion between our rational and irrational natures, exemplified by the positive and negative sides of our astrological chart.

As the chart is a blueprint of the soul, the two-chart technique allows the astrologer to pinpoint and clarify irrational behavior patterns and to direct the soul to her innate positive nature, ideally leading to the transformation of the lower nature. Inherent in every astrological chart, inborn in every soul, is the way out of every problem. It is always a matter of freewill choice which direction we take.

Ficino himself strove to live a Christian life, one in which he used music, medicine, astrology, art and ritual to achieve a lifestyle focused on the higher nature of the soul, thereby living a happy, peaceful and soul-centered existence.

Seeing beyond a Two-Dimensional Existence

The purpose of Ficino's life and work was to help people see beyond the material, two-dimensional existence of man into the deeper meaning of life. And through this journey one would connect with the higher essence of his soul, bringing him closer to God and closer to finding the happiness and peace that Ficino believed was inherent in everyone. He saw spirit or soul in every aspect of life, and he used this knowledge to help others to reconnect with the inner essence of their own soul.

In today's society we have separated the spirit from the physical. People don't always feel their connection with nature. They are trapped in their minds with the thoughts and burdens of everyday life. When people desire to reconnect with nature, to go to a mountain lake or stream where it is peaceful, quiet and far away from the stress of daily life, they are practicing the very kind of natural magic Ficino encouraged.

Today we may see a book as an inanimate object, lifeless and without soul. However, to Ficino, a book would be filled with the spirit of the message of its author. It would not be an inanimate object. It would be the reflection of its author, a creation alive with the author's spirit.

There is no real separation between what is within (the invisible world of thoughts and emotions) and what is without (the visible world of physical, inanimate objects). The separation is an illusion we have created by the condition of duality in time and space. The closer we come to resolving this split, this separation from God, the more we will be aware of the oneness of all life.

Modern physics echoes this understanding in the concepts of quantum and chaos theory, through which scientists have come to the conclusion that all life is interconnected. The illusion of separation comes from the split in our own beings, which is the result of the soul's separation from her source—Spirit, or God. That split created the dual nature of the rational and irrational elements of the soul.

For Ficino, all matter is infused with the spirit of the soul of life, our life, God's life. There is no separation between body and spirit or the physical microcosm and the spiritual macrocosm. Everything is alive with the energy infused in it by God and man.

"We Are They, They Are Us"

Ficino teaches that we are part of the planets and they are part of us. They, like ourselves, are part of the spiritual, animating force of life created by God and altered by free will as man's rational and irrational nature is radiated to the planets and reflected back to him in a constant yet changing dynamic of life.

Yet, like man, the World Soul through the planets contains the Spirit of God that is perfect, divine and unchanging. It is therefore constantly reflecting back to the soul her true place in the universe. This Spirit, from whence we came, is the divine state of perfection to which Ficino encourages us to return.

Ficino himself sums it up very well:

"In summary, consider that those who by prayer, by study, by manner of life, and by conduct imitate the beneficence, action, and order of the celestials, since they are more similar to the gods, receive fuller gifts from them."[29]

Revelation to the Soul

This remarkable understanding of the interplay of the soul and the starry heavens has been a revelation to my own soul. As a modern-day psychologist of the soul, I echo Karen Drye's closing comment:

> In my focus on the works of Ficino, Hermes Trismegistus and Plato, I can witness to Ficino's practice of philosophy and contemplation as leading the soul to higher knowledge. I have come to understand the soul and the deeper meanings of the concepts that Ficino teaches in a way I have never understood before. It seems that Ficino's spirit can still touch us through his written works and that he is still practicing as the physician of the soul.[30]

In the spirit of Ficino, Karen and I would like to leave you with a passage from *Meditations on the Soul.* In this book, a collection of Ficino's personal letters, he shares his daily prayer with a dear friend. Here is a portion of his inspiring communion with God:

> Rid us, dear Father, of what has separated us from You for so long: distrust, despair, and indifference. Give back to us, dear Father, what unites us to You: true faith, firm home, and burning love. Give these back to us, O light of lights and life of the living, lest separated from You and left to ourselves we should, like the dead, at once sink into outer darkness.
>
> May we who have lived for You devotedly now live for You spiritually, as far as we are able. May we dwell in Your very being forever. In You may we shine and burn, may we blaze and be made joyful. May we rejoice in bliss without end, beyond the measure of our desires.
>
> May we, without distraction, infinitely love Your infinite beauty. May we without surfeit eternally enjoy Your infinite good.[31]

12

Ascending the Mountain of Selfhood

There are three lessons I would write,
Three words as with a burning pen,
In tracings of eternal light
Upon the hearts of men.

—FRIEDRICH VON SCHILLER
"Hope, Faith and Love"

Many courageous souls who originally embodied on earth are now ascended masters. They forged that victory by learning to discern subtle forms of evil, being careful not to misuse power, and by treating others compassionately. And they kept their hand in God's hand in the darkest of circumstances.

These warriors of the Spirit ensouled the divinity of the Father-Mother God and embodied the light in the face of darkness. Their earthly lives and teachings offer guidance and inspiration for our own ascent of the mountain of selfhood.

On June 30, 1995, Elizabeth Clare Prophet gave invaluable teaching about the evolution of souls on earth that helps us understand our own journey in time and space. She also discussed the role of the ascended masters who guide us and described some of their spiritual retreats in the etheric octave:

> The souls in the first three evolutions that came to earth remained in the etheric octave, attained their perfection through fourteen thousand years and returned to the heart of God in the victory of the ascension. Then came the fourth, fifth and sixth root races.[1]
>
> The fourth root race was compromised by fallen angels, laggards, individuals who led them astray from their divine destiny. Consequently, many of the fourth root race made extensive karma with those of the dark side. And many of the fourth root race, if not the majority, are in embodiment today.
>
> The same took place with the fifth root race. And two thousand years ago, the sixth root race began to embody. They are the newest souls in the earth.
>
> So the fourth and fifth root races are very old souls who are totally familiar with the teachings of East and West and have a deep, instantaneous understanding of the paths of East and West.
>
> The Great Divine Director will usher in the seventh root race, which is to embody in South America. And the God and Goddess Meru, Manus* of the sixth root race, have their focus over Lake Titicaca, on the border between Peru and Bolivia. The terms *God* and *Goddess* denote that they are cosmic beings who ensoul the God consciousness of their office. God Meru has explained that the names God and Goddess Meru have come down from ancient Lemuria, where their twin flames guarded the light of the Motherland.
>
> The physical focus of the Mother flame was lost when Lemuria sank beneath the Pacific. That was the

*Each root race embodies under the aegis of a Manu (Sanskrit, "progenitor" or "lawgiver"), who embodies the Christic image for the race.

most ancient continent that we are aware of, although there are civilizations that predate Lemuria.

The God and Goddess Meru have enshrined the Mother flame at their retreat on the etheric plane to make up for the loss of the focus of the Mother flame on Lemuria. This vast retreat, the Temple of Illumination, is located over Lake Titicaca, high in the Andes Mountains. . . .

The Great Divine Director, Manu of the seventh root race, presides spiritually over the continent of South America, where the seventh root race is destined to incarnate in the Aquarian age.

In a dictation delivered through Mark Prophet on April 2, 1961, the Great Divine Director said: "Today in South America . . . there now arises a transcendent and beautiful beginning in the land of Brazil. In the city of Brasilia there has been created a beautiful setting and climate for the government over which we will preside during the reign of the seventh root race."

The Great Divine Director is the ascended master whose attainment of cosmic consciousness qualifies him to ensoul the flame of divine direction on behalf of earth's evolutions and untold lifewaves beyond. His name, as Saint Germain has explained, "is the title of an office in the cosmic hierarchy given to the one who, by virtue of diligent application over the aeons, presently focuses within his causal body the formula of the ascension for the children of God and the sons and daughters of the Most High evolving in this cosmos."[2]

The Great Divine Director has said, "I pray . . . that you will call to me, for I have within my consciousness . . . the scroll of the divine plan for every living soul on Terra [earth] and in the vast beyond."[3]

That is a great invitation to call to the great blue causal body of the Great Divine Director to receive your

> divine plan for the remainder of your incarnations on earth.
>
> The Great Divine Director is a member of the Darjeeling Council[4] and also serves as a member of the Karmic Board,[5] on which he represents the first ray, the will of God. He has two retreats in the etheric octave: the Cave of Light in the heart of the Himalayas in India and the Rakoczy Mansion in the Carpathian Mountains in Transylvania.[6]

Mrs. Prophet explained that these retreats are in the etheric plane; thus we do not see them with the naked eye. However, if we are near those mountains and sensitive to higher vibration, we might very well sense the presence of the retreats. I have experienced that exhilarating higher vibration in Jackson Hole, Wyoming, where another retreat, the Royal Teton Retreat, is congruent with the Grand Teton.

We can also ask to be taken to these retreats in our finer bodies while we sleep at night. After doing so, we often awaken refreshed and with a renewed enthusiasm for meeting the tasks of the day from a higher perspective, a more rounded point of view.

This is a major purpose of the ascended masters and bodhisattvas who guide the souls evolving on earth. They have dedicated themselves to helping us raise our consciousness so that we, too, may pass our tests and win our ascension.

Raising our consciousness is particularly important now, since the seventh root race is preparing for their earthly journey at a time when the evolutions of earth are at a spiritual crossroads. We will either choose to evolve spiritually or continue to descend into the nightmare of ongoing terrorist activity, international conflict, economic crisis and the underlying threat of nuclear war.

Many people have an inner awareness of this worldwide dilemma, and we see a return to spirituality of people who may not have been as attentive to their spiritual journey in the past. Thus we see crowds cheering the Pope, audiences praising God at Benny Hinn services, and a widespread awareness of Buddhist, Jewish and Muslim faiths. In addition, many New Age movements are spiritually oriented.

Whether we are ordinary people nurturing hearth and home and going to our jobs every day or adepts holding the balance in the heights of the Andes, we are experiencing a strong inner drive to move onward and upward to higher consciousness. This is the spiritual propelling of the winds of Aquarius.

Invoking Divine Direction for Your Life

In order to raise our consciousness and win our victory of the ascension in the light, we need divine direction. We know that Jesus talked to his Father in heaven in the Garden of Gethsemane. And the angels came to strengthen him. We know that saints throughout the ages have walked and talked with God, and thereby received divine direction. And even today we have reports of angelic guidance and visitations. How can we directly ask for this kind of intervention?

Saint Germain, sponsor of the Aquarian age, asked his students to do a thirty-three-day meditation with the Great Divine Director in order to get the guidance they needed.

He said:

> Day by day the cosmic computer of the mind of God adjusts the formula of the path according to the individual patterns of living, being, acting on the stage of life. For every action there is a corresponding reaction in the cosmos—an adjustment for the increase or decrease

of light in manifestation, which is the result of the individual application of free will.

According to the choices you make daily, your divine plan is adjusted, and in the blueprint of your soul's evolution, adjustments are made for the balance of cycles. Thus the equation of living on Terra can be stated: The law plus you plus karma and dharma equals the divine plan manifest as circumstance in time and space.... Daily choices to accelerate the divine plan, to make the most of life, to do one's best and better than one's best, must be made....

Souls cry out: "We know not the way to go! We know not how to make the choices, though choices we would make." This year [and every year] mankind face the collective karma of their failure to make right choices in all past ages.... There is a plan for you. For every child of the light, for every chela of the law, there is a divine way. But there is always the human alternative....

I bid you make the choice of entering into a novena to... define the path of your own Self-realization....

Begin by placing yourself at a desk, clean and cleared, where you will not be disturbed. Take a blank sheet of white paper, and with pen in hand commune with the innermost light of your being. You can meditate upon your divine plan by visualizing a white sphere before you. Approximately two feet in diameter, this sphere is the symbol of your own cosmic consciousness which you contact in meditation.

Now address the Lords of Life, saying: "In the name of my own Real Self, the I AM THAT I AM, and the Christed one of my being, I call forth from the reservoir of my cosmic consciousness the divine plan of my life, the blueprint of being. I call to the Lords of Life, to the Great Divine Director, and to Saint Germain to assist me now in the implementation of the law of cosmos as it applies to my individual identity, to my karma and my dharma, and to the circumstances of my life in time and space."

Light a candle and consecrate it to the spark of divinity which is your very own opportunity to fulfill your cosmic destiny. Let the flame be the focus of the threefold flame of love, wisdom, and power that burns on the altar of your heart. Let it be a focus of untapped resources, of energies available, idling in the nexus of decision, waiting for your command to descend as flowing fire for the crystallization of the God flame within you.

Now take your pen and set forth in your own handwriting upon the white page before you, symbolizing the white page that God has given to you as the gift of life, the goals that you desire to accomplish while the sands of opportunity yet fall in the hourglass.

Measuring moment by moment the choices that you make in time and space, write down your fondest hopes, your impossible dreams, your heart's longings, your desire for soul fulfillment, your educational goals, your spiritual and material expectations, the service you desire to render unto God and man, the mark of mastery and the record of victory that you have determined to leave behind for those who will follow you on the path of initiation.

You may write and rewrite this outline of your life, examining it for purity of motive, for its practicality, its probability, your own ability, your own willingness to summon from the God flame within the energies of commitment, co-measurement, and constancy.

When you have set forth to your own satisfaction a realistic as well as an idealistic set of goals, make two copies. Place one between the pages of your Bible [or other sacred text] and consign the other to the flame of the Holy Spirit—that is, put it in the physical fire in the ritual of the ancient alchemist, that it might be secured in the etheric level of your consciousness and conveyed to the Great Divine Director and the Lords of Karma for the necessary ratification of the law of cosmos.

With your left hand on the Bible, take in your right hand the mantra for divine direction . . . and give it fourteen times. Repeat this exercise for thirty-three days. Each day at the conclusion of your meditation and mantra, take your pen and write upon another white page the thoughts of your mind, the feelings of your heart that come to you as a means to augment and to implement the goals you have set forth and to bring them into alignment with the goal of life for your lifestream held in the causal body of the Great Divine Director.

Do not strain to hear the word of God when the answer to your call is the bliss of the Great Silence. Do not fret when the clarity of divine direction does not manifest to your outer consciousness; for as sure as I live —and I am Saint Germain—the alchemy of divine direction is at work within you like the leaven which the "woman took and hid in three measures of meal till the whole was leavened."[7]

Even so, the alchemy begins at the fiery core of being in the center of your heart flame; and it works hour by hour, day by day, from the within to the without. As you give the mantra and the meditation, you are planting seeds of your own cosmic consciousness at conscious and subconscious levels of being. These seeds will germinate and push through to the surface by the light of your own I AM Presence and by the watering of the living word of your own Christ Self.[8]

THE GREAT DIVINE DIRECTOR'S MANTRA

1. Divine Director, come,
   Seal me in thy ray—
   Guide me to my home
   By thy love I pray!

Refrain: (repeat after each verse)

Thy blue belt protect my world,
Thy dazzling jewels so rare
Surround my form and adorn
With essence of thy prayer!

2. Make us one, guard each hour
   Like the sun's radiant power—
   Let me be, ever free
   Now and for eternity!

3. Blessed Master R,
   You are near, not far—
   Flood with light, God's own might
   Radiant like a star!

4. Divine Director dear,
   Give me wisdom pure—
   Thy power ever near
   Helps me to endure!

5. Shed thy light on me,
   Come, make me whole—
   Banner of the free,
   Mold and shape my soul!

And in full faith I consciously accept this manifest, manifest, manifest! (repeat three times) right here and now with full power, eternally sustained, all-powerfully active, ever expanding and world enfolding until all are wholly ascended in the light and free! Beloved I AM! Beloved I AM! Beloved I AM![9]

The Dark Night of the Soul

As inner spiritual acceleration intensifies, the soul approaches the first phase of spiritual purgation, known as the "dark night of the soul."[10] Saints, adepts and bodhisattvas have passed through this period of inner contemplation and seeming darkness. And ordinary people walking the spiritual path also encounter this testing of the mettle of the soul.

What enables the soul to win the victory is faith in God and the acceleration of light. Yet that very acceleration brings to the surface whatever darkness lurks at unconscious or subconscious levels of being. Even advanced souls experience a certain measure of anxiety, depression and hopelessness during the dark night.

The sixteenth-century mystic Saint John of the Cross (1542–1591), in his classic, *Dark Night of the Soul,* goes into depth in describing both the dark night of the soul and the dark night of the Spirit. He also gives a brief description of these two phases of darkness and purgation:

> This night, which, as we say, is contemplation, produces in spiritual persons two kinds of darkness or purgation, corresponding to the two parts of man's nature—namely, the sensual and the spiritual. And thus the one night or purgation will be sensual, wherein the soul is purged according to sense, which is subdued to the spirit; and the other is a night or purgation which is spiritual, wherein the soul is purged and stripped according to the spirit, and subdued and made ready for the union of love with God.
>
> The night of sense is common and comes to many: these are the beginners; and of this night we shall speak first. The night of the spirit is the portion of very few, and

> these are they that are already practised and proficient, of whom we shall treat hereafter.[11]

The ascended masters explain that the dark night of the soul ("the night of sense") is our encounter with the return of personal karma, which, if we have not kept our "lamps" (chakras) trimmed with light,[12] may eclipse the light (Christ consciousness) of the soul and therefore her discipleship under the Son of God. This initiation precedes the dark night of the Spirit, the supreme test of Christhood, when the soul is, as it were, cut off from the I AM Presence and must survive solely on the light garnered in the heart while holding the balance for planetary karma.

In a dictation to Elizabeth Clare Prophet, Archeia Holy Amethyst described these periods of testing as a choice between the sorrowful way and the glorious way:

> The road of return [to God] has two aspects: the sorrowful way and the glorious way. It all depends upon your perspective; for the bliss of the divine reunion is experienced within—even in the moment of agony, through the dark night of the soul and on the cross.
>
> The sixty-ninth Psalm of David contains three cycles of twelve. In thirty-six verses David reveals the experiences of one who passed through the dark night of the soul to the full realization of the Christ consciousness.
>
> You who have determined to pass through the dark night of both the soul and the Spirit would do well to ponder the meditations of David and then to apply yourself diligently to the invocations of the sacred fire, especially to the violet flame that is the concentrated energy of the Holy Spirit in the forgiveness of sin, the righting of all wrong, and the bringing of the four lower bodies into alignment with the original blueprint of creation.[13]

The dark night of the soul is also the story of the biblical character Job, Saint John of the Cross, Padre Pio and many other individuals who have passed this initiation with flying colors. In this dark night, the soul is inundated by her karma and there is a purging of the senses as one by one the human ego's possessions and material comforts go their way.

Jesus taught his disciples the difficulty of this testing of the soul. When a rich young man came to Jesus and asked him what he needed to do to have eternal life, Jesus replied:

> If thou wilt be perfect, go and sell that thou hast, and give to the poor, and thou shalt have treasure in heaven: and come and follow me.
>
> But when the young man heard that saying, he went away sorrowful: for he had great possessions.
>
> Then said Jesus unto his disciples, Verily I say unto you, That a rich man shall hardly enter into the kingdom of heaven.
>
> And again I say unto you, It is easier for a camel to go through the eye of a needle, than for a rich man to enter into the kingdom of God.[14]

Spiritually, Jesus' point was not that it is a sin to be rich, but that the soul must put God before earthly riches. This redemptive process is also known as the "stripping of the garments," in which the devotee is pressed by circumstances into a posture of nonattachment to human desires and possessions and the need for human support.

During this period of testing and initiation, we are called to surrender all of the trappings of our human ego to the divine ego, our Higher Self. We are impelled to "let go and let God," to surrender our human desires and our attachment to our possessions. As we do so, we gradually experience the spiritual love and blessings that come from surrendering the lesser self.

What actually occurs as we go through this remarkable initiation? The biblical story of Job is a dramatic example of the dark night of the soul. As you may remember, Job was a man who revered God and shunned evil. He had seven sons and three daughters and thousands of sheep, camels, oxen and donkeys. He was a wealthy householder in his day.

Job was tested in many ways. His servants were slain, his animals carried off and his sons and daughters killed. Yet Job continued to be reverent before his God. As the Bible records it, he "rent his mantle, and shaved his head, and fell down upon the ground, and worshiped. And said, Naked came I out of my mother's womb, and naked shall I return thither: the LORD gave, and the LORD hath taken away; blessed be the name of the LORD. In all this Job sinned not, nor charged God foolishly."[15]

Job did not curse God, nor did he resist the stripping of his possessions. Even when he broke out in boils all over his body, Job continued to be faithful to God. And when his wife shamed him by saying, "Dost thou still retain thine integrity? Curse God, and die," he rebuked her: "Thou speakest as one of the foolish women speaketh. What? Shall we receive good at the hand of God, and shall we not receive evil?"[16]

Job received further harassment from friends who came to commiserate with him but ended up making matters worse. His first friend, a religious dogmatist, said many things that were true but did so in a hard and cruel way. The second friend thought Job was a hypocrite because if he were really pure and upright, God would not have allowed these disasters to come upon him. And the third friend decided Job was both a hypocrite and a liar and if he would repent God would take away his burdens.[17]

Through all of this, Job despaired but did not falter in his faith in God. He understood the platitudes and hypocrisy of his friends, but he did not curse them or God. He simply confronted the friends about their accusations, explained his spiritual understanding and told them he would talk to God about it.

The friends continued to scorn, rebuke and persecute him, but Job never wavered in his faith. At one point he declared, "For I know that my redeemer liveth, and that he shall stand at the latter day upon the earth: And though after my skin worms destroy this body, yet in my flesh shall I see God."[18]

God answered Job, rebuked his friends and ordered them to do a burnt offering for their sins and accusations. He told them he would accept only Job's prayers on their behalf because of their folly. Chastened, they went away and did as God commanded them.

Following this testing of the dark night of the soul, God gave Job twice as much as he had before. And he was given seven more sons and three daughters. Job lived to be 140 years old and saw four generations of his progeny.

Thus we see that although we may fear to surrender, when we do so, God is waiting to claim us as his own. The dark night of the soul is about letting go of our human desires and attachments and becoming one with the consciousness of God. And as we do this, we experience oneness with all that is good and beautiful in the universe.

It's actually kind of peculiar, isn't it, to fear surrendering ourselves to God when God lives right where we stand? When we think of the reality of all this, there's a hint of the ridiculous in fearing to let go. Yet that fear can keep us from embracing our love for God and our soul's divine destiny until we choose otherwise.

This process of faith and perseverance is both spiritual and psychological. So we keep our attention on God. We take courage to recognize our fear. We observe those fearful thoughts and feelings from a point of detachment. We refuse to be moved. We put our hand in God's hand and take practical action to address difficult circumstances. We work on transforming fear by love and mindfulness, wisdom and inner strength. And we keep on moving!

Ultimately, according to karmic cycles and our own determination and righteous effort, we catch a glimpse of the realm of Reality. Invigorated by the light of God, we pass through the long, dark night, and a new day begins to dawn.

The Dark Night of the Spirit

Now let's look at the second dark night, the "dark night of the Spirit," the experience of feeling total separation from God. This is an advanced spiritual testing of the soul striving for union with God—it is a giant step beyond the dark night of the soul.

Saint John of the Cross describes the dark night of the Spirit:

> Since the divine extreme strikes in order to renew the soul and divinize it (by stripping it of the habitual affections and properties of the old man to which it is strongly united, attached, and conformed), it so disentangles and dissolves the spiritual substance—absorbing it in a profound darkness—that the soul at the sight of its miseries feels that it is melting away and being undone by a cruel spiritual death; it feels as if it were swallowed by a beast and being digested in the dark

> belly, and it suffers an anguish comparable to Jonas's when in the belly of the whale [Jon. 2:1–3]. It is fitting that the soul be in this sepulcher of dark death in order that it attain the spiritual resurrection for which it hopes.[19]

This second dark night frequently comes quite some time after the first purgation. This is God's mercy, by which the soul is given additional time and space to grow in grace and attainment before undergoing more advanced testing. In this interim period, the soul grows in sweetness and interior communion with God, yet the sensual aspect of the soul may endure frailties and sufferings and be fatigued in spirit. Soul and spirit are being inwardly trained to be unmoved by either extreme—rapture or torment.

With the advent of the dark night of the Spirit, the awareness of the presence of God is temporarily suspended and the soul achieves union with God through total surrender. In this dark night, we meet the darkness with our Christ attainment as our only succor.[20] We must stand upon our attainment, internalized in the threefold flame, and not be dependent on any outer source.

This is the experience Jesus had on the cross when he momentarily felt that separation from God and cried out, "Eloi, Eloi, lama sabachthani?" that is to say, "My God, my God, why hast thou forsaken me?"[21] He faced that final initiation where all he had to go on was his own spiritual adeptship and attainment. And with his last breath, he surrendered to his God and his ultimate victory: "Father, into thy hands I commend my spirit."[22]

We who would become one with God will come to that moment. We will meet that sense of total darkness and emptiness, of seemingly being forsaken by God. Some have called this experience "the void." And what we have to go on in this dark night is our faith and devotion and what we have claimed of God within ourselves—which comes about through union with our Higher Self.

How have the saints made it through? They have kept their focus on the light at the end of the tunnel. And that's what we want to do. So we take courage and keep moving toward the light. With Gautama Buddha, we say, "I am awake!"[23] We move by faith, by holy intuition and the alertness of our spiritual faculties.

Think of the dark night of the Spirit as an adversary that God in you will conquer. And fill that void with a faith, wisdom and love of God that knows no boundaries. Stand up and shout to the universe, "I know that God lives in me! I AM one with the unbounded light and love of Almighty God!"

Affirm to the universe: "The light of God never fails! (repeat three times) And the beloved, mighty I AM Presence is that light!"

The Eastern Path of the Bodhisattva

In Buddhism, there are two paths that the disciple may pursue toward enlightenment. As Huston Smith explains in *The Religions of Man:*

> [These are the paths of] the *Arhat,* the perfected disciple who strikes out on his own for Nirvana and with prodigious concentration makes his way unswervingly toward that pinpointed goal, and the *Bodhisattva,* who, having brought himself to the brink of Nirvana, voluntarily renounces his prize that he may return to the world to make it accessible to others. . . .
>
> The difference between these two types is illustrated in the story of four men who, journeying across an immense desert, come upon a compound surrounded

> with high walls. One of the four determines to find out what is inside. He scales the wall and on reaching the top gives a whoop of delight and jumps over. The second and third do likewise.
>
> When the fourth man gets to the top of the wall, he sees below him an enchanted garden with sparkling streams, pleasant groves, and delicious fruit. Though longing to jump over, he resists the impulse. Remembering other wayfarers who are trudging the burning deserts, he climbs back down and devotes himself to directing them to the oasis. The first three men were *Arhats,* the last was a *Bodhisattva,* one who vows not to desert this world "until the grass itself be enlightened."[24]

Thus, when a bodhisattva attains enlightenment, he or she remains in the world, often looking like any ordinary person but devoting his or her attention to relieving suffering and helping others attain enlightenment. These remarkable people choose to share and bear the burden of world suffering.

A bodhisattva has divine pity and concern for the welfare of all beings; thus, these stalwart souls dwell in a consciousness of divine wisdom, compassion and inner strength. They dedicate their higher faculties to helping others carry the burdens of karma; they are living examples of enlightenment and mercy.

Why do they do this? They have such great love for humanity that they have vowed to remain until all beings are free. They do their best to rescue humanity from physical and moral sickness, ignorance of spiritual laws, infirmity of soul and spirit, and the cycles of death and rebirth. The bodhisattvas offer knowledge and enlightenment to humanity, compassionately laying down their lives in perpetual service to God and mankind.

The sacrificial blessing of the bodhisattva is his renunciation of blissful reunion with God in order to bring divine illumination and understanding to others. He may forgo his ascension for thousands of years or until the last man, woman and child on earth wins his victory.

The ascended masters teach that many great saints and sages (who yet retain the physical body and are known as "unascended masters") dwell in inaccessible reaches of the Himalayas, holding the balance of light for the planet. However, there are also bodhisattvas in the ascended realm. They are ascended masters who have vowed not to go on to cosmic service until all earth's evolutions are free.

The vow of the bodhisattva to stand with humanity is truly a sacred labor. However, the ascended masters have cautioned us against taking that vow unless we thoroughly understand the calling. They have encouraged us to help mankind from the ascended realm after we have won the victory of the ascension. Thus, the bodhisattva vow is a freewill choice we can make once we reach that level of attainment.

Kuan Yin: Bodhisattva of Compassion

Kuan Yin, the bodhisattva of compassion, is an ascended lady master. She is known and loved as the Goddess of Mercy in both East and West, and she has kept that flame of mercy for the people of China and of every nation and continent.

As Chinese Saviouress and Mother of Mercy's Flame, Kuan Yin has been called the guiding spirit of Buddhism. Still very much a part of Eastern culture, she has awakened interest in her path and teaching among a growing number of Western devotees.

To many of her followers, Kuan Yin in her role as bodhisattva embodies the great ideal of Mahayana Buddhism—a being of wisdom and compassion who is destined to become a Buddha. According to legend, as Kuan Yin was about to enter heaven, she paused to listen to the cries of the world.

Her name means "She who hearkens to the cries of the world." And she has been venerated by many people, ranging from simple fishermen to Taoist sages in their mountain hermitages to Buddhist lay people in the East and West. In Tibet she has been identified with Tara, the White Goddess.

Kuan Yin is also considered to be the feminine form of the Indian and Tibetan Avalokiteshvara, the masculine bodhisattva who ensouls the God flame (attribute) of compassion. Kuan Yin is depicted in early iconography as this masculine polarity but has found her place of honor in popular religion as the Goddess of Mercy—bestower of children, guardian of sailors, a very personal presence in time of trouble.

Ancient texts tell of the bodhisattva's miraculous power to save any and all who call to her for help. Today in many parts of Asia there are likely innumerable temples and household shrines dedicated to the Lady Kuan Yin.

The ascended masters teach that Kuan Yin had numerous embodiments on earth prior to her ascension thousands of years ago. In a dictation, Kuan Yin stated:

> I am the Goddess of Mercy—so named by Alpha and Omega, for I have tended the God flame of mercy for an incomparable span of time and space. Long ago in another system of worlds, in the evolution of the brothers and sisters of a particular planet, I perceived the need for mercy, for the ark that provides the way of escape for the evolving consciousness. . . .
>
> And so I said to myself, indeed there is no quality more precious than the mercy of God. I would become that mercy, and I would be that mercy on behalf of all.

> For, precious hearts, when I saw the difference between those who were given mercy through intercessory prayer and those who had not that mercy, I could not withhold my service. I could not set my hand to another task. I must be there. I must walk by the side of each one. I must have and hold and be the cup of mercy.
>
> God in his infinite goodness has again and again listened to the pleas of my angels, of my office, of Mary the Mother and other lady masters who have journeyed to the courts of heaven to make intercession on behalf of a wayward humanity. "Just a little while longer!" we have pleaded. "For mankind, if they but knew the Law, would do the works of that Law in action."[25]

Kuan Yin explained a unique aspect of the little juggler who juggled before the statue of Mother Mary, offering his only gift. She likened this to one on the path of initiation, who must juggle his karma at the same time he puts on the robes of divinity.

When an ascended being kneels in prayer to invoke mercy from the heart of God on behalf of those who are having difficulty managing this juggling act, they receive help and encouragement. This comes in the form of a temporary setting aside of a portion of their karma from past embodiments until they become stronger and more ready to advance on the Path.

This action of setting aside of karma for a time gives an individual the opportunity to seek God, to find the Holy Spirit and to unite with his or her Higher Self. Of course, once the person accomplishes this, the karma that has been temporarily deferred comes full circle to be balanced. For this is cosmic law: whatever we send out ultimately returns to us—as blessing or burden, as the case may be.

The law of forgiveness has also been called the law of

containment. Through forgiveness our misdeeds and debts to life are set aside, contained temporarily, until we receive enough knowledge of the law and are strong enough to pay the piper. Then we receive the karmic return.

Thus, when we feel a sense of injustice because of problems in our lives while a friend or neighbor seems to be moving along unscathed, it may be because we have set our feet firmly on the path of the ascension. If so, our soul may very well have asked for the opportunity to balance the remaining karmic debts quickly. The one who seems to be leading such a charmed life may not yet have embarked on an accelerated path of initiation.

Kuan Yin describes the virtue of mercy by saying that within mercy are faith, hope and charity. Faith is the knowing that perfection will ultimately manifest; hope is holding the immaculate concept until it appears; and charity is that love that refuses to let go of the loved one until eternal perfection manifests.

As the bodhisattva of compassion Kuan Yin tells us, mercy is a love that smoothes the rough places of life and heals the wounds of the etheric body. Mercy mends the cleavages of mind and feelings and clears away the debris of sin and sense of struggle before they manifest in our physical body as disease, decay, disintegration and death.

Kuan Yin says:

> The power of mercy is the intensity of love that will dissolve all fear, all doubt, all recalcitrance and rebellion. . . . The mercy of the Law is sometimes very stern, but it is always patient, always tolerant, and it sees the flame within the heart rising, rising, rising to meet the Christ. . . . Mercy is the strongest power in the universe. It is the power of the will of God.[26]

By the flame of mercy we have the opportunity between lives to go to etheric retreats where we learn the way to balance whatever wrongs we have committed. By mercy's flame many cycles can be set aside so that our soul can achieve her victory. And sometimes mercy is a quick return of our karma so that we learn a necessary lesson in a timely way. Always, mercy is an aspect of the divine love of our Father-Mother God.

Kuan Yin is also a member of the Karmic Board, a council of justice composed of eight ascended beings who mediate mankind's karma, dispensing opportunity, mercy and the true and righteous judgments of the LORD. Kuan Yin works with the evolutions of this planet and solar system, teaching them to balance their karma and fulfill their divine plan by loving service to life and the application of the violet flame—God's great dispensation of mercy delivered to his people through their exercise of the Science of the Spoken Word.

As hierarch of the etheric Temple of Mercy over Peking (Beijing), China, Kuan Yin focuses the flame of mercy and forgiveness for the children of the ancient land of Chin and the souls of humanity.

Babaji: Unascended Master of the Himalayas

Babaji is an unascended master in the Himalayas who embodies the bodhisattva ideal. His name means "revered father," and in the East he is known as an *avatara.** Babaji has become well-known in the West through the writings of Paramahansa Yogananda.[27]

Yogananda has written about Babaji's close relationship with Christ Jesus:

*In Hindu scriptures *avatara* signifies the descent of Divinity into physical form.

> Babaji is ever in communion with Christ; together they send out vibrations of redemption and have planned the spiritual technique of salvation for this age. The work of these two fully illumined masters—one with a body, and one without a body—is to inspire the nations to forsake wars, race hatreds, religious sectarianism, and the boomerang evils of materialism.[28]

Thus Jesus Christ sends forth the light of God from higher realms while Babaji anchors the light of God on earth. He remains in a body of flesh and dwells high in the Himalayas, yet he is able to dematerialize his body at will.[29] Babaji is a part of the Great White Brotherhood in the lineage of the unascended brotherhood of the Himalayas.

Mighty Victory, a cosmic being,[30] has described the service of these unascended masters. He said:

> [They are] unascended souls of magnificent countenance who have stood with the evolutions of Terra, who have stood with the saints and as the sages. They have stood to retain that flame at the etheric level to give comfort to life. . . . They are the consciousness of the ascension, yet unascended.
>
> "You might say they have reached that plane of samadhi, of eternal communion with Mother light, and from that communion [they have] drawn forth even the light of nirvanic planes, anchoring that light here below. They are the perpetuation of the Word. . . . They stand to ennoble the race.[31]

According to Yogananda, Babaji has never disclosed his family origin, birthplace or birth date. He can converse with ease in any language, although he usually speaks in Hindi. Yogananda describes Babaji's appearance:

> [Babaji,] the deathless guru, bears no mark of age on his body; he appears to be a youth of not more than twenty-five. Fair-skinned, of medium build and height, Babaji's beautiful, strong body radiates a perceptible glow. His eyes are dark, calm, and tender.[32]

Yogananda's Sanskrit tutor, who had spent time with the master in the Himalayas, said of Babaji:

> The peerless master moves with his group from place to place in the mountains.... After Babaji has been in one locality for some time, he says... "Let us lift our camp and staff."... His words are the signal for moving with his group instantaneously to another place.... Sometimes he goes on foot from peak to peak.
>
> Babaji can be seen or recognized by others only when he so desires. He is known to have appeared in many slightly different forms to various devotees.... His undecayable body requires no food.[33]

One of Babaji's disciples explained why Babaji has kept a physical body for so long. One night when Ram Gopal, Lahiri Mahasaya and Babaji's sister, Mataji, were kneeling at the great Guru's feet, Babaji said: "Blessed Sister, I am intending to shed my form and plunge into the Infinite Current."

Mataji asked, "Why should you leave your body?" Babaji replied, "What is the difference if I wear a visible or an invisible wave on the ocean of my Spirit?"

Mataji responded, "Deathless Guru, if it makes no difference, then please do not ever relinquish your form."

"Be it so," said Babaji solemnly. "I shall never leave my physical body. It will always remain visible to at least a small number of people on this earth."[34]

During a dictation at the Royal Teton Ranch, the ascended

master Surya explained that Babaji had been suspended within the hall for some time, "floating in the lotus posture, beaming intense and fiery love.... Remaining at the interval and the nexus between the crystal spheres of the Spirit-Matter cosmos, this unascended master of the Himalayas does come to demonstrate to you what is the victory of the Mother flame, how ascension's flame as a buoyant fount of light may become the lotus pad."[35]

Babaji has spoken on behalf of the Brotherhood of the Himalayas, urging his students to take up the path of the violet flame.[36] He has also told them not to avoid but to face the problematic drama of life on earth. He says, "Get over your desire to be the removed one set apart and in meditation and in unreality when there is a victory to be won and a battle to enter."[37]

Babaji says to all of us, "Ask me and I will come into your life!"[38]

Question: To Be a Bodhisattva or an Ascended Master?

How does the path of the bodhisattva relate to the initiation of the ascension? The messenger Mark L. Prophet gave a lecture in which he explained both paths and encouraged his students to pursue the path of the ascension:

> I believe that clarification of these two pathways [bodhisattva and ascension] is sometimes important to those sincere students who want to know those little details that can have an impact upon goal-fitting....
>
> We prefer the path of the ascension as the choicest goal for the student of the light. But remember, if we skim off all the cream from society, we will have a very thin skimmed milk left....

The pathway leading to the ascension is one of degrees spiritually attained and mastery of the self by the individual. This includes complete emotional and mental control.... Mastery is a divine achievement, and the accreditation of the one aspiring to cosmic mastery is determined by the Brotherhood according to their tenets. It has nothing to do with human opinion of what a person is.

And this is why many of you have met masters on the street, unascended beings, of course, but adepts and masters nonetheless, and have not known them.... So don't be too quick to judge others. Don't decide that because somebody uses a word of slang, or somebody does something that you wouldn't do, that they are immediately cast down in your mind from that pedestal you have placed them on, in ruins on the marble floor. Because we really cannot judge outwardly. And we ourselves ought not to judge ourselves outwardly.

Instead of that, we ought to have a mounting aspiration toward the ascension. We ought to be lost in the clouds of glory surrounding goal-fittedness and not be trapped by the dying flowers along the pathway—the flowers of illusion that hold us more or less enamored with their jewel-like quality and then their fading. These are meaningless. What really counts is the process of overcoming—true adeptship, true mastership, true overcoming, true victory....

A bodhisattva is one who has overcome, who has attained mastership.... As a rule they remain here, and by their vibration, the force of their divine thought, they affect millions of the evolutions of this planet benignly. They do work for the Brotherhood at inner levels, and they identify themselves with the planet.

Regardless of what human beings do in this world,

> the bodhisattvas continue to maintain a high state of cosmic immutability in their physical bodies; and their physical bodies do not deteriorate, but are charged with liquid light. . . .
>
> These bodhisattvas are of great assistance to the hierarchy as far as maintaining a vibrational contact upon the planetary body. That is very stabilizing to the planet. I think sometimes that the earth would probably split in two if it were not for the pure and holy Christlike vibrations of the bodhisattvas. . . .
>
> However, I think that the bodhisattva ideal should not become the goal of the average person in the Western world and my opinion is that few in the Eastern world should follow it. I think we should try to obtain our ascension. This is the real goal of humanity and the one we should prefer.[39]

The Ascension as the Goal of Life

The ascension is the ultimate goal of life. It is the victorious return to God from whence we came. In reality we are flaming spirits who descended into physical form to master the conditions and trials of life on earth. When we have successfully overcome our human will, human ego and human intellect and replaced them with their divine components, we can ascend back to the heart of God—as victors over time and space.

Jesus fulfilled the ritual of the ascension so that we could follow his example. And the Bible records a few of the many who have ascended into the light: Enoch, the seventh from Adam, "walked with God: and he was not; for God took him."[40] Elijah ascended "by a whirlwind into heaven."[41]

Melchizedek, Mary the Mother of Jesus, John the Beloved, Gautama Buddha, Zarathustra, Confucius, Saint

Thérèse of Lisieux and Pope John XXIII are only a few of the many ascended beings in heaven. The masters have explained that there are many more ascended and cosmic beings than there are men and women in physical embodiment.[42]

Serapis Bey, the ascended master who sponsors us on the path of the ascension, teaches that the love of God infuses life, frees life and is inherent within life. That love is the energy that raised Christ in the resurrection and ultimately propelled him into the heavens in the ascension in the light. All of us can follow him in the ritual of the ascension. That is the goal of our soul and spirit!

As Serapis says:

> It is the soul purified, consecrated, and fired after the fashion of the image most holy that must come before the altar of the ascension flame as a bride adorned for her husband, prepared for the marriage of the Lamb. The soul must present itself a living sacrifice if it expects God and his Spirit to present itself unto the soul as the living testifier of the testimony of the Law.[43]

Even though the angels and ascended beings are ready and willing to give us all the assistance possible, we need to ask for that help. God and his divine helpers are the authority in the ascended octave, but we have asked for and been given the responsibility of fulfilling the law of our being in the physical world. Thus heaven does not intervene unless we have the inner desiring, make the call and do our part to resolve whatever karmic circumstances we have created.

Serapis tells us, "The future is what you make it, even as the present is what you made it."[44] If we are not happy with our circumstances, God has provided a way out. And that way is through invoking divine assistance and walking the path to the ascension. This is the way we ultimately return to the heart of God in the currents of the ascension flame.

Candidates for the Ascension

The ascended masters teach that to achieve our divine destiny of the ascension we must balance at least 51 percent of our karma. This means serving the light of the Christ in ourselves, our loved ones, our friends and neighbors and those we meet on life's pathway. We are also called to master our spiritual lessons on earth and to balance our karma with those we may have injured or dissuaded from the spiritual path.

These are the realities our soul considers if we would be candidates for the ascension. Thus we benefit by contemplating, What gifts can I offer to family, friends and people in need? What spiritual lessons do I need to learn? What karmic debts do I owe? How can I settle them?

The messenger Mark L. Prophet ascended from earth's schoolroom in 1973 and is now the ascended master Lanello. In his first dictation after his ascension, he stated:

> I say, you are *all* candidates for the ascension if you choose to be.... There is no need to tarry. There is no need to go back to the old ways of the human consciousness. I say, your Christed awareness, your Christed being, is the *blazing* reality of your consciousness! It is the new day dawning within you! It is your potential of victory! It is your purity *now!*
>
> And I say, you do not have to wait for that carnal mind to evolve, for the carnal mind will never evolve, precious hearts. It will *never* become the Christ. It must be put off and cast into the flame! You have to trade in the old model and take out the new. How long will you

dwell with that old model? Some of you are more tolerant of your former selves than you are of your cars that you trade in every year, but you forget to trade in the carnal mind for the Christ mind that is in the height of fashion in the courts of heaven!

And so, precious hearts, I say that of all of the warnings and all of the prophecies that I might prophesy this night, it is this one key of Christhood, and salvation through Christhood, that can give you the ultimate victory. And it is with ultimate victories that we are concerned—not with the skirmishes that are lost or won each hour and each day.

Nevertheless, these do count as the great Keeper of the Scrolls makes his mark in the Book of Life. But I say, sometimes when you lose in the fray, it is a lesson that needs to be learned. And a temporary loss may mean the ultimate victory, for the lesson that is gained is a measure toward perfection.

And so I say, count the experiences that you have been through as the past that is prologue. . . . I say, the saga of your lives—of many of you—is beautiful to behold. For you have indeed won in small ways and in great ways. And until the last tally is taken, you never know how the Lord looks upon the balance of power within you. So keep on striving for the light, striving for the right. And know that I, Lanello, walk with you each step of the way. . . .

If there is one thought that I desire to impress upon your minds in this fireside chat, it is this: Go forth and fulfill your high calling. Let no mortal, no family, no friends, no earthly loves take you from the Christ or take you from letting him reign as king, as queen within your consciousness. . . .

I say to you, whatever you have done in the past,

> forsake the past! Leave it behind! And let the light of mercy triumph within you, for our God is a God of mercy and his mercy endureth forever. Therefore, take a step forward this night, and consider that in taking that step you are stepping out of the skins of the former man and into the raiment of the Christ.[45]

Mother Mary says:

> If you could but reach out your hand and touch mine! You can almost feel that there is very little between us, beloved ones. Very little is the line between the angelic hosts and mankind. As you give your prayers, as you are in your beds at night, realize that simply by a touch, by a thought, by a point of light we are in your presence.
>
> And if you will ask, beloved ones, that the Electronic Presence of the master of your choice be superimposed over your form before you go to sleep at night, you will find that throughout the hours of rest, all of the momentums of light of that ascended being can be absorbed into your consciousness, into your four lower bodies, by the power of the electrode upon the spine—the ascending and descending currents of God that formulate the magnetic forcefield which is the focus of the great cycles of Infinity within your very own Presence.[46]

The Initiation of the Ascension

What then are the requirements of the ascension? In addition to balancing 51 percent of our karma, it is necessary to fulfill our divine plan and balance our threefold flame.

In the process we will be aligning our four lower bodies so they can be pure chalices for the light, achieving self-mastery on the seven rays of the Christ, gradually raising up the Mother light of the kundalini, and transmuting the energies of the electronic belt. Serapis Bey tells us that we also need to desire the ascension—not as an escape from worldly duties but as the culmination of a life of service.[47]

Saint Germain has promised that everyone who sincerely tries can make his ascension in this lifetime or the next if there are extenuating circumstances that require another incarnation. And in that case, at the time of passing from the screen of life, the soul will be taken to temples of the Brotherhood and tutored so that the succeeding embodiment can be victorious.

Serapis Bey also emphasizes the need for true humility, and cites the Master Jesus as the perfect example:

> I recall full well when the Master Jesus came to Luxor as a very young man that he knelt in holy innocence before the Hierophant, refusing all honors that were offered him and asking to be initiated into the first grade of spiritual law and spiritual mystery. No sense of pride marred his visage—no sense of preeminence or false expectation, albeit he could have well expected the highest honors. He chose to take the low road of humility, knowing that it was reserved unto the joy of God to raise him up.
>
> To raise an individual is a glorious thing when that individual lies prone in hope, in faith, and in charity, awaiting an act of God to reconsecrate the self to the simple quality of humility. For there is an act of false pride which manifests as false humility and causes individuals to appear humble whereas in reality they reek with pride. This false humility is often manifest in subtle ways, and it is a mockery of the real....
>
> I urge upon all, then, that they seek the banner of divine humility. If the masters and the Divine Presence of men through the mediatorship of the Christ have ever

> recognized any of the errors of men that have hindered them from becoming that which they long to become, they have recognized their pride. Pride takes many forms and true humility but one.
>
> True humility must be worn eternally. It is not a garment you place upon yourself for a moment, for a day or for a year, or [during periods] when passing a test. It is an undergarment with which God himself is clothed; and unless it surround thee, thy hopes of attainment are slim indeed.[48]

With his usual touch of humor Mark Prophet shared his view on the ascension two years before he became the ascended master Lanello:

> I want to tell you that the ascension is a glorious attainment. . . . It is not a process of just dissolution of the elements of the body. In other words, it's not like a cremation. But what actually takes place is that the Spirit of the Father accepts the total being of the Son in this cloud that receives him out of human sight. And in effect, man is then found everywhere at the same time, just like God is.
>
> Heaven is the place within ourselves in consciousness. It is not a physical place in space somewhere. It can be anywhere and probably is everywhere. So in effect, when Jesus went up on Bethany's hill and disappeared from physical view he assumed the posture of Spirit. And he became—if you can compare the universe to a sponge—he became like the water that is absorbed by the sponge. . . .
>
> Now, this is no desecration, by the way, in any sense, microcosmic or macrocosmic. Right now you're a little sponge, maybe five or six feet high. And you have absorbed a spark of God's life in yourself. And when you came out of your mother's womb, you were a little bit of

a shaver. And you grew. But that's all relative.

And, in effect, what happens is that in the process of the ascension, the being of man and his consciousness is absorbed by the Godhead and he gets into a bigger sponge. So the body of all cosmos, in effect, becomes his. Master of cosmos, he is then possessed with the ability at will to transfer himself to any point in space or time where he can appear at will to anyone he wishes to. . . .

The general idea here is that an ascended being is not some sort of a God-king in the sense of the world's Caesarian concepts. He doesn't just sit on a throne somewhere and order people around. Here we're dealing with a cosmic being. But now remember that this cosmic being in reality is a member of a great Brotherhood.

And please understand the Fatherhood of God. God is the Spirit. The Brotherhood is made up of other consciousnesses. . . . The only way that the divine lightning can strike in human affairs is by the permission of the human will. Therefore every son of heaven that receives this fire that leads him to the goal of his ascension receives it in the same way and is traveling the same road. And ultimately he will become as masterful as God himself. But he's going to find when he gets a little higher in the divine peerage that there are those who have been there before [him].[49]

And some final words of instruction from Serapis Bey, hierarch of the Ascension Temple, who tells us we ascend daily:

You need not expect, precious ones, that as the swoop of a great bird of paradise, heaven will come down to you and raise you instantly up into the light. Each day you weave a strand of light substance back to the heart of your Presence by the shuttle of your attention.

Each strand strengthens the anchor beyond the veil

> and thus draws you into a state of consciousness wherein God can use you more as an effective instrument for good.[50]...

Thus we need not feel that we are being selfish if we decide to pursue the path of the ascension rather than to remain as a bodhisattva with the evolutions of earth. The victory of each individual contributes to the victory of all, for as each soul ascends, an increment of the ascension light is anchored on Terra.

In the words of Serapis, "The ascension is the fulfillment of the will of God for every man."[51]

On the Homeward Journey: Twelve Steps to Inner Peace and Harmony

1. Cultivate an upbeat attitude. Make the best of things. When working with others, do your best. Serve the Christ in others by asking yourself, What would Jesus do? What would Mother Teresa do?

2. Write down unresolved situations in your life and strive for peaceful resolution. Instruct your four lower bodies to come into alignment with your Higher Self by saying, "Peace, be still and know that I AM God!" Through your Higher Self, you are the authority over all elements of your lower self.

3. Forgive and ask to be forgiven even when you think you are not in the wrong. Do this because you live by the code of forgiveness. Perhaps you know that someone else needs to be forgiven or to forgive. By bringing up the subject tactfully and kindly, you will make it easier for the other person to take right action.

4. Determine that you will not be moved from your God-centeredness of love and peace, come what may, even in trifling matters. For have not small incidents ruined friendships and separated families?

5. Examine your heart. The heart needs perfecting, as does every other chakra. Expand your heart's love by practicing loving-kindness toward yourself and others.

6. Be humble before your God. Have a sense of holiness in the presence of another's Higher Self. And judge not. When we judge others we engage in pride —and pride goeth before a fall.

7. Forsake any harshness, abruptness or negative words idly spoken.

8. Spend some time each day in silence, focusing on the wonders of nature, joyful remembrances or inspiring ideals.

9. Intensify the light in your chakras, organs and all elements of your being. Remember that God created you as a being of light.

10. Correct the flaws in the jewel of your being. If someone tells you that you have a fault, they may be right and they may be wrong. But always consider it. We often learn the most important lessons about ourselves from those we have thought to be our adversaries.

11. Keep your harmony and make it a point to create harmony and peace in your interactions with others.

12. Make this fiat your byword: "I shall not be moved from oneness with my Higher Self and my God!"[52]

APPENDIX

Alchemical Formulas for Soul Liberation

The inner power that dethrones the dweller-on-the-threshold is the spiritual fire of God, which we release through the throat chakra. Archangel Michael and all the ascended masters and angels release that fire when we call them into action in our lives and the lives of others.

You can prepare yourself for the action of binding the dweller by invoking the light of God to cleanse and uplift your consciousness. First, take several deep breaths, exhaling slowly, as you focus your attention on your heart. Then envision a shower of brilliant white light enfolding you, descending from your I AM Presence* into your aura, consciousness, being and world as you give the following mantra:

---

*For a pictorial representation of your I AM Presence, Christ Self and soul, see the Chart of Your Divine Self, p. 312.

VIOLET FIRE AND TUBE OF LIGHT DECREE

O my constant, loving I AM Presence, thou light of God above me whose radiance forms a circle of fire before me to light my way:

I AM faithfully calling to thee to place a great pillar of light from my own Mighty I AM God Presence all around me right now today!

Keep it intact through every passing moment, manifesting as a shimmering shower of God's beautiful light through which nothing human can ever pass. Into this beautiful electric circle of divinely charged energy direct a swift upsurge of the violet fire of freedom's forgiving transmuting flame!

Cause the ever expanding energy of this flame projected downward into the forcefield of my human energies to completely change every negative condition into the positive polarity of my own Great God Self!

Let the magic of its mercy so purify my world with light that all whom I contact shall always be blessed with the fragrance of violets from God's own heart in memory of the blessed dawning day when all discord—cause, effect, record and memory—is forever changed into the victory of light and the peace of the ascended Jesus Christ.

I AM now constantly accepting the full power and manifestation of this fiat of light and calling it into instantaneous action by my own God-given free will and the power to accelerate without limit this sacred release of assistance from God's own heart until all men are ascended and God-free in the light that never, never, never fails![1]

Now invoke Archangel Michael's blue-fire power and protection:

LORD MICHAEL

1. Lord Michael, Lord Michael,
   I call unto thee—
   Wield thy sword of blue flame
   And now cut me free!

Refrain: Blaze God-power, protection
   Now into my world,
   Thy banner of faith
   Above me unfurl!
   Transcendent blue lightning
   Now flash through my soul,
   I AM by God's mercy
   Made radiant and whole!

2. Lord Michael, Lord Michael,
   I love thee, I do—
   With all thy great faith
   My being imbue!

3. Lord Michael, Lord Michael
   And legions of blue—
   Come seal me, now keep me
   Faithful and true!

Coda: I AM with thy blue flame
   Now full-charged and blest,
   I AM now in Michael's
   Blue-flame armor dressed! (3x)*

*Repeat the coda three times to complete your recitation of the decree. Give this decree as often as you like to reinforce Archangel Michael's protection.

Once you have invoked your "Tube of Light" and Archangel Michael's protection, you are ready to give a fiery decree for the angels to bind the dweller-on-the-threshold. This is an alchemical formula for casting out the conglomerate of inner darkness.

The dweller decree is a dynamic prayer that liberates us from layers of unreality—the scar tissue of bygone traumas that needs to be cleared for our soul's resurrection. When we give this decree, we champion our soul and defend our right to be who we are as our Real Self.

Center in your heart and envision the angels binding and casting out the dweller-on-the-threshold and freeing your soul as you give the decree:

"I CAST OUT THE DWELLER-ON-THE-THRESHOLD"

In the name of my beloved mighty I AM Presence and Holy Christ Self, Archangel Michael and the hosts of the LORD, in the name Jesus Christ, I challenge the personal and planetary dweller-on-the-threshold, and I say:

You have no power over me! *You* may not threaten or mar the face of my God within my soul. *You* may not taunt or tempt me with past or present or future, for I AM hid with Christ in God. I AM his bride. I AM accepted by the LORD.

You have no power to destroy me!

Therefore, be *bound!* by the LORD himself.

Your day is *done!* You may no longer inhabit this temple.

In the name I AM THAT I AM, be *bound!* you tempter of my soul. Be *bound!* you point of pride of the original fall of the fallen ones! You have no power, no reality, no worth. You occupy no time or space of my being.

You have no power in my temple. You may no longer steal the light of my chakras. You may not steal the light of my heart flame or my I AM Presence.

Be *bound!* then, O Serpent and his seed and all implants of the sinister force, for *I AM THAT I AM!*

I AM the Son of God this day, and I occupy this temple fully and wholly until the coming of the LORD, until the New Day, until all be fulfilled, and until this generation of the seed of Serpent pass away.

Burn through, O living Word of God!

By the power of Brahma, Vishnu and Shiva, in the name Brahman: I AM THAT I AM and I stand and I cast out the dweller.

Let him be bound by the power of the LORD's host! Let him be consigned to the flame of the sacred fire of Alpha and Omega, that that one may not go out to tempt the innocent and the babes in Christ.

Blaze the power of Elohim!

Elohim of God—Elohim of God—Elohim of God.

Descend now in answer to my call. As the mandate of the LORD—as Above, so below—occupy now.

Bind the fallen self! *Bind* the synthetic self! Be *out* then!

Bind the fallen one! For there is no more remnant or residue in my life of any, or any part of that one.

Lo, I AM, in Jesus' name, the victor over death and hell! (repeat two times)

Lo, *I AM THAT I AM* in me—in the name of Jesus Christ—is *here and now* the victor over death and hell!

Lo! it is done.

After giving the dweller call, invoke the violet flame to transmute any residual debris or sense of burden:

VIOLET FLAME FROM THE HEART OF GOD

Violet flame from the heart of God, (3x)*
Expand thy mercy through me today! (3x)
Violet flame from the heart of God, (3x)
Transmute all wrong by forgiveness ray! (3x)
Violet flame from the heart of God, (3x)
Blaze into action through all to stay! (3x)
Violet flame from the heart of God, (3x)
O mercy's flame, fore'er hold sway! (3x)
Violet flame from the heart of God, (3x)
Sweep all the earth by Christ-command! (3x)
Violet flame from the heart of God, (3x)
Thy freeing power I now demand! (3x)

Take dominion now,
To thy light I bow;
I AM thy radiant light,
Violet flame so bright.
Grateful for thy ray
Sent to me today,
Fill me through and through
Until there's only you!

I live, move, and have my being within a gigantic fiery focus of the victorious violet flame of cosmic freedom from the heart of God in the Great Central Sun and our dearly beloved Saint Germain, which forgives, transmutes, and frees me forever by the power of the three-times-three from all errors I have ever made.

*Repeat each line three times when the notation (3x) appears.

Seal the alchemical action of your mantras and decrees by accepting and amplifying the light you have called forth:

> And in full faith I consciously accept this manifest, manifest, manifest! (repeat three times) right here and now with full power, eternally sustained, all-powerfully active, ever expanding and world enfolding until all are wholly ascended in the light and free! Beloved I AM! Beloved I AM! Beloved I AM!

Complete the transformational process by affirming your higher qualities and the victory of your soul's mission:

I AM AFFIRMATIONS

I AM a soul of light.
I AM walking the path home to God.
I AM the will of God manifesting in my life.
I AM the wisdom of the Christ and the Buddha.
I AM the compassion of the Divine Mother.
I AM the purity of my Higher Self.
I AM one with the flame of Truth.
I AM the servant of the Christ in all.
I AM joyfully balancing my karma.
I AM lovingly obedient to my Real Self.
I AM passing my soul initiations.
I AM winning my ascension.

SEALING BENEDICTION

May the words of my mouth and the meditation of my heart be acceptable in thy sight, O LORD, my strength and my redeemer.

THE CHART OF YOUR DIVINE SELF

The Chart of Your Divine Self

The reason we can call to God and he will answer is because we are connected to him. We are his sons and daughters. We have a direct relationship to God and he has placed a portion of himself in us. In order to better understand this relationship, the ascended masters have designed the Chart of Your Divine Self.

The Chart of Your Divine Self is a portrait of you and of the God within you. It is a diagram of yourself and your potential to become who you really are. It is an outline of your spiritual anatomy.

The upper figure is your "I AM Presence," the Presence of God that is individualized in each one of us. It is your personalized "I AM THAT I AM." Your I AM Presence is surrounded by seven concentric spheres of spiritual energy that make up what is called your "causal body." The spheres of pulsating energy contain the record of the good works you have performed since your very first incarnation on earth. They are like your cosmic bank account.

The middle figure in the chart represents the "Holy Christ Self," who is also called the Higher Self. You can think of your Holy Christ Self as your chief guardian angel and dearest friend, your inner teacher and voice of conscience. Just as the I AM Presence is the presence of God that is individualized for each of us, so the Holy Christ Self is the presence of the universal Christ that is individualized for each of us. "The Christ" is actually a title given to those who have attained oneness with their Higher Self, or Christ Self. That's why Jesus was called "Jesus, the Christ." *Christ* comes from the Greek word *christos,* meaning "anointed"—anointed with the light of God.

What the Chart shows is that each of us has a Higher Self, or "inner Christ," and that each of us is destined to become one with that Higher Self—whether we call it the Christ, the Buddha, the Tao or the Atman. This "inner Christ" is what the Christian mystics sometimes refer to as the "inner man of the heart," and what the Upanishads mysteriously describe as a being the "size of a thumb" who "dwells deep within the heart."

We all have moments when we feel that connection with our Higher Self—when we are creative, loving, joyful. But there are other moments when we feel out of sync with our Higher Self—moments when we become angry, depressed, lost. What the spiritual path is all about is learning to sustain the connection to the higher part of ourselves so that we can make our greatest contribution to humanity.

The ribbon of white light descending from the I AM Presence through the Holy Christ Self to the lower figure in the Chart is the crystal cord (sometimes called the silver cord). It is the "umbilical cord," the lifeline, that ties you to Spirit.

Your crystal cord also nourishes that special, radiant flame of God that is ensconced in the secret chamber of your heart. It is called the threefold flame, or divine spark, because it is literally a spark of sacred fire that God has transmitted from his heart to yours. This flame is called "threefold" because it engenders the primary attributes of Spirit—power, wisdom and love.

The mystics of the world's religions have contacted the divine spark, describing it as the seed of divinity within. Buddhists, for instance, speak of the "germ of Buddhahood" that exists in every living being. In the Hindu tradition, the Katha Upanishad speaks of the "light of the Spirit" that is concealed in the "secret high place of the heart" of all beings.

Likewise, the fourteenth-century Christian theologian and mystic Meister Eckhart teaches of the divine spark when he says, "God's seed is within us." There is a part of us, says Eckhart, that "remains eternally in the Spirit and is divine. . . . Here God glows and flames without ceasing."

When we decree, we meditate on the flame in the secret chamber of our heart. This secret chamber is your own private meditation room, your interior castle, as Teresa of Avila called it. In Hindu tradition, the devotee visualizes a jeweled island in his heart. There he sees himself before a beautiful altar, where he worships his teacher in deep meditation.

Jesus spoke of entering the secret chamber of the heart when he said: "When thou prayest, enter into thy closet, and when thou hast shut thy door, pray to thy Father which is in secret; and thy Father which seeth in secret shall reward thee openly."

The lower figure in the Chart of Your Divine Self represents you on the spiritual path, surrounded by the violet flame and the protective white light of God, the "tube of light." The soul is the living potential of God— the part of you that is mortal but that can become immortal.

The purpose of your soul's evolution on earth is to grow in self-mastery, balance your karma and fulfill your mission on earth so that you can return to the spiritual dimensions that are your real home. When your soul at last takes flight and ascends back to God and the heaven-world, you will become an "ascended" master, free from the rounds of karma and rebirth.

The high-frequency energy of the violet flame can help you reach that goal more quickly.

Notes

Introduction

1. Mark L. Prophet and Elizabeth Clare Prophet, *Morya I* (Corwin Springs, Mont.: The Summit Lighthouse Library, 2001), pp. xvii–xviii.
2. Sir Edwin Arnold, trans., *The Song Celestial, or Bhagavad-Gita* (London: Routledge & Kegan Paul, 1948), p. 9.
3. Initiation refers to the spiritual testing that we encounter on the Homeward path, that strait gate and narrow way that leadeth unto life (Matt. 7:14).
4. A messenger is one who is trained by an ascended master to receive and deliver the teachings, messages and prophecies of the Great White Brotherhood for a people and an age. The Great White Brotherhood is a spiritual fraternity of ascended masters, archangels and other advanced spiritual beings. The term *white* refers not to race but to the aura of white light that surrounds these immortals.
5. Mark L. Prophet and Elizabeth Clare Prophet, *Understanding Yourself: A Spiritual Approach to Self-Discovery and Soul-Awareness* (Corwin Springs, Mont.: Summit University Press, 1999), pp. 1, 2, 7–8.

Chapter One • *The Merry-Go-Round of Time and Space*

1. Elizabeth Clare Prophet, "Karma, Reincarnation and Christianity 1," in 1992 *Pearls of Wisdom,* vol. 35, no. 11, pp. 132–34.

2. To put this in context, El Morya has said: "What is the mastery of the self? To properly answer this question, we must first define the self. Know, O chela of the light, that you are what you are regardless of what you think you are. The affirmation of the Real Self of every man and woman—the declaration of being and consciousness—is I AM WHO I AM." See El Morya, *The Chela and the Path: Keys to Soul Mastery in the Aquarian Age* (Corwin Springs, Mont.: Summit University Press, 1976), p. 24.
3. The term *subconscious* refers to mental activities just below the threshold of awareness, e.g., what we mean when we say, "It's just on the tip of my tongue." Psychoanalysts use the term *subconscious* to describe the zone between the unconscious and conscious levels of consciousness. The ascended masters teach that the subconscious is also the repository of the "electronic belt," an energy field that contains the cause, effect, record and memory of the negative aspects of our karma.
4. Prophet and Prophet, *Morya I,* pp. xiii–xiv.
5. Gal. 6:7.
6. The movie *The Lord of the Rings: The Fellowship of the Ring* was released in December 2001.
7. See J. R. R. Tolkien, *The Fellowship of the Ring,* part 1 of *The Lord of the Rings* (New York: Ballantine Books, 1965), opening quotation.
8. Lord Acton, *Letter to Bishop Mandell Creighton,* April 5, 1887.
9. A decree is a dynamic form of spoken prayer used to direct God's light into individual and world conditions. As Job 22:28 says, "Thou shalt also decree a thing, and it shall be established unto thee: and the light shall shine upon thy ways." Short decrees are called fiats, e.g., "Let there be light" (Gen. 1:3, the original fiat of the Creator). See Mark L.

Prophet and Elizabeth Clare Prophet, *The Science of the Spoken Word* (Corwin Springs, Mont.: Summit University Press, 1991).

10. In a dictation delivered October 29, 1966, the ascended master Saint Germain explained, "The self is a mountain of holy treasure, and within the domain of the self, joy must be brought forth and multiplied. And joy is indeed the motor of life, which when properly understood and harnessed will cause the regenerative processes within the forcefield of individuals to amplify the light energy within the cells. Thus, a renewal of the power of eternal youth occurs within the dimension and forcefield of the individual because God is there and pours out his limitless light, even as the sun gives forth her energy."

11. Rev. Annice Booth writes: "There could be no question about the fact that Mark was a devotee, and yet he was firmly grounded on earth. El Morya once remarked that 'your spirituality is expressed by your practicality.' Mark was a very practical man who had a tender concern and loving care for every person on his staff and, in fact, for everyone he met.

    "I have often thought that Will Rogers' observation, 'I never met a man I didn't like,' applied equally well to Mark Prophet. He would show his concern for others on an everyday practical level and yet be able to inspire them to seek a higher level of spiritual attainment." This quote is taken from Annice Booth's delightful book *Memories of Mark: My Life with Mark Prophet* (Corwin Springs, Mont.: Summit University Press, 1999), p. 2.

12. The "unconscious," or "personal unconscious," is the arena of our personal memories, wishes and impulses not directly accessible to conscious awareness but impacting our thoughts, feelings and actions. The "collective unconscious," which we all share, is the repository of archetypal images that reflect mankind's historical experience.

Chapter Two • *Ready or Not, Here I Come!*

1. Annice Booth, *The Path to Your Ascension: Rediscovering Life's Ultimate Purpose* (Corwin Springs, Mont.: Summit University Press, 1999), p. 139.
2. We know from the classic work of Maria Montessori, Jean Piaget and early childhood research that during the first five or seven years of our lives we actually learn by absorbing and interacting with everything around us. See Lesley Britton, *Montessori Play and Learn: A Parent's Guide to Purposeful Play from Two to Six* (New York: Crown Publishers, 1992). For the original source, see Maria Montessori, *The Absorbent Mind* (Madras, India: The Theosophical Publishing House, 1949). Also see Thomas Armstrong, Ph.D., *Awakening Your Child's Natural Genius: Enhancing Curiosity, Creativity, and Learning Ability* (New York: Jeremy P. Tarcher/Perigee, 1991).
3. Wayne Muller, *Legacy of the Heart: The Spiritual Advantages of a Painful Childhood* (New York: Simon & Schuster, Fireside, 1993), pp. xiii, xiv.
4. *The Miracle Worker,* a three-act play by William Gibson, portrays the moving story of Anne Sullivan's work with young Helen Keller. In 1962 the story became an award-winning film of the same title, starring Anne Bancroft and Patty Duke.
5. Helen Keller's poem is courtesy of the American Foundation for the Blind, Helen Keller Archives.
6. Elizabeth Clare Prophet, "The Abortion of the Divine Plan of a Soul," lecture delivered in Corwin Springs, Montana, March 30, 1991.
7. Mark L. Prophet and Elizabeth Clare Prophet, *Climb the Highest Mountain: The Path of the Higher Self,* 2d ed. (Corwin Springs, Mont.: Summit University Press, 1986), pp. 38–39.
8. Luke 23:34.
9. Muller, *Legacy of the Heart,* p. 181.

10. Kuan Yin is revered as the bodhisattva of compassion (see pp. 285–89 this volume for more about this beloved Saviouress in Buddhism and in the teachings of the ascended masters). Maitreya is known as the Coming Buddha and the "Loving One." His name actually derives from the Sanskrit word *maitri,* which translates as loving-kindness, benevolence and friendliness. As the first disciple of Gautama Buddha, Maitreya comes to teach all who have departed from the way of the Great Guru Sanat Kumara, from whose spiritual lineage he and Gautama descended.
11. See Prophet and Prophet, *Science of the Spoken Word,* pp. 71–74.
12. A fiat is an authoritative decree, sanction, order; a pronouncement; a short dynamic invocation or decree usually using the name of God, I AM, as the first word of the fiat. Fiats are always exclamations of Christ-power, Christ-wisdom and Christ-love consciously affirmed and accepted in the here and now. See "Definitions of the Spoken Word," in Prophet and Prophet, *Science of the Spoken Word,* pp. xix–xxii.
13. See Elizabeth Clare Prophet, *The Creative Power of Sound: Affirmations to Create, Heal and Transform* (Corwin Springs, Mont.: Summit University Press, 1998), p. 87; and Prophet and Prophet, *Science of the Spoken Word,* p. 95.
14. Serapis Bey, *Dossier on the Ascension: The Story of the Soul's Acceleration into Higher Consciousness on the Path of Initiation* (Corwin Springs, Mont.: Summit University Press, 1979), pp. 176–77.

Chapter Three • *Setting Sail on a Healing Journey*

1. Robert Assagioli, *Psychosynthesis, A Manual of Principles and Techniques* (New York: Hobbs, Doorman & Company, 1965), pp. 17–18.

2. Carl Gustav Jung, *The Practice of Psychotherapy* (London: Routledge & Kegan Paul, 1966), p. 169.
3. Piero Ferrucci, *What We May Be: Techniques for Psychological and Spiritual Growth* (Los Angeles: J. P. Tarcher, 1982), pp. 43–45.
4. For further understanding of psychosynthesis, I recommend Ferrucci's book cited above. For information on spiritual psychology, check my web site: www.spiritualpsychology.com.
5. *Saint Germain On Alchemy: Formulas for Self-Transformation* (Corwin Springs, Mont.: Summit University Press, 1993), p. 350.
6. Sharon Salzberg, *Lovingkindness: The Revolutionary Art of Happiness* (Boston: Shambhala Publications, 1995), p. 30.

Chapter Four • *Transforming the Inner Critic*

1. See Hal Stone, Ph.D., and Sidra Stone, Ph.D., *Embracing Your Inner Critic: Turning Self-Criticism into a Creative Asset* (HarperSanFrancisco, 1993).
2. See John Bradshaw, *Healing the Shame That Binds You* (Deerfield Beach, Fla.: Health Communications, 1988).
3. See Ps. 139:7.
4. Paul the Venetian, dictated to Mark L. Prophet, given at Dodge House in Washington, D.C., January 13, 1963.
5. Kuthumi, "The Vessel of Kindness," May 5, 1991, in 1991 *Pearls of Wisdom,* vol. 34, no. 33, pp. 403, 404.
6. Muller, *Legacy of the Heart,* pp. 178–80.
7. Steps 4, 5, and 6 of this exercise are adapted from HeartMath. See Doc Lew Childre, *Freeze Frame®: A Scientifically Proven Technique* (Boulder Creek, Calif.: Planetary Publications, 1994), pp. 27–33.
8. The 1946 movie *It's a Wonderful Life* became a Christmas movie classic due to repeated television showings at Christ-

mastime. Frank Capra, the director, regarded the film as his own personal favorite. It was also Jimmy Stewart's favorite of all of his feature films.

9. Mark L. Prophet and Elizabeth Clare Prophet, *The Lost Teachings of Jesus 1,* pocketbook ed. (Corwin Springs, Mont.: Summit University Press, 1994), pp. 3, 13–14, 15.
10. Muller, *Legacy of the Heart,* p. 182.

Chapter Five • *Encounters with Dragons and Dwellers*

1. Elizabeth Clare Prophet, lecture given October 7, 1974, at Summit University.
2. Elizabeth Clare Prophet, "Christ and the Dweller," in 1983 *Pearls of Wisdom,* vol. 26, no. 38, pp. 432, 433.
3. See Acts 7:58–60; 8:2–3; 9:1–31; 13–28.
4. Prophet, "Christ and the Dweller," pp. 436–37.
5. John 14:30.
6. *Tibet's Great Yogi Milarepa: A Biography from the Tibetan,* 2d ed., ed. W. Y. Evans-Wentz (New York: Oxford University Press, 1969).
7. According to Buddhist teachings, drunkenness is a deplorable evil and productive of bad karma. See *Tibet's Great Yogi Milarepa,* p. 61, footnote.
8. *Tibet's Great Yogi Milarepa,* p. 70.
9. Ibid., p. 87.
10. Ibid.
11. Elizabeth Clare Prophet, "The Path of the Bodhisattva: The Guru-Chela Relationship: Marpa and Milarepa," lecture given November 6, 1988.
12. *Tibet's Great Yogi Milarepa,* p. 135.
13. Prophet, "The Path of the Bodhisattva."
14. John 10:30.

15. See *The Man Who Would Be King and Other Stories,* by Rudyard Kipling (New York: Dover, 1994).
16. Prophet, "Christ and the Dweller," pp. 438, 441, 442.

Chapter Six • *The Quest for Enlightenment*

1. This teaching on mystery schools was given by Elizabeth Clare Prophet, December 31, 1976, during the conference *Energy Is God,* held in Pasadena, California.
2. Mark L. Prophet gave this teaching on January 10, 1971.
3. Elizabeth Clare Prophet analyzed act II of Wagner's *Parsifal* in her lecture on February 18, 1979.
4. Ibid.
5. Elizabeth Clare Prophet, "The Lost Years and the Lost Teachings of Jesus Christ," lecture delivered at the Penta Hotel in New York City, October 4, 1987.
6. See Hans Jonas, *The Gnostic Religion* (Boston: Beacon Press, 1958).
7. Prophet, "The Lost Years and the Lost Teachings of Jesus Christ."
8. Ibid.
9. These poetic stanzas from the "Hymn of the Pearl" are taken from G. A. Gaskell's *Gnostic Scriptures Interpreted* (London: The C. W. Daniel Company, 1927), pp. 46–68. The translation of the poem is by G. R. S. Mead.
10. Ibid., p. 64.

Chapter Seven • Dilemmas of Soul and Spirit

1. See Matt. 7:12; Luke 6:31.
2. The source of this biographical material is a summary of the video *J.C. Penney: Main Street Millionaire.* The videotape can be ordered through the Internet: http://store.aetv.com/html/catalog/

3. Elizabeth Clare Prophet, June 3, 1977, in unpublished lecture "Padre Pio, the Stigmatist."
4. William Shakespeare, *King Henry the Sixth,* Part III (1591), act 3, scene 1, lines 62–65.
5. Robert Greene, *Farewell to Folly* (1591), stanza 1.
6. See Matt. 19:16–26.
7. Elizabeth Clare Prophet, *How to Work with Angels* (Corwin Springs, Mont.: Summit University Press, 1998), pp. 106–7.

Chapter Eight • Curing the Angst of the Soul

1. During the winter months a certain percentage of people suffer from the SAD (Seasonal Affective Disorder) syndrome. "The prevalence of SAD in the United States has been found to increase with increasing latitude and has been estimated to range from 1.4 percent in Florida to 9.7 percent in New Hampshire" (L. M. Rosen, S. D. Targum, M. Terman, et al., "Prevalence of Seasonal Affective Disorder at Four Latitudes," *Psychiatry Res.* 1989; 31:131– 44). This malady led to the development of special sunlamps that give the dosage of artificial sunlight the physical body needs for a person to feel a certain sense of well-being throughout the dark winter months. For further information or a reprint of "Diagnosis and Treatment of Seasonal Affective Disorder," by Norman E. Rosenthal, M.D., *Journal of the American Medical Association,* vol. 270, no. 22 (December 8, 1993), contact the Section on Environmental Psychiatry, Clinical Psychobiology Branch, National Institute of Mental Health, Bldg. 10, Room 4S-239, 9000 Rockville Pike, Bethesda, MD 20892 (Dr. Rosenthal).
2. W. Walter Menninger, M.D., "Challenges to Providing Integrated Treatment of Anxiety Disorders" in *Bulletin of the Menninger Clinic: A Journal for the Mental Health Professions* 59, no. 2, Supplement A (spring 1995), pp. A86, A87.
3. I Cor. 9:26.

4. *Saint Germain On Alchemy,* pp. 219, 221, 222, 223–24, 225–26.
5. Kuthumi, "Remember the Ancient Encounter," January 27, 1985, in 1985 *Pearls of Wisdom,* vol. 28, no. 9, p. 91.
6. For an in-depth understanding of dreams through techniques of spiritual psychology, see my book *Dreams: Exploring the Secrets of Your Soul* (Corwin Springs, Mont.: Summit University Press, 2001).
7. Elaine Pagels, *The Gnostic Gospels* (New York: Vintage Books, 1981), p. 162.
8. Ibid., p. 152.
9. Peter Slater, "The Relevance of the Bodhisattva Concept for Today," in *The Bodhisattva Doctrine in Buddhism,* ed. Leslie S. Kawamura (Waterloo, Ontario: Canadian Corporation for Studies in Religion, 1981), p. 1.
10. Elizabeth Clare Prophet, "Lecture on Gnosticism," July 6, 1986.
11. Edward Conze, ed., *Buddhist Texts through the Ages* (New York: Harper & Row, Harper Torchbooks, 1964), p. 181.
12. Pagels, *The Gnostic Gospels,* p. 161.
13. Ibid., p. xix.
14. James M. Robinson, ed., *The Nag Hammadi Library in English,* 3d ed. (HarperSanFrancisco, 1988), p. 129.
15. John 8:12.
16. Matt. 5:14, 16.

Chapter Nine • *The Living Flame of Love*

1. Mark 10:15.
2. *Bits and Pieces,* August 8, 2002, p. 3.
3. Maha Chohan, "The High Rope," April 1, 1994, in 1994 *Pearls of Wisdom,* vol. 37, no. 15, p. 143.
4. See *Saint Germain On Alchemy,* pp. 351–52.

5. Rom. 12:9.
6. Dictation from Chamuel and Charity, given through Elizabeth Clare Prophet, October 12, 1973, in Santa Barbara, California.
7. For further teaching, see "Praise to the Enemies," in *Shambhala: In Search of the New Era,* by Nicholas Roerich (Rochester, Vt.: Inner Traditions International, 1990), pp. 150–55.
8. Jesus and Kuthumi, *Corona Class Lessons: For Those Who Would Teach Men the Way* (Corwin Springs, Mont.: Summit University Press, 1986), p. 77.
9. Rom. 8:26, 27.
10. John 21:22.
11. I Cor. 12:4–11; 13.
12. Maha Chohan, "The High Rope," pp. 142–44, 147, 152–53.

Chapter Ten • *Karma and Reincarnation*

1. Elizabeth Clare Prophet with Erin L. Prophet, *Reincarnation: The Missing Link in Christianity* (Corwin Springs, Mont.: Summit University Press, 1997), p. 19, quoting Carl Van Doren, *Benjamin Franklin* (New York: Viking Press, 1938), p. 124.
2. Phylos the Thibetan, *A Dweller on Two Planets, or The Dividing of the Way* (New York: Harper & Row, 1974). As the write-up on the back cover states, "Through his amanuensis Frederick S. Oliver, [Phylos] seeks to enrich human life with timeless truths. At the heart of this work is a recounting of the history, politics, religion, customs, and technological achievements of Poseid (Atlantis)."
3. "Letter from Phylos, Author of This History," January 1886, in Amanuensis Preface in *A Dweller on Two Planets,* by Phylos the Thibetan.

4. Elizabeth Clare Prophet, "The Psychology of Zailm: A Study of Reincarnation and Karma," part 1, lecture given on December 29, 1990.
5. Matt. 24:22; Mark 13:20.
6. Prophet, "The Psychology of Zailm."
7. Ibid.
8. Ibid.
9. Ibid.
10. Phylos, *A Dweller on Two Planets,* p. 140.
11. Prophet, "The Psychology of Zailm."
12. Psychologically, how a boy relates to his mother (or a mother figure) sets the stage for his relationships with women. And his relationship with his father (or father figure) builds his sense of masculine identity. In a similar way, how a girl relates to her father (or father figure) sets the tone for her relationships with men. And her relationship with her mother (or mother figure) shapes her identity as a woman.
13. Prophet, "The Psychology of Zailm."
14. Phylos, *A Dweller on Two Planets,* p. 128.
15. Ibid., p. 74.
16. Prophet, "The Psychology of Zailm."
17. Elizabeth Clare Prophet, "The Psychology of Zailm," part 2, December 31, 1990.
18. Phylos, *A Dweller on Two Planets,* pp. 159, 160.
19. Ibid., pp. 164–65. Phylos refers to the Maxin Light as the "Fire of Incal." Elizabeth Clare Prophet explains that this is the unfed, all-consuming fire of God.
20. Ibid., p. 176.
21. Ibid., p. 195.
22. Ibid.
23. Ibid., p. 238.

24. James 1:22.
25. Phylos, *A Dweller on Two Planets,* p. 374.

Chapter Eleven • *The Soul's Connection with the Stars*

1. I Cor. 14: 8.
2. *Saint Germain On Alchemy,* pp. 210–13, 215.
3. See Dr. Barrick's best-selling book, *Emotions: Transforming Anger, Fear and Pain* (Corwin Springs, Mont.: Summit University Press, 2002), available in Barnes & Noble and other fine bookstores; also available through www.b&n.com, www.amazon.com and www.summituniversitypress.com.
4. For further information on the study of spiritual astrology, contact Karen Drye through her web site: www.spiritual astrology.com.
5. This research paper was written by Karen Drye for her course work at Kepler College of Astrological Arts and Sciences, 4630 200th Street SW, Suite A-1, Lynnwood, Washington, 98036; www.kepler.edu.
6. See Patrick Curry, *A Confusion of Prophets: Victorian and Edwardian Astrology* (London: Collins & Brown, 1992), pp. 122–59.
7. S. J. Tester, *A History of Western Astrology* (Woodbridge, Suffolk, Great Britain: Boydell & Brewer, Boydell Press, 1990), p. 204.
8. Elizabeth Clare Prophet and Patricia R. Spadaro, *Your Seven Energy Centers: A Holistic Approach to Physical, Emotional and Spiritual Vitality* (Corwin Springs, Mont.: Summit University Press, 2000), pp. 4, 5.
9. Frances A. Yates, *Giordano Bruno and the Hermetic Tradition* (Chicago: University of Chicago Press, 1964), p. 20.
10. Ibid., pp. 27–28.
11. Ibid.

12. Uranus, Neptune and Pluto were not yet discovered during the time of Ficino. These planets are considered "outer planets," more impersonal and separate in distinction from the seven inner planets.
13. Thomas Moore, *The Planets Within: The Astrological Psychology of Marsilio Ficino* (Great Barrington, Mass.: Lindisfarne Books), opening quotation.
14. Plato, *The Republic and Other Works,* trans. B. Jowett (Garden City, N.Y.: Doubleday, Anchor Press, 1973), p. 130.
15. Yates, *Giordano Bruno,* pp. 27–28.
16. In Gautama Buddha's first sermon following his enlightenment, he outlined the Four Noble Truths and the Eightfold Path. He explained that by following this path and avoiding the extremes of self-indulgence and self-mortification, one gains knowledge of the Middle Way. The Four Noble Truths state that (1) life is *dukkha,* "suffering," (2) the cause of suffering is inordinate desire, (3) freedom from suffering is in the attainment of nirvana, and (4) the way to this liberation is through the Eightfold Path. The Eightfold Path gives eight precepts for right living: (1) Right Understanding (or Right Views), (2) Right Aspiration (or Right Thought), (3) Right Speech, (4) Right Action, (5) Right Livelihood, (6) Right Effort, (7) Right Mindfulness, and (8) Right Concentration (or Right Absorption of God). For further understanding of how these teachings relate to our emotions, see *Emotions: Transforming Anger, Fear and Pain,* by Marilyn C. Barrick, Ph.D.
17. Prophet and Spadaro, *Your Seven Energy Centers,* p. 3. In relation to Ficino's teachings, the irrational expression of the seven chakras relates to the seven deadly sins: pride, envy, anger, avarice, gluttony, lust and sloth.
18. Ibid., p. 4.
19. Marsilio Ficino, *Platonic Theology,* vol. 1, bks. 1–4, trans.

Michael J. B. Allen with John Warden (Cambridge: Harvard University Press, 2001), p. 79.

20. Ibid.
21. Ibid., p. 81.
22. Heb. 9:27.
23. Plato, *The Republic and Other Works,* p. 126.
24. Marsilio Ficino, *Three Books on Life,* trans. Carol V. Kaske and John R. Clark (Tempe, Ariz.: Arizona Board of Regents for Arizona State University, 1998), p. 331.
25. Ibid., p. 259.
26. See Zane B. Stein, *Essence and Application: A View from Chiron* (Lansford, Penn.: Zane B. Stein, 1995); to order, see Stein's website: www.geocities.com/adamlink/chiron.htm. See also Robert von Heeren, *The Seven-Centaur-Ephemeris: 1850–2050* (Amsterdam, Netherlands: Symbolon, 2001).
27. Melanie Reinhart, *Chiron and the Healing Journey: An Astrological and Psychological Perspective,* updated ed. (London: Penguin Books, Arkana, 1998), p. 23.
28. Marsilio Ficino, *Meditations on the Soul: Selected Letters of Marsilio Ficino,* trans. members of the Language Dept. of the School of Economic Science, London (Rochester, Vt.: Inner Traditions International, 1996), p. 152.
29. Ficino, *Three Books on Life,* p. 369.
30. Conclusion of Karen Drye's research paper written for course work at Kepler College of Astrological Arts and Sciences, March 5, 2002.
31. Ficino, *Meditations on the Soul,* p. 150.

Chapter Twelve • *Ascending the Mountain of Selfhood*

1. A root race is a group of souls (or an evolution, or lifewave) who embody together and have a unique archetypal pattern, divine plan and mission to fulfill on earth or on other

systems of worlds. According to esoteric tradition, there are seven primary root races on earth. The ascended masters teach that the first three root races have won their immortal freedom and ascended from earth. Members of the fourth, fifth and sixth root races (the latter not entirely descended into physical incarnation) remain in embodiment on earth. The seventh root race is destined to incarnate on the continent of South America in the Aquarian age.

Each root race embodies under the aegis of a Manu (Sanskrit, "progenitor" or "lawgiver"), who embodies the Christic image for the race. Lord Himalaya and his divine complement are the Manus for the fourth root race; Vaivasvata Manu and his consort are the Manus for the fifth root race; the God and Goddess Meru are the Manus for the sixth root race; and the Great Divine Director and his divine complement are the Manus for the coming seventh root race. See Mark L. Prophet and Elizabeth Clare Prophet, *Climb the Highest Mountain: The Path of the Higher Self,* 2d ed., pp. 72–80, 84–87, 493–96; and glossary in *Saint Germain On Alchemy,* s.v. "Manu." See also H. P. Blavatsky, *The Secret Doctrine,* vol. 2 (1888; reprint, Pasadena, Calif.: Theosophical University Press, 1952).

2. Saint Germain, "Divine Direction for the Path of Your Choosing," August 10, 1975, in 1975 *Pearls of Wisdom,* vol. 18, no. 32, p. 160.
3. Great Divine Director, "Let Us Implement the Plan of Hierarchy," July 6, 1975, in Elizabeth Clare Prophet, *The Great White Brotherhood in the Culture, History and Religion of America* (Corwin Springs, Mont.: Summit University Press, 1987), p. 323.
4. The Darjeeling Council is a council of the Great White Brotherhood consisting of ascended masters and unascended chelas whose objective is to train souls for world service in God-government and the economy, through international

relations and the establishment of the inner Christ as the foundation for religion, education, and a return to golden-age culture in music and the arts.

5. The Karmic Board is composed of ascended beings who dispense justice to this system of worlds, adjudicating karma, mercy and judgment of behalf of every lifestream.
6. Elizabeth Clare Prophet, "Background on the God and Goddess Meru, the Great Divine Director, Babaji, Ishvara and Vajrasattva," lecture given June 30, 1995.
7. Matt. 13:33.
8. Saint Germain, "Divine Direction for the Path of Your Choosing," pp. 160–62; also published in *The Crystallization of the God Flame,* vol. 1, no. 13 (1976), pp. 10–12.
9. See 1975 *Pearls of Wisdom,* p. 164.
10. See the classic in the literature of mysticism, *Dark Night of the Soul,* by St. John of the Cross. I recommend the translation by E. Allison Peers (New York: Doubleday, Image Books, 1990), pp. 21–90.
11. Ibid., p. 61.
12. Matt. 25:1–3. The esoteric interpretation of the "lamps of the wise virgins" is that the lamps represent the chakras.
13. Archeia Holy Amethyst, "The Initiation of the Judgment," November 30, 1975, in 1975 *Pearls of Wisdom,* vol. 18, no. 48, p. 259. To learn more about the violet flame and for additional decrees and mantras to the violet flame, see the following by Elizabeth Clare Prophet, published by Summit University Press: *Violet Flame to Heal Body, Mind and Soul,* pocket guide; *Saint Germain's Prophecy for the New Millennium,* pocketbook, chaps. 13–15; *Spiritual Techniques to Heal Body, Mind and Soul,* 90-min. audiotape; and *Save the World with Violet Flame! by Saint Germain 1,* 90-min. audiotape.
14. Matt. 19:21–24.

15. Job 1:20–22.
16. Job 2:9, 10.
17. Job, chaps. 3–11.
18. Job 19:25–26.
19. *The Collected Works of St. John of the Cross,* trans. Kieran Kavanaugh and Otilio Rodriguez (Washington, D.C.: ICS Publications, 1979), p. 337.
20. The Dark Night of the Spirit is also discussed in Saint John of the Cross's *Dark Night of the Soul;* see book 2, chapter 1 (in Peer's translation, pp. 91–93).
21. Mark 15:34.
22. Luke 23:46.
23. "I am awake" refers to the experience of becoming spiritually enlightened. Gautama Buddha attained the enlightenment of the Buddha twenty-five centuries ago, a path he had pursued through many previous embodiments culminating in his seven-day (or forty-nine-day, according to some accounts) meditation under the Bo tree. During his soul's evolution, Gautama went through many initiations. In his final initiation, as he sat under the Bo tree in deep meditation, Mara, the emissary of evil, assailed him with hurricanes, flaming rocks, a storm of deadly weapons, even warriors to pierce him with spears and voluptuous maidens to entice him. The aspiring Buddha felt all of this in his physical body but remained unmoved and nonattached. As a last resort, Mara challenged the aspiring Buddha's right to be doing what he was doing and demanded he get up from his seat, claiming it as his own. The Buddha-to-be calmly tapped the earth, and the earth rumbled in ratification of his victory. Thus Gautama passed his final initiation and became the Buddha. Mara had no power over him because his mind and heart were completely focused on God.
24. Huston Smith, *The Religions of Man* (New York: Harper & Row, Perennial Library, 1965), p. 137.

25. Kuan Yin, "A Vial of Mercy's Flame," June 30, 1973, in 1973 *Pearls of Wisdom,* vol. 16, no. 43, pp. 183–84.
26. Kuan Yin's dictation was given October 10, 1969, at the *Pyramid Conference,* held in Colorado Springs, Colorado.
27. See Paramahansa Yogananda, *Autobiography of a Yogi* (Los Angeles: Self-Realization Fellowship, 1974), pp. 345–70.
28. Ibid., p. 347.
29. Ibid., p. 369.
30. A cosmic being is (1) an ascended master who has attained cosmic consciousness and ensouls the light/energy/consciousness of many worlds and systems of worlds across the galaxies, (2) a being of God who has never descended below the level of the Christ, never taken physical embodiment, never made human karma.
31. Mighty Victory, "Victory's Torch Passed unto the Messengers of Truth in Science and Religion," December 31, 1976, in 1977 *Pearls of Wisdom,* vol. 20, no. 21, p. 92.
32. Yogananda, *Autobiography of a Yogi,* p. 348.
33. Ibid., pp. 348–49.
34. Ibid., pp. 352–53.
35. Dictation from ascended master Surya, "Passing Through," January 2, 1988, delivered through the messenger Elizabeth Clare Prophet; see 1988 *Pearls of Wisdom,* vol. 31, no. 5, p. 50.
36. See dictation from Babaji, delivered through the messenger Elizabeth Clare Prophet, June 17, 1979, in 1987 *Pearls of Wisdom,* vol. 30, no. 51, p. 464.
37. Ibid., p. 463.
38. Ibid., p. 464.
39. Excerpts from lecture by Mark L. Prophet, "The Ascension versus the Bodhisattva Ideal," April 9, 1971, in *The Crystallization of the God Flame,* vol. 1, no. 21 (1977), pp. 10, 12.

40. Gen. 5:24.
41. II Kings 2:11.
42. See *The Crystallization of the God Flame,* vol. 1, no. 20 (1977), p. 5.
43. Serapis Bey, "The Opening of the Temple Doors IV," April 1, 1973, in 1973 *Pearls of Wisdom,* vol. 16, no. 13, p. 51.
44. Serapis Bey, *Dossier on the Ascension,* p. 89.
45. Lanello, "The Wonders of Purity and Victory," April 20, 1973, in 1973 *Pearls of Wisdom,* vol. 16, no. 32, pp. 136, 135.
46. Dictation by Mother Mary, December 31, 1967.
47. See Serapis Bey, *Dossier on the Ascension,* pp. 164–70.
48. Ibid., pp. 33, 34.
49. Mark L. Prophet, "The Ascension versus the Bodhisattva Ideal," pp. 11–12.
50. Serapis Bey, *Dossier on the Ascension,* pp. 166–67.
51. "Introducing the Ascended Master Serapis Bey," in *The Crystallization of the God Flame,* vol. 1, no. 21 (1977), p. 15.
52. Adapted from "10 Tips for Keeping the Peace from Elohim Peace and Aloha," a leaflet published by Church Universal and Triumphant, 2001.

Alchemical Formulas for Soul Liberation

1. All of the mantras and decrees in this section are taken from Mark L. Prophet and Elizabeth Clare Prophet's *Science of the Spoken Word,* published by Summit University Press.

Bibliography

Armstrong, Thomas, Ph.D. *Awakening Your Child's Natural Genius: Enhancing Curiosity, Creativity, and Learning Ability.* New York: Jeremy P. Tarcher/Perigee, 1991.

Arnold, Sir Edwin, trans. *The Song Celestial, or Bhagavad-Gita.* London: Routledge & Kegan Paul, 1948.

Assagioli, Robert. *Psychosynthesis, A Manual of Principles and Techniques.* New York: Hobbs, Doorman & Company, 1965.

Barrick, Marilyn C., Ph.D. *Dreams: Exploring the Secrets of Your Soul.* Corwin Springs, Mont.: Summit University Press, 2001.

Barrick, Marilyn C., Ph.D. *Emotions: Transforming Anger, Fear and Pain.* Corwin Springs, Mont.: Summit University Press, 2002.

Barrick, Marilyn C., Ph.D. *Sacred Psychology of Change: Life as a Voyage of Transformation.* Corwin Springs, Mont.: Summit University Press, 2000.

Barrick, Marilyn C., Ph.D. *Sacred Psychology of Love: The Quest for Relationships That Unite Heart and Soul.* Corwin Springs, Mont.: Summit University Press, 1999.

Blavatsky, H. P. *The Secret Doctrine,* vol. 2. 1888. Reprint, Pasadena, Calif.: Theosophical University Press, 1952.

Booth, Annice. *Memories of Mark: My Life with Mark Prophet.* Corwin Springs, Mont.: Summit University Press, 1999.

Booth, Annice. *The Path to Your Ascension: Rediscovering Life's Ultimate Purpose.* Corwin Springs, Mont.: Summit University Press, 1999.

Bradshaw, John. *Healing the Shame That Binds You.* Deerfield Beach, Fla.: Health Communications, 1988.

Britton, Lesley. *Montessori Play and Learn.* New York: Crown Publishers, 1992.

Butterworth, Eric. *Life Is for Loving.* New York: Harper & Row, 1973.

Childre, Doc Lew. *Freeze-Frame®: A Scientifically Proven Technique.* Boulder Creek, Calif.: Planetary Publications, 1994.

Conze, Edward, ed. *Buddhist Texts through the Ages.* New York: Harper & Row, Harper Torchbooks, 1964.

Curry, Patrick. *A Confusion of Prophets: Victorian and Edwardian Astrology.* London: Collins & Brown, 1992.

Delaney, John J. *Dictionary of Saints.* Garden City, N.Y.: Doubleday & Company, 1980.

El Morya. *The Chela and the Path: Keys to Soul Mastery in the Aquarian Age.* Dictated to Elizabeth Clare Prophet. Corwin Springs, Mont.: Summit University Press, 1976.

Evans-Wentz, W. Y., ed. *Tibet's Great Yogi Milarepa: A Biography from the Tibetan.* New York: Oxford University Press, 1969.

Ferrucci, Piero. *What We May Be: Techniques for Psychological and Spiritual Growth.* Los Angeles: J. P. Tarcher, 1982.

Ficino, Marsilio. *Meditations on the Soul: Selected Letters of Marsilio Ficino.* Translated by members of the Language Department of the School of Economic Science, London. Rochester, Vt.: Inner Traditions International, 1996.

Ficino, Marsilio. *Platonic Theology.* Translated by Michael J. B. Allen with John Warden. Vol. 1. Cambridge: Harvard University Press, 2001.

Ficino, Marsilio. *Three Books on Life.* Translated by Carol V. Kaske and John R. Clark. Arizona Board of Regents for Arizona State University, 1998.

Gaskell, G. A. *Gnostic Scriptures Interpreted.* London: C. W. Daniel Company, 1927.

Heeren, Robert von. *The Seven-Centaur-Ephemeris: 1850–2050.* Amsterdam, Netherlands: Symbolon, 2001.

Jesus and Kuthumi. *Corona Class Lessons: For Those Who Would Teach Men the Way.* Corwin Springs, Mont.: Summit University Press, 1986.

John of the Cross, St. *Dark Night of the Soul.* Translated by E. Allison Peers. New York: Doubleday, Image Books, 1990.

Jonas, Hans. *The Gnostic Religion.* Boston: Beacon Press, 1958.

Jung, Carl G. *Collected Works* 16, *The Practice of Psychotherapy.* New York: Pantheon Books, 1954.

Kavanaugh, Kieran, and Otilio Rodriguez, trans. *The Collected Works of St. John of the Cross.* Washington, D.C.: ICS Publications, 1979.

Kawamura, Leslie S., ed. *The Bodhisattva Doctrine in Buddhism.* Waterloo, Ontario: Canadian Corporation for Studies in Religion, 1981.

Kipling, Rudyard. *The Man Who Would Be King and Other Stories.* New York: Dover, 1994.

Moffatt, BettyClare. *Soulwork: Clearing the Mind, Opening the Heart, Replenishing the Spirit.* Berkeley, Calif.: Wildcat Canyon Press and San Rafael, Calif.: Berkeley Press, 1994.

Montessori, Maria. *The Absorbent Mind.* Madras, India: The Theosophical Publishing House, 1949.

Moore, Thomas. *The Planets Within: The Astrological Psychology of Marsilio Ficino.* Great Barrington, Mass.: Lindisfarne Books, with permission of Associated University Presses, 1982.

Muller, Wayne. *How Then, Shall We Live? Four Simple Questions That Reveal the Beauty and Meaning of Our Lives.* New York: Bantam Books, 1996.

Muller, Wayne. *Legacy of the Heart: The Spiritual Advantages of a Painful Childhood.* New York: Simon & Schuster, 1992.

Muller, Wayne. *Sabbath: Finding Rest, Renewal, and Delight in Our Busy Lives.* New York: Bantam Books, 1999.

Pagels, Elaine. *The Gnostic Gospels.* New York: Vintage Books, 1981.

Phylos the Thibetan. *A Dweller on Two Planets, or The Dividing of the Way.* San Francisco: Harper & Row, 1974.

Plato, *The Republic and Other Works.* Translated by B. Jowett. Garden City, N.Y.: Doubleday, Anchor Books, 1973.

Prophet, Elizabeth Clare. *The Creative Power of Sound: Affirmations to Create, Heal and Transform.* Corwin Springs, Mont.: Summit University Press, 1998.

Prophet, Elizabeth Clare. *The Great White Brotherhood in the Culture, History and Religion of America.* Corwin Springs, Mont.: Summit University Press, 1987.

Prophet, Elizabeth Clare. *How to Work with Angels.* Corwin Springs, Mont.: Summit University Press, 1998.

Prophet, Elizabeth Clare. *The Lost Years of Jesus: Documentary Evidence of Jesus' 17-Year Journey to the East.* Corwin Springs, Mont.: Summit University Press, 1984.

Prophet, Elizabeth Clare. *Violet Flame to Heal Body, Mind and Soul.* Corwin Springs, Mont.: Summit University Press, 1997.

Prophet, Elizabeth Clare with Erin L. Prophet. *Reincarnation: The Missing Link in Christianity.* Corwin Springs, Mont.: Summit University Press, 1997.

Prophet, Elizabeth Clare, and Patricia R. Spadaro. *Your Seven Energy Centers: A Holistic Approach to Physical, Emotional and Spiritual Vitality.* Corwin Springs, Mont.: Summit University Press, 2000.

Prophet, Elizabeth Clare, with Patricia R. Spadaro and Murray L. Steinman. *Saint Germain's Prophecy for the New Millennium.* Corwin Springs, Mont.: Summit University Press, 1999.

Prophet, Mark L., and Elizabeth Clare Prophet. *Climb the Highest Mountain: The Path of the Higher Self.* 2d ed. Corwin Springs, Mont.: Summit University Press, 1986.

Prophet, Mark L., and Elizabeth Clare Prophet. *The Lost Teachings of Jesus I.* Corwin Springs, Mont.: Summit University Press, 1986.

Prophet, Mark L., and Elizabeth Clare Prophet. *Morya I.* Corwin Springs, Mont.: The Summit Lighthouse Library, 2001.

Prophet, Mark L., and Elizabeth Clare Prophet. *The Science of the Spoken Word.* Corwin Springs, Mont.: Summit University Press, 1991.

Prophet, Mark L., and Elizabeth Clare Prophet. *Understanding Yourself: A Spiritual Approach to Self-Discovery and Soul-Awareness.* Corwin Springs, Mont.: Summit University Press, 1999.

Reinhart, Melanie. *Chiron and the Healing Journey: An Astrological and Psychological Perspective.* London: Penguin Books, Arkana, 1998.

Reinhart, Melanie. *To the Edge and Beyond.* London: The Centre for Psychological Astrology Press, 1996.

Robinson, James M., ed. *The Nag Hammadi Library in English.* 3d ed. HarperSanFrancisco, 1988.

Roerich, Nicholas. *Shambhala: In Search of the New Era.* Rochester, Vt.: Inner Traditions International, 1990.

Saint Germain On Alchemy: Formulas for Self-Transformation. Recorded by Mark L. Prophet and Elizabeth Clare Prophet.

Corwin Springs, Mont.: Summit University Press, 1993.

Salzberg, Sharon. *Lovingkindness: The Revolutionary Art of Happiness.* Boston: Shambhala Publications, 1995.

Serapis Bey. *Dossier on the Ascension: The Story of the Soul's Acceleration into Higher Consciousness on the Path of Initiation.* Corwin Springs, Mont.: Summit University Press, 1979.

Smith, Huston. *The Religions of Man.* New York: Harper & Row, Perennial Library, 1965.

Stein, Zane B. *Essence and Application: A View from Chiron.* Lansford, Penn.: Zane B. Stein, 1995.

Stone, Hal, Ph.D., and Sidra Stone, Ph.D. *Embracing Your Inner Critic: Turning Self-Criticism into a Creative Asset.* New York: HarperCollins, 1993.

Tester, S. J. *A History of Western Astrology.* Woodbridge, Suffolk, England: Boydell & Brewer, Boydell Press, 1987.

Timmerman, Felix. *The Perfect Joy of St. Francis.* Translated by Raphael Brown. New York: Doubleday, 1952.

Tolkien, J. R. R. *The Fellowship of the Ring.* Part 1 of *The Lord of the Rings.* New York: Ballantine Books, 1965.

Van Doren, Carl. *Benjamin Franklin.* New York: Viking Press, 1938.

Yates, Frances A. *Giordano Bruno and the Hermetic Tradition.* Chicago: University of Chicago Press, 1964.

Yogananda, Paramahansa. *Autobiography of a Yogi.* Los Angeles: Self-Realization Fellowship, 1974.

Zukav, Gary. *The Seat of the Soul.* New York: Simon & Schuster, 1989.

Emotions
Transforming Anger, Fear and Pain

ISBN: 0-922729-77-8
Trade Paperback $14.95

Scientists have demonstrated the link between emotional balance and physical and mental well-being. When we learn how to handle our emotions, we can achieve balance in body, mind and soul. In *Emotions: Transforming Anger, Fear and Pain,* Dr. Marilyn Barrick, a transformational psychologist, takes the study of our emotions—and how to deal with them—to the next level.

In *Emotions,* you will discover how to release anger, guilt and grief in a healthy way to experience inner joy. The author shares techniques such as trauma-release therapy, peaceful self-observation and using nature as healer to help us realize loving-kindness, mindfulness and tolerance. She also shares successful spiritual techniques she has developed in her practice.

In these uncertain times, *Emotions: Transforming Anger, Fear and Pain* is an invaluable guide to creating heart-centeredness in a turbulent world.

"Marilyn Barrick is on the mark. While we search for the understanding of our physical, mental and spiritual selves, we often forget the source of the balance between all of them—our emotional self. This book addresses the issue magnificently. Read it and grow."

—DANNION BRINKLEY, N.Y. *Times* best-selling author of *Saved by the Light* and *At Peace in the Light*

"Emotions *is a wise, heartfelt and deeply spiritual path that can lead you from fear to courage, anger to joy, and helplessness to effectiveness—whatever challenges you may be facing. I have found it tremendously helpful."*

—MARTIN L. ROSSMAN, M.D., author of *Guided Imagery for Self-Healing*

"Written in an easily understandable style, Emotions: Transforming Anger, Fear and Pain *offers a wealth of information. Dr. Barrick provides excellent methods for freeing ourselves from some of our most destructive emotions—thus opening the door to improved health at all levels. This book is deserving of wide reading and rereading."*

—RANVILLE S. CLARK, M.D., psychiatrist, Washington, D.C.

Dreams
Exploring the Secrets of Your Soul

ISBN: 0-922729-63-8
Trade Paperback $14.00

Everyone and everything in our dreams is part of us . . . We spend one-third of our lives asleep—and most of that time we are dreaming. Dr. Marilyn Barrick's fascinating work shows that our dreams are not only meaningful and connected with events in our lives, but they also hold valuable keys to our spiritual and emotional development. In fact, our souls are great dramatists and teachers, and the scripts of our dreams often contain profound and valuable guidance.

Dreams: Exploring the Secrets of Your Soul discusses Tibetan sleep and dream yoga, lucid dreaming and techniques to help you more clearly remember and understand your dreams. Learn how to interpret your dreams through the powerful insights in this book and the author's visionary analysis of actual dreams. And discover how to decode the metaphorical messages of your own soul.

"This unique book on dreams integrates the soul's development on the spiritual path with personal dream work. . . . It invites us to consider a greater potential of the self beyond life's ordinary conflicts and helps us open up to a greater understanding of the purpose of life."

—RALPH YANEY, M.D.,
psychiatrist/psychoanalyst and author of *10,001*

"Dreams. . . *helps the reader unlock hidden secrets thereby opening new vistas to awareness, understanding, healing and finally, higher consciousness. . . . Dr. Barrick carefully, cogently and expertly enables the reader to understand the dream messages psychologically and spiritually."*

—RICHARD FULLER, senior editor, *Metaphysical Reviews*

Sacred Psychology of Change

ISBN: 0-922729-57-3
Trade Paperback $14.95

Catch the vision of your role in the 21st century. *Sacred Psychology of Change* shows how you can welcome cycles of change and even chaos as transformational opportunities. It is jam-packed with helpful information from cutting-edge change theories, psychology and spirituality.

Dr. Marilyn Barrick teaches us how to envision and explore the future while living productively in the present. Discover the importance of a creative mind-set, an open heart and the maturing of soul to successfully navigate the waves of change. Learn how to meet the challenges of endings and beginnings and emerge from the darkness of grief and loss into a bright new day.

The storytelling chapters and exercises bring your personal journey to life and suggest practical approaches to the challenging scenarios of our fast-moving world.

"This book asks us to 'focus our attention on the higher intelligence of our heart' and then describes in loving detail ways of doing just that. Those interested in the heart's ability to heal will find encouragement in these pages."

–RUTH BLY, licensed psychologist, Jungian analyst, author

"A profound treasure of spiritual truths and their practical application based on the author's many successful years of personal and professional experience. Written in the language of the heart and with remarkable clarity and sensitivity, this book will lead you, chapter by chapter and step by step, to a profoundly healing dialogue with yourself—and through an exciting spiritual and psychological journey of change."

–KENNETH FRAZIER, L.P.C., D.A.P.A., A.C.P.E.

Sacred Psychology of Love

ISBN: 0-922729-49-2
Trade Paperback $12.95

Searching for your perfect love? *Sacred Psychology of Love* unfolds the hidden spiritual and psychological dramas inherent in friendships, love relationships and marriage. It tells the story of each one's inner beloved and offers tender ways to spark divine love in your relationships.

After 35 years as a clinical psychologist and relationship counselor, Dr. Barrick is uniquely qualified to reveal the impact of childhood experiences upon adult relationships and to awaken us to the benefits of the reflecting mirror of the beloved. She shows the key role your inner "other half" plays in the eternal dance of love and gives practical self-help exercises to guide you on your quest for relationships that unite heart and soul.

"A wonderful marriage of the mystical and practical, this soul-nourishing book is beautiful, healing and thought-provoking."

–SUE PATTON THOELE,
author of *Heart-Centered Marriage*

"In our search for the Beloved, whether inner or outer, we seek that mysterious blend of beauty and practicality which Dr. Marilyn Barrick masterfully conveys on every page. Synthesizing her knowledge of sacred text, her clinical expertise and her life's wisdom, she has written a book for anyone seeking to love or to be loved. With compassion and humor, she gives us an important tool for enriching relationships."

–ANNE DEVORE, Jungian analyst

Marilyn C. Barrick, Ph.D., is the author of a seven-book series on sacred psychology, a synthesis of her knowledge of sacred text, her clinical expertise and life's wisdom. The first five books, published in English and Spanish, highlight personal and spiritual growth through understanding the ins and outs of love, change, dreams, emotions, and the soul.

Dr. Barrick will complete the series with two books offering her professional and spiritual insights on children and family and on past lives.

FOR MORE INFORMATION

Summit University Press books are available at fine bookstores worldwide and at your favorite on-line bookseller.

For a free catalog of our books and products or to learn more about the spiritual techniques featured in this book, please contact:

Summit University Press
PO Box 5000
Corwin Springs, MT 59030-5000 USA
Telephone: 1-800-245-5445 or 406-848-9500
Fax: 1-800-221-8307 or 406-848-9555
E-mail: info@summituniversitypress.com
www.summituniversitypress.com

MARILYN C. BARRICK, Ph.D., minister, psychologist and transformational therapist, is the author of a seven-book, self-help series on spiritual psychology. The first four books are *Emotions: Transforming Anger, Fear and Pain; Dreams: Exploring the Secrets of Your Soul; Sacred Psychology of Change: Life as a Voyage of Transformation;* and *Sacred Psychology of Love: The Quest for Relationships That Unite Heart and Soul.*

In her fifth book, *Soul Reflections: Many Lives, Many Journeys,* Dr. Barrick takes the reader on a spiritual-psychological journey—the journey of the soul from heaven to earth and back again. She skillfully interweaves karma and reincarnation, psychological interpretation, client stories and self-help exercises. She introduces the magic of Milarepa, the heroism of Parsifal, the ancient and modern lives of Phylos the Thibetan, plus stories of modern-day saints and heroic figures, such as Padre Pio and Helen Keller.

In addition to her private practice as a clinical psychologist, Dr. Barrick conducts seminars and workshops in the U.S.A., Canada and Europe. Over her 38-year professional career, she has consulted as a psychological expert to schools, churches, government agencies, professional advisory boards and mental health facilities. She has also taught graduate psychology courses and served as a Peace Corps training development officer and field counselor.

As a minister in a church that integrates the spiritual teachings of the world's major religions, Dr. Barrick integrates her considerable psychological expertise with a broad spiritual perspective.

Visit Dr. Barrick's web site at www.spiritualpsychology.com.